HOME

HOME

A Place in the World

Edited by Arien Mack

NEW YORK UNIVERSITY PRESS

NEW YORK AND LONDON

New York University Press wishes to acknowledge the Trustees of the Imperial War Museum in London for the wartime poster by Frank Newbould; Rijksmuseum-Stichting for the frontispiece drawing for *Plaisante Plaetsen* by Claes Jansz Visscher, for the *Huis te Kleef* by Jan van de Velde after Pieter Saenredam, for river scene and *The Forts at Tholen* by Esaias van de Velde, for *Jeremiah Lamenting the Destruction of Jerusalem* by Rembrandt; Musée du Louvre for *Egmond-aan-Zee* by Jan van Goyen, *Melancholy* by Chaperon; Staatliche Kunsthalle for *Ein Bauer auf der Rast* by Roelandt Savery; the Amon Carter Museum, Fort Worth for *The Hunter's Return* 1983.156 by Thomas Cole; the Metropolitan Museum of Art, Gift in memory of Jonathan Sturges by his Children, 1895 (95.13.1) for *In the Woods* by Asher Durand; Museum Boymans—van Beunungen for *Night Attack on a Village* by Esaias van de Velde; Réunion des Musées Nationaux-Paris for *Melancholy* by Feti.

NEW YORK UNIVERSITY PRESS
New York and London

Library of Congress Cataloging-in-Publication Data
Home : a place in the world / edited by Arien Mack.
p.   cm.
Includes bibliographical references and index.
ISBN 0-8147-5483-X (alk. paper)
1. Home.   2. Home in literature.   3. Family.   4. Family in literature.   I. Mack, Arien.
HQ503.H75   1993
306.85—dc20   92-44279
                         CIP

New York University Press books are printed on acid-free paper, and their binding materials are chosen for strength and durability.

c 10 9 8 7 6 5 4 3 2 1

*'Home is the place where, when you have to go there,
They have to take you in.'*
*'I should have called it
Something you somehow haven't to deserve.'*

—From "Death of the Hired Man" by
Robert Frost

Contents

Contributors

BREYTEN BREYTENBACH, a novelist born in South Africa and now living in Paris, wrote *True Confessions of an Albino Terrorist* (1985). His most recent novel is *Memory of Snow and Dust* (1989).

DAVID BROMWICH, professor of English at Yale University, is author, most recently, of *Choice of Inheritance: Self and Community from Edmund Burke to Robert Frost* (1989).

SANFORD BUDICK is director of the Center for Literary Studies at the Hebrew University of Jerusalem. His most recent book is *The Dividing Muse: Images of Sacred Disjunction in Milton's Poetry* (1985).

STANLEY CAVELL is Walter M. Cabot Professor of Aesthetics and the General Theory of Value at Harvard University. His most recent book is *Conditions Handsome and Unhandsome: The Constitution of Emersonian Perfectionism* (1990).

MARY DOUGLAS taught anthropology at the University of London, Northwestern University, and Princeton University. Her most recent book is *How Institutions Think* (1986).

TAMARA K. HAREVEN is Unidel Professor of Family Studies and History at the University of Delaware. Her books include *Family Time and Industrial Time* (1982).

ERIC HOBSBAWM, Emeritus University Professor of Politics and Society at Cambridge University, is now a member of the Graduate Faculty of the New School for Social Research. His most recent book is *The Age of Empire* (1989).

JOHN HOLLANDER is A. Bartlett Giamatti Professor of English at Yale University. His most recent books are *Melodious Guile* (1988), criticism, and *Harp Lake* (1988), poetry.

KIM HOPPER is a research scientist at the Nathan Kline Institute for Psychiatric Research and visiting professor of anthropology at the New School for Social Research.

GEORGE KATEB is professor of politics at Princeton University and author of *Hannah Arendt: Politics, Conscience, Evil* (1984).

ALEXANDER KEYSSAR, associate professor of history at Duke University, wrote *Out of Work: The First Century of Unemployment in Massachusetts* (1986).

STEVEN MARCUS is George Delacorte Professor in the Humanities at Columbia University. His most recent book is *Freud and the Culture of Psychoanalysis* (1984).

ORLANDO PATTERSON is professor of sociology at Harvard University. His book, *Freedom: Vol I: Freedom in the Making of Western Culture* won the 1991 National Book Award for Non-Fiction.

JOSEPH RYKWERT is Paul Philippe Cret Professor of Architecture at the University of Pennsylvania. His books include *The First Moderns* (1980).

SIMON SCHAMA, professor of history at Harvard University, is the author of *The Embarrassment of Riches: An Interpretation of Dutch Culture in the Golden Age* (1987) and *Citizens: A Chronicle of the French Revolution* (1989).

ALAN TRACHTENBERG, Neil Gray Jr. Professor of English and American Studies at Yale University, is the author, most recently, of *Reading American Photographs: Images as History from Mathew Brady to Walker Evans* (1989).

GWENDOLYN WRIGHT is professor of architecture and history at Columbia University and author of *Building the Dream: A Social History of Housing in America* (1983).

Introduction

I_N the fall of 1990, *Social Research* and the New School for Social Research organized a multi-institutional collaboration around the idea of Home. The timeliness of this project is obvious. We live at a time when the idea of home has become problematic. We are confronted every day with painful images and stories about the growing numbers of homeless people, about criminal violence toward children, and about the plights of those exiled from their homelands. And all of this coexists with the persistent images of home as a place of comfort, safety and refuge.

This project was the second in a continuing series organized by *Social Research* around critical contemporary issues, the first of which was *In Time of Plague: The History and Consequences of Lethal Epidemic Diseases.*[1] Our collaborators in the Home Project were five major New York City museums—The Bronx Museum of the Arts, the Brooklyn Children's Museum, the Cooper-Hewitt Museum, the Jewish Museum and the Studio Museum in Harlem. A series of public programs and exhibits on the theme of Home: A Place in the World were presented at these museums and at The New School with the aim of interpreting and focusing attention on key aspects of this fundamental and complex concept.

A national conference, Home: A Place in the World, a central part of the Home Project, was held at The New School in October 1990. It was designed to explore the ideology of home, its meaning as a central human idea as well as the crises engendered by its loss in homelessness and exile and by the experi-

---

[1] The proceedings of this project appear in *In Time of Plague: The History and Social Consequences of Lethal Epidemic Disease*, edited by Arien Mack (New York: New York University Press, 1991).

ence of loss suffered in alienation. The papers from this conference appear in this volume accompanied by illustrations
taken from the exhibits. We hope that the sustained reflections
to be found in these papers which range from "Landscape as
Home" and "Alienation and Belonging to Humanity" to "A
Curse to Themselves and a Menace and Injury to the City:
Homelessness in New York City History" and "The Long March
from Hearth to Heart" will begin to unravel the intellectual,
the moral, the historic and cultural tangles in which the idea of
home is embedded. It is our belief that in so doing we will
engender a deeper understanding of what it means not to
belong, and not to have a home at a moment when that condition has become so widespread and urgent that it demands an
effective and humane response.

Many people helped to make this project possible. We are
grateful to all of them. In particular, we acknowledge with
gratitude the support of the National Endowment for the Humanities, the Rockefeller Foundation and the Ford Foundation.

THE IDEA OF HOME

The idea defined. The idea of home has a deep resonance for us that is not fully captured by its use as a social and political slogan. What is its history and ideology? What has it meant and how has its meaning changed?

Introduction
BY STANLEY CAVELL

P ART OF MY particular interest in the topic of this conference, "Home: A Place in the World"—beyond sharing the sense of the fascination and the urgency of issues raised by it—is my anticipation of help in making clearer to me why and how the concept of home has increasingly provided a focus around which my work in philosophy has revolved. This means, for example, making more explicit the conditions expressed in Novalis's saying: "Philosophy is essentially homesickness—the universal impulse to be home."

I find this idea taken on in the two figures of this century whose work, for better or worse, has seemed, for many people, the most compelling exemplifications of philosophy—Martin Heidegger and Ludwig Wittgenstein, for each of whom, in something like opposite ways, the intervention of philosophy in Western culture is at the cause, if possibly it will be for the solace, of the human being's self-alienation (let's say) from its rightful habitat. Their affinity on this ground might remind one of their each having responded, as their generation of intellectuals was apt to respond, to the teaching of Oswald Spengler, whose *Decline of the West* contains in an early note the declaration that "home" is a profound word "which obtains its significance as soon as the barbarian becomes a culture-man and loses it again [with] the civilization-man."

In my case, making explicit a philosophical preoccupation with home, hence with home lost and home left, means making connection between such European thinkers and the fact that a philosophical masterpiece on these themes, matching their achievements, was made in the American nineteenth century— think of Thoreau's *Walden* on the topic of the building of a house, and its idea, shared with Emerson, that owning or belonging to a place is the promise and power of leaving it, say of staking one's name. From here, I have gratefully to add, my case means making further connection with the education my generation growing up in America acquired from serious attendance at the movies. I think of the memorable *Stella Dallas,* King Vidor's film of 1937, in which a daughter climactically, with hammering irony, appeals to her mother not to send her away, instructing her in what "belonging" someplace means, saying in particular that it does not mean just having fun, but crying together; and I think of that mother, or rather of Barbara Stanwyck who plays Stella Dallas there, some fifteen years later, in Fritz Lang's film (from the play by Clifford Odets) *Clash by Night,* saying to a man, a stranger, "Home is where you go when you run out of places."

The papers we are to hear this afternoon are wonderful new beginnings of the education I seek; they sketch out an expansive region from which to inspire our discussions over the next three days. John Hollander virtuosically lays out lines along which to derive a series of inflections of our meaning when we invoke the name of home, opening the question of why and how it is that thinking about home will take the form of remembering, and constructing, aphorisms of home, as of enclosures of sudden familiarity. Joseph Rykwert's reflections span an aesthetic-spiritual distance from the claim that finding a home can be managed in the absence of a constructed dwelling to sustain and express it, to the claim that we are making of our world one whose constructions are unfit to sustain and express the longing for a home. Simon Schama introduces historical and national contours into his fascinating tracing of the evolution of Western sensibility in the representation of landscape—differences specifically in and of the idea of a land as an idea or allegory of the people of that land.

Homelands

BY SIMON SCHAMA

In the most difficult and uncertain days of the Second World War, Frank Newbould, the greatest virtuoso of the patriotic poster, did his bit for Britain. His posters projected an image of the country as sempiternally sweet and pure—rolling downs, lyrically lit, gently peopled by loyal dogs and obedient sheep, a stone-walled village, "nestling," as the railway photographs always had it, at the base of undulating hills (Plate 1). The countryside was a homology of the people's own idea of themselves—devoid of extravagance, unromantic, understated, moderate, enduring. On the radio, John of Gaunt's dying speech from *Richard II,* "the scepter'd isle," was repeated countless times in the accents of Churchillian fortitude.

Across the North Sea the Third Reich had an equally (if not more) powerful sense of landscape and people as composed from one material, or rather two: blood and soil. Painters who responded eagerly to the state's call for regenerate rather than degenerate art obligingly produced works that drew on ancient allusions to work and redemption (plowing and growing) and titled their works *Steaming Furrow* (Max Bergmann) or *German Earth and Spring* (Werner Peiner; Plate 2). Together they created a mystical definition of homeland: illimitable fecund acres tilled by men and beasts of the same potent stock. If the ruling paradigm for patriotic topography in Britain was pastoral, in Germany it was fundamentally eugenic and zoological.

The claim that landscape and people are morphologically akin, constructed, as it were, from common clay, and that they constitute in some primal cultural sense the nature of each other—that land and homeland may be interchangeable—is now a familiar commonplace. "America the Beautiful" is

Plate 1.   A wartime poster by Frank Newbould.

Plate 2. Werner Peiner, *Furrows*.

meant to speak of the distinctiveness, the providentially blessed character of the whole culture through a topographical inventory. But for much of Western history this sort of association was not at all axiomatic. Land defined social and legal status, provided subsistence, could be praised as touched by diligent godliness, plowing and sowing being used as Christian emblems of hope and resurrection, aestheticized in Virgilian georgic—but never appropriated to define and celebrate the particular qualities of a culture or a state.

When did that type of association, then, begin? In image making, at least, I think the date can be given quite precisely: the late Renaissance in northern Europe and in the Netherlands; in other words, at the moment when the concept of landscape as an autonomous form, rather than as the auxiliary of sacred or classical narrative, was being invented. The word itself, coined as "landskip" by Edward Norgate's *Art of Limning*, was first used to describe the kind of things turned out by Dutch artists. More than just the generic northern view uncomplicated by narrative, history, or allegory, however, it was the rejection of what Otto Benesch called the "universal" cosmology, say, of Pieter Brueghel's topographical encyclopedism—towering mountains and boiling sea coasts beside which demure Flemish villages have been improbably inserted. In place of these macrocosmic constructs, the microcosmic Dutch world: sand and mud, sea and fish, highly particular, low-horizoned, indeed rectangular in format, monochrome in hue, reproduced by painters like van Goyen in hundreds for the market (rather than in singles or discrete sets for a single patrician connoisseur, like Niclaes Jonghelinck, for whom Brueghel's *Seasons* were executed).

The moment of alteration from the universal to the particular, from world to home, may even be specified further in the career of a single, very great artist, Hendrik Goltzius. It is precisely because so much of his career was shaped by the international philosophies of the time—humanist and mannerist, to which his grand history paintings showed undeviating allegiance—that the implications of what Goltzius did in this 1603 series of drawings seems so radical. With no precedent, other than a few drawings of Brueghel as his possible inspiration, Goltzius produced the prototypes of Dutch landscapes with low horizons, gently indicated horizontal features, ambulatory impressions of the countryside beyond Haarlem—images, in other words, of a rural home.

This innocent, domestic parochialism becomes all the more striking given Goltzius's own epically nomadic history—born in Germany, taught engraving by the great humanist writer and politician Coornhert, a direct student of another cosmopolitan intellectual, Erasmus, forced on his wanderings by the tides of war, to the border town of Xanten, and finally returning to a Haarlem that was recovering from the trauma of a brutal Spanish siege, occupation, and mass executions. It was in this self-consciously ancestral town of Dutch culture that the group around Goltzius—Carel van Mander, Cornelis van Haarlem— produced, in different ways and genres, work that celebrated the local traditions of the Netherlands. Van Mander wrote the first anthology of Netherlands artists' lives; Cornelis offered a *Massacre of the Innocents* to replace the altarpiece by Maarten van Heemskerk destroyed in the occupation, and Goltzius produced prints alluding to the heroes of the war and the destruction of tyrants.

Even though some of their subject matter concerned the defense of hearth and home, the form in which those concerns were communicated seldom broke with the international vocabulary of late mannerism (the Cornelis *Massacre* being a case in point). In recovering a much more domestic and vernacular language, suggested only in Brueghel's drawings and the 1559 series of views of Brabant published by Hieronymus Cock, Goltzius was self-consciously setting a private parochial language against the public rhetoric of mannerism. Yet it was only when this kind of view of landscape (figuratively and metaphorically) was re-engraved, by Claes Jans, Visscher and Willem Buytewech, and Jan van de Velde

(in other words, by the *next* generation), that it could effectively
supersede the international by the domestic, empire by
homeland.

   There is nothing explicitly patriotic or political in series like
Buytewech's *Verscheiden Landschapjes* or Visscher's *Plaisante
Plaetsen,* yet the timing of their publication—at the beginning
and the end of the brief nine-year truce in the Dutch war with
Spain—speaks, I think, to the celebration of local virtues, to
the specific connection between home and territory, that colors
the series. The frontispiece to Visscher's series (Plate
3) foregrounds Haarlem's coat of arms, its recent history in the
motto (virtue overcomes force) with the supporters of
diligence and time. The views which follow in the series
represent (in the tradition of Brueghel) bucolic pursuits and
fishing, but embody precisely those peaceful activities which
Dutch literature, hymns, and poetry now opposed to the
invasive brutalities of the Spanish soldiery. And the pastime of
suburban walks into the surrounding countryside, which David

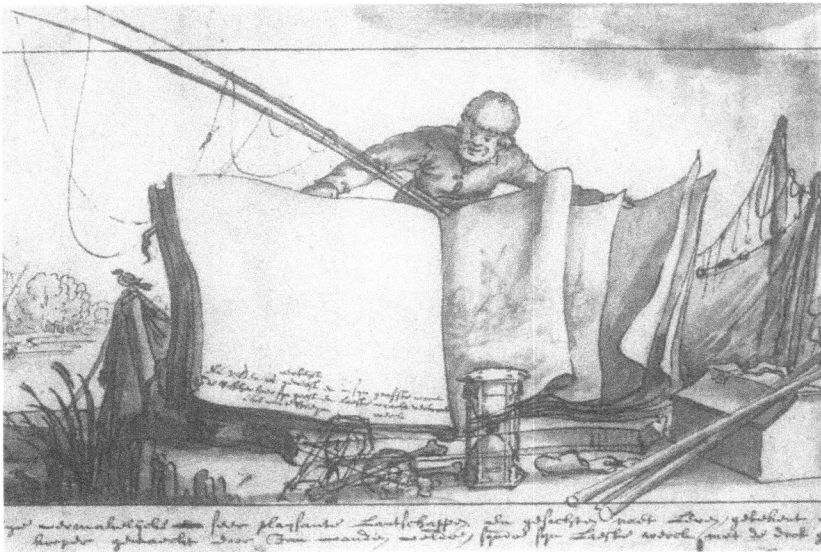

Plate 3. Claes Jansz Visscher, frontispiece drawing for *Plaisante Plaetsen*.

Freedberg has emphasized were the social counterpart of these little series, itself presupposed a hard-won safety that could allow such extramural recreation.

So it should not surprise us to find in other series published in the early years of the renewal of war reminders of all these connections between history, landscape, and freedom. For if during the first period of the Dutch revolt—between 1572 and 1609—there had been no coherent sense of where the homeland might be, in any religious, territorial, or political sense (the Dutch after all offered sovereignty to Queen Elizabeth and the duke of Anjou), the second phase from 1621 onward was marked by a much more decisive sense of the defense of a homeland (and the futile effort to recover those parts of it in the south that had been sealed off by the Spanish armies and the river barriers). Thus Buytewech's landscape prints feature views and commentaries on Bredero Castle and the Huis te Kleef, both blown up by the Spanish armies (Plate 4). In the same sense, when the artist usually (and rightly)

Plate 4. Jan van de Velde after Pieter Saenredam, *The Huis te Kleef.*

identified as the founder of the new, distinctively vernacular manner of Dutch landscape painting, Esaias van de Velde, produced, at the same time, his own landscape prints and paintings, he was also painting alarming documents of the war such as one where the satanic hosts bear down on Dutch shooters seen in defense of a home (Plate 5).

There was one type of landscape (if it can be classified as such) which must especially have spoken of this idealized local community and which was painted over and again by the first generation of northern Netherlands artists: the fishing village. Can it be altogether a matter of random simultaneity that at the time when the fishing villages of Zeeland and the North Sea coast were taking brutal losses from the Dunkirk privateers, fighting for Spain, artists like Arent Cabel (himself from a simple fishing background), Avercamp, Esaias and Jan van de Velde were producing little paintings that represented the men and their homes as a kind of Netherlandish idyll—frugal, industrious, brave, and pious (Plate 6). Indeed,

Plate 5. Esaias van de Velde, *Night Attack on a Village*.

Plate 6. Esaias van de Velde, river scene.

some specific places like the coastal village of Egmond-aan-Zee
with its ruined abbey became an extraordinary sort of canon, a
touchstone of collective self-perception, painted innumerable
times throughout the Dutch tradition by Jan van Goyen, Jacob
van Ruisdael, Adriaen van de Velde (Plate 7). Other paintings
of river scenes often included subtle suggestions (in watchtow-
ers, river forts, and batteries) of the relationship between
domestic security—the watch over the home—and local
prosperity (Plate 8).

It has even been argued (and convincingly) that cattle pieces
like those by Paulus Potter might have spoken to the
traditional emblematic associations of the *Hollandse koe:* the
symbol of a domestic farm animal, deliberately used in
contravention of the traditional heraldic bestiary of eagles and
lions, to symbolize the providentially allotted fecundity of the
Netherlands. And it hardly needs saying that the strength of
these associations owed a great deal to the shared conviction
(and indeed historic truth) that Dutch land had been

Plate 7. Jan van Goyen, *Egmond-aan-Zee.*

self-created and was thus accountable only to the Creator himself rather than any feudal suzerain from whom it had been held on conditions. That was, in effect, why the landscapes of the books of hours of the Limbourg brothers represent not home but the daunting reality of social power embodied in the manorial system. Nothing could be further away than images like Esaias's where the laborer's cottage occupies the central place allotted to the castle.

It does seem to me, then, that it was in the Netherlands that the concept developed of an explicitly domestic landscape, something that should be visualized without the stylizations and formulaic (often, of course, Virgilian) conventions of the classical and pastoral traditions, traditions that still dominated landscape representation in France and Italy. Low horizons; ruins from the recent rather than the classical past; unadorned representations of farmers and fishermen rather than bucolically ingratiating accounts of shepherds and milkmaids—all presupposed a view of homeland that was uncompromisingly

Plate 8. Esaias van de Velde, *The Forts at Tholen.*

down-home. There were, at the same time, we are always reminded, painters for whom this was not enough, who needed, like Seghers and Rembrandt, Both and Berchem, a grander poetic language of invention. But it was the more artisanal, home-grown manner which, from the mid-1620s for at least two decades, flooded the market with literally thousands of often rapidly painted (one is tempted to say reproduced, so formulaic did they become) images.

What these images were *not* is perhaps at least as interesting as what they were. For the implicit culture from which all of this visual parochialism differentiated itself was, as I have already suggested, universalist and imperial. Politically, the Habsburg empire against which the Dutch fought extended, in two dominions, from the Danube to Peru. Ideologically, especially in the Thirty Years War, its apologists and propagandists (like Pieter Paul Rubens) still thought of a Pax Hispanica as a benign international arbitration, the heir of the reforming Neoplatonism, of the Erasmian ecumenism, of the

previous century. And when that war was finished in 1648 and
the Dutch separate homeland acknowledged, they had, almost
immediately, to come to grips with two other versions of
universalism: the Protestant universalism embodied in Oliver
Cromwell's startling offer to melt their own sovereignty into a
single republican state; and not long after that, the universalist
pretensions of the next great expanding force, Louis XIV's
France. (The list as a perennial counterpoint to Dutch national
life could be almost indefinitely extended—against British
naval imperialism, Bonapartist universalism.)

Almost all of these universalist claims to religious, political,
and territorial indivisibility aspired to be the heirs of Rome.
And it was similarly against this Roman universalism that a
second and, for the future of the landscape-home idea, still
more powerful type was invented: that of the forest home.

Paradoxically, of course, the concept was virtually invented—or at least transmitted to posterity—by a Roman,
though one whose allegiance to imperial absolutism was, to say
the least, qualified: Tacitus. Not just in the *Germania* but also in
the *Histories* and the *Annales* (in the brutal battles between
Arminius and Germanicus), Tacitus offered an implied (or
more than implied) critique of the Roman state, of the
discrepancy between its perennial pretensions and the reality
of its decadence. He does this by counterpointing Roman
decay with a kind of primitive ethnography of the German
tribes, a method that owed a great deal to Herodotus, and one
in which the forest landscape, the concept of a patrimonial
home and the conditioning of manners and laws, was
paramount. The most telling distinction from the basic axioms
of Roman life comes in chapter 16, where the sentence "It is
well known that none of the German tribes live in cities"
occurs. The distinction here was between *silva*, the ancestral
woodlands which, according to Virgil, provided the birth of
Rome itself and which in the Republic and Empire supplied
forage and material for its armies and navies, a woodland for

the state, and, on the other hand, the impenetrable forest, *horridum et deserta,* the abode of the barbarian tribe.

And though Tacitus's portrait is by no means always flattering (grudging, horrified admiration might be the better characterization), his emphasis on their closeness to nature— wearing the skins of wild animals—is linked to their relative immunity from the kind of social corruptions that had eaten away at Roman vigor and virtue. Thus in his account, "the marriage tie is strict"; their life one of "fenced-off chastity . . . adulteries are very few for the number of people; punishment is prompt . . . the children in every house growing up amid nakedness and squalor into that girth of limb and frame which is to our people a marvel. Its own mother suckles each at her breast; they are not passed on to nursemaids and wet-nurses"; masters and servants impossible to differentiate by clothes or manners, "they live in the company of the same cattle and the same mud floor." And though he does not explicitly repeat Livy's pious nostalgia for a primitive Rome, indeed for the Romulan hut, a place built with shingles and timbers, where the first Senate was itself a timbered affair, Tacitus's invidious contrasts are full of an implied moral cycle that travels from wooden virtue to imperial masonry.

The philologist Robert Ulrey has made it clear that some German monasteries, connected with Fulda, had manuscript copies of the *Germania* as early as the ninth century. But it was not until the late fifteenth century that printed editions were first produced through the enthusiasms of German humanists like Conrad Celtis. More remarkable still, of all Tacitus's works it was the *Germania* which first made its way into print and on which there were four commentaries by the early sixteenth century, some of them by Protestants like Philip Melanchthon. The tribal war leader Arminius was adopted by contemporary German epitomes of *Ritterschaft* like Ulrich von Hutten (who called Arminius the "most German of Germans") as a legitimate precedent for outright revolt against both the sacerdotal and imperial Rome. A whole generation of sixteenth-century cosmographers—beginning with the happily named Aenius Silvius (the Piccolomini who became Pope Pius II but who conceived a project of a *Germania Illustrata* to set against the familiar *Italia Illustrata*); Johannes Aventius (*Bavarian Chronicle*); Sebastian Munster; Beatus Rhenanus in Basel; Johann Rauw—reworked Tacitus as well as Strabo and Pliny to invent an entire arboreal world that, although not at all coterminous with all of Germania, was in every sense represented as its earliest, formative home, not just a home but a cradle of culture.

Topography was fleshed out with ethnography. In printed representations of the German forest home (some of them, significantly, done in woodcuts, a craft tradition, combining, as it does, the sacred, the organic, and the mystique of a patrimony which goes right through to the woodcut landscapes of Die Brücke), like these taken from Philip von Cluver's (Cluverius) *Germania Antiqua,* all the classic Tacitean virtues were given precise embodiment: clothing made from skins; sacred groves for worship; houses made exclusively from timber; even weapons—clubs and shields—that were wooden. Territorially, *Teutschlands Baumen*—the German forest home— was now said to have stretched indivisibly from the Elbe to the Rhine and had only been broken up by the arbitrary invasions and interruptions of Rome and her successors.

Some German courts were especially hospitable to the development of an ethnic type in which landscape and manners were seen as symbiotic. Both the Protestant Elector Palatine Frederick III and the highly unorthodox Catholic Emperor Rudolf II at Prague gathered groups of scholars and artists deeply committed to imagining a German world of primeval virtues. They included a number of figures from the borderlands of the Netherlands and Germany, two of whom, Gillis Coninxloo and Roeland Savery, made the forest primeval a major theme of their work. Some time during the first decade of the seventeenth century Savery produced the definitive image of the Bohemian *Waldmann,* dressed in rustic simplicity, posed against the ruins of antiquity that have been enveloped by the irrepressible organic greenery (Plate 9). The antithesis between classicism and organicism is at the precise pole from Italian pastoral landscapes where the architectural remains of antiquity are set in harmony with landscape itself and shepherds and woodsmen are aestheticized to a maximum degree of refinement.

The stereotype of the forest home as a benevolently presocial space, somewhere protected from, or in active resistance to, urban, Roman concepts of civility, law, and the state, was not the exclusive property of Germanic tradition,

Plate 9. Roeland Savery, *The Waldmann.*

though it was there that it was most insistently revived. The English literary creation of Greenwood, the forest home and dwelling place of Robin Hood, that flourished from the fourteenth to the nineteenth century, imagined another place set against the arbitrary world of statutory enforcement, a place where social wrongs (done to bankrupted knights, cast-off friars) could be redressed by a clan that, just like the primitive Germans, recognized among themselves a brotherhood and no other sovereignty than direct fealty to their king. However the countless versions of the Hood saga varied, they all had in common a crucial narrative in which Robin encounters (indeed, often engages in a chivalric contest with) a disguised king who sees in the world of the Greenwood the primitive equities he is supposed to uphold but which have been alienated, usurped, and corrupted by the actual institutions of the fiscal court and state.

Similarly, the French Revolutionary cult of the liberty tree owed a great deal (in its more spontaneous, less managed phase) to the *mais sauvages*—the may trees that turned Drudical rites of vernal rebirth into more generalized symbols of that crucial revolutionary obsession, regeneration (cf. the idea of the living cross).

With whatever justice or not, the Napoleonic empire was seen to proclaim the classical Roman ideal of universal empire, constituted from a legally indivisible and topographically indiscriminate expanse from the Polish marshes to the Bay of Biscay. And against such modern ecumenism, romantic nationalism—in which the mystique of landscape played an essential role—set up its opposition. In the German case, as we have seen, there was already a rich literary and historical tradition of the homeland, refreshed in the eighteenth century by the Göttingen circle of the Hainbund with its emphasis on the oak in bud as the symbol of rebirth from dormancy, by the history of Justus Moser that differentiated once more the artificial, institutional imperial German past from an authentic, popular, tribal inheritance, and by the already popular connections made (most famously by goethe at Strasbourg cathedral) between the organic cathedral of the trees and the inspirational architecture of Christian gothic. A number of Caspar David Friedrich's most rhetorically powerful works— the chasseur in the forest; the tomb of Arminius— consummated these patrimonial associations of immemorial sacredness, patriotic immanence, an organic bond between place and people.

Rome did not, however, lose its way in the immensity of the forest quite as much as Friedrich's painting of the haplessly overawed hussar suggests. Indeed, in the shape of the nineteenth-century *Macht-und-Rechstaat*, be it Bismarck's or Gladstone's or Lincoln's, the pieties of an ancestral home were directly confronted and in fact overwhelmed by the imperatives of the state. As fuel for industry, urbanization, railways, newsprint, and war, forests were seen primarily as providentially offered resource rather than sacred patrimony. In some cultures like Sweden, in fact, the superabundance of timber was recast as indicating the potency of the industrial future, rather than an endless resurrection of the Nordic-Viking past. It was the sawmill rather than the stand of firs, the dynamic rather than the inert, that received the epic treatment from Nordic artists.

Nowhere were these paradoxes more self-conscious than in North America. Though the painters who would most explicitly transfer associations of sacred immemoriality to the American forests—Asher Durand and Albert Bierstadt—were either themselves German or had studied in Germany, these themes of the advance of empire against the sacred patrimonial landscape home were already much in evidence in the formative work of Thomas Cole and his epigone, Frederick Church. Cole, who came from the British industrial Midlands (where whole forests like Deane were synonyms for the immense expansion of industrial power), was the most adamant, indeed occasionally apocalyptic, in opposing "civilization" to "nature." His most ambitious cycle on "The Course of Empire" set out the by-now-banal cycle of an imperial history that proceeded relentlessly from an Edenic pastoral through violent and voluptuous hubris to ruins that were once more significantly and redemptively overgrown. For much of Cole's life, the sound of the ax was the beginning of the end, yet he could hardly himself deny that the spaces it opened were, in fact, the permitting conditions of his own work. The most he conceded, toward the end of this life in *Home in the Woods* or *The Hunters Return* (Plate 10), was a simplified georgic idyll where house was necessarily made of wood, the clearing isolated and solitary rather than part of any organized settlement, and a clear reciprocity established between the landscape and family harmony.

In the same year, Cole published his famous warning in *The Literary World* reminding landscape painters that

> they have a high and sacred mission to perform and woe betide them or their memories if they neglect it. The axe of civilization is busy with our old forests and artisan ingenuity is fast sweeping

Plate 10. Thomas Cole, *The Hunters Return*.

away the relics of our national infancy. What were once the wild and picturesque haunts of the Red Man and where the wild deer roamed in freedom, are becoming abodes of commerce and seats of manufactures. Our inland lakes, once sheltered and secluded in the midst of noble forests are now laid bare and covered with busy craft and even the old primordial hills once bristling with shaggy pine and hemlock like old Titans as they were are being shorn of their locks and left to blister in the cold nakedness of the sun.

In response to this summons, Frederick Church produced as his representation of the subject set by the New York Sketch Club, "Too Soon," an image of *Main Street and Family Store* (urban America exemplified in the architectural form of the classical villa) absurdly cut into the landscape of the virgin forest.

In the decade that followed, the same period when Francis Parkman recast himself away from the Great Plains and took up his self-appointed vocation as historian of the American forest, the periodical *The Crayon* ran a fourteen-part series on the wilderness and its waters, and Asher Durand's "Letters on Landscape Painting" made explicit appeals for American artists to return to native scenery. Durand's *In the Woods* (Plate 11) can be taken as the exact analogy to his summons to evoke an American nature as yet "spared from the pollutions of civilization."

Franklin Kelly and other historians have suggested that the years following the Civil War saw a waning of the "national landscape." But in fact, like much else of the persistent formative motifs in creating a mythology of American national identity, the idea of the forest home merely moved west. The discovery of Yosemite and the first representations of the great sequoias in the Mariposa and Calaveras groves of the Sierra Nevada were immediately colored by associations of a primeval American past. It was all the more helpful to protagonists of American distinctiveness, since the immensity of both size and years supplied heroic archetypes that could be said to have both predated and surpassed the European classical past.

Plate 11. Asher Durand, *In the Woods.*

Writer after writer pointed out the pregnant significance that only in the heart of the American west were there trees whose lives literally corresponded to the Christian era. As the *Boston Daily Advertiser* (1869) put it,

> What lengths of days are here. His years are the years of the Christian era; perhaps this is how when the angels saw the Star of Bethlehem standing in the East this germ broke through the tender sod and came out into the air of the upper world.

In this sense at least, Albert Bierstadt's woodsman, dwarfed by the *Great Grizzly* (a painting produced for the Philadelphia Centennial of 1876; Plate 12), was the linear descendant of

Plate 12. Albert Bierstadt, *The Great Grizzly*.

Savery's rustic: both self-evidently at home in the forest. And our own generation is facing all over again (and with much the same rhetoric) in the California Forests Forever ballot question, in the bitter struggle over clear-cutting in the north Pacific forests, exactly the same issue of the arboreal home. Only today the edicts of the new Rome are issued as much by the Japanese timber market. In the classical world, of course, the owl of Minerva was the attribute of wisdom; in the Dutch tradition it became the symbol of short-sightedness. Just whether the fate of the spotted owl of the Pacific redwoods will come to symbolize the protection or the destruction of our own forest home is still hard to predict.

It All Depends

BY JOHN HOLLANDER

"IT ALL DEPENDS on what you mean by home." Mary, the farmer's wife in Robert Frost's "The Death of the Hired Man," may as well raise one of our central questions for us this afternoon. We will remember that, in the poem, a former farmhand—and one of variable efficiency—who had left their employ in somewhat strained circumstances, shows up at the house in extremely debilitated condition:

> 'Warren,' she said, 'he has come home to die
> You needn't be afraid he'll leave you this time.'

> 'Home,' he mocked gently.

>   'Yes, what else but home?
> It all depends on what you mean by home.
> Of course he's nothing to us any more
> Than was the hound that came a stranger to us
> Out of the woods, worn out upon the trail.'

This occasions that celebrated exchange between man and wife that used to be so well known to readers of my generation; the husband's formulation—

> 'Home is the place where, when you have to go there,
> They have to take you in.'

—is followed by his wife's rejoinder:

>   'I should have called it
> Something you somehow haven't to deserve.'

At first glance, the dialogue seems to privilege the contrast

between these views—the husband defines home with respect
to the responsibilities, specifically of the other persons who
constitute a household, while the wife talks the language of
rights, rather than responsibilities, and of a possession, a place
in particular. Frost himself, amusingly and quite trivially,
highlighted this difference by giving it a reductive reading of
his own:

> In "The Death of the Hired Man" [he remarked in an interview
> with his greatest critic, Richard Poirier] that I wrote long, long
> ago, long before the New Deal, I put it two ways about home.
> One would be the manly way: "Home is the place where, when
> you go there, they have to take you in." That's the man's feeling
> about it. And then the wife says, "I should have called it /
> Something you somehow haven't to deserve." That's the New
> Deal, the feminine way of it, the mother way. You don't have to
> deserve your mother's love. You have to deserve your father's.
> He's more particular. One's a Republican, one's a Democrat.
> The father is always a Republican toward his son, and his
> mother's always a Democrat.[1]

But the art of this poet has been ultimately to make us hear
these definitions as profoundly complementary. The husband's remark unfolds in a line of monosyllables, with
displaced syntax, slowly and as if framed with some difficulty;
his wife's answer completes a half line and trips musically
along. She has the last word; but her "I should have called it
. . ." might ultimately just as well be put as "That is to say, it's /
Something you somehow . . . ," for they are ultimately
paraphrases of the same notion. You have to get taken in by
them whether you deserve it or not; you don't have to deserve
to be there (and, consequently, to oblige them to acknowledge
this by taking you in). This complementarity, rather than a
more aggressively arrayed antithetical quality, marks the
relation of the masculine and feminine definitions. Poirier has
remarked on how these two are like Milton's Adam and

---

[1] Richard Poirier, *Robert Frost: The Work of Knowing* (New York: Oxford University
Press, 1977), pp. 254–255.

Eve—but, we should add, before the Fall (in *Paradise Lost,* book 9). Afterward, their debate might have been trivialized, and the fallen Eve, now a merely human housewife, might have muttered in return, "I know, and we're / The 'they' who're always stuck with having to" or even (He) "Home is the place where, when I finally get there / My supper will be hot." (She) "And yet Shaw called it / 'Home . . . the girl's workhouse and the woman's prison.'" Yet in this antithesis, the caustic force of the last word is primarily directed not toward what's wrong with having a home, but with a false or partial way of construing it. One bad construction deserves another. But let us return to the prelapsarian one.

Something you somehow haven't to deserve . . . Therefore not an earned right, or desert, but a natural one, to be acknowledged along with one's personhood or humanity. Still, *"it all depends on what you mean by home,"* and thereby some home, somewhere, or any particular home (which might certainly lead to conflicts, if two people claim the right to the same home as theirs, and with some exclusivity). Is a right to some home, then, like some sort of extension of rights to and in one's body? An entity one claims as one's home may indeed coincide with some particular piece of property, rights in which, by law, one has in some way to deserve.

But this is surely not the point. The ultimately unspecified, not-quite-repressed definition of home evoked by the end of "The Death of the Hired Man" is as the human point of ultimate return. Perhaps the poet-in-the-reader might add, "*I* should have called it / The place you always come to when you die," the grave being what figured, in the King James Version's queer translation of the great passage in Ecclesiastes (12.5) about the decay of the body, as you'll remember: ". . . and the grasshopper shall be a burden, and desire shall fail: because man goeth to his long home, and the mourners go about the streets." And to that extent we are all delinquent farmhands of the earth, coming back to it when we return in the cyclic movement of dust (primordial mud and/or adamic clay) to dust. We will return to this text a bit further on, noting only at this point a particularly central instance of one way that we use the word "home" in modern English to mean "a place of origin returned to." I cannot help but notice the name of the Macintosh function key in front of me, pressing which will take me back to the top of my document: "HOME." In the more profoundly general case of death, the English language reinforces the sense of a particular enclosure with two associated names with the rhymes—almost a commonplace in the Renaissance—on "womb" and "tomb" (as if the *-omb* were the general human home).

It all depends on what you mean by home. This central issue—as I take it to be—for today's observations can apply variously to the word and the concept, to a matter of linguistics in English and to a matter of deep human consciousness. I wish to consider the ways in which these are interestingly related; but from the outset we may feel that the latter of these plagues the process of definition. My self, my body, my home—I don't know if this series should show some intervening terms; but it is clear that "home" belongs toward the very beginning of it, rather than toward the end occupied by "my favorite chair," "sandwich," "my [half-read] newspaper." But "it all depends on what you mean by home" could also be a lawyer's remark, in re, say, the law's word for "home"—not unoccluded access to a somehow privileged place, nor the acknowledgment of its privileged relation to you by others, but where simply you are at legally, as a citizen, as a social agent.

The active word here is "domicile." "Domicile" is defined by *Black's Law Dictionary* as "That place where a man has his true, fixed, and permanent home and principal establishment, and to which whenever he is absent he has the intention of returning. . . . The permanent residence of a person or the place to which he intends to return though he may reside elsewhere." This intention to return—perhaps marked by possessions left at a residence with intent to return to them—is crucial to the legal notion of *necessary domicile,* "that kind of domicile which exists by operation of law, as distinguished from voluntary domicile or domicile of choice."[2] In other words, "Home is the place where, for its jurisdiction / A court says where you're from." The *domicile of choice* alluded to is what we construe a home to be: "Home is the place where, when you want to stay there / They have to say you are." For the law, necessary domicile can frequently prevail over domicile of choice, and in a larger sense, we might say that our bodies-in-the-world are our domicile of choice. (This is vainly opposed to Nature's overriding claim that we are mere sojourners in them, merely residing there, while our true domicile is the earth.)

Also to be distinguished are two more metaphorical instances of legal home: *Corporate domicile,* "the center of corporate affairs and place where its functions are discharged" (corporations "have" homes in a very different sense from persons having them), or—to follow the paradigm—"Home is the place that's haunted by that ghost / We call a corporation." More relevant to the present discussion perhaps is that other institutional concept, *matrimonial domicile,* "Wherever either one may be, home's where / The marriage always is" (perhaps it's more a matter of *in rem*).

And finally, there is that most mythologically pregnant among the distinctions drawn by legal language, the *domicile of origin,* defined as "the home of the parents," or "Home is the place which you were been born into / Wherever else you go." The ways in which domicile of choice ceases to be coextensive with domicile of origin are part of the story of the developing

---

[2] Domicile for purposes of jurisdiction of a court would be an instance of this. Thus (from *Mas v. Perry,* 489 F2d 11396 95th Circ. 1974) a woman who formerly lived in Mississippi goes to Louisiana to graduate school, then moves to Illinois; she intends to move back to Louisiana so that her husband can complete a degree, and has no idea where she will live after that. The court holds that she is domiciled in Mississippi, for all that. Or, hypothetically, X moves from his home in New York to California to be with a terminally ill parent, renting an apartment nearby, hoping to stay there until the parent's death, then return to New York. But he is necessarily domiciled in California, since he can't predict the exact date of the death and of his consequent return.

and growing self in modernity. Many of our modern fables deal with the child's need for a domicile of choice, however small, located within the larger circumference of the parental home; in the past, when reading led to both knowledge and imagination and hence to freedom, the child's own home was often the place where he or she could be alone with a book, a place both walled in with privacy and far outrunning, in imaginative space and possibility, the walls of the household that could protect, but not contain, it. The central dialectic of the wall as boundary (rather than as bearing structural member) involves the price paid, in the hard cash of being walled in, for walling out the unwanted. Here emerges the important relation of safety and freedom that Simon Schama aligns, in his discussion of seventeenth-century Dutch culture, with the concept of home and world.[3]

Many of the questions of "what you mean by home" depend upon specification of locus and extent, in what might be likened to a set of Emersonian conceptual concentric circles. The outermost one, for the time being, let us call the surface of the planet, which can certainly qualify as being home realm—what in German is called *Heimat*, or native land— enough for any returning astronaut. The law's "necessary domicile" will almost invariably designate a state or a county in the United States, without specifying any smaller enclosure of space, rights to use that space (acquired by ownership or rental or whatever), etc. Construing "home" often entails considering concentricities radiating outward, starting from a smallest central point—in modernity it is the body as a home for the self (indeed, perhaps even a temple of that self, built to enclose its cult image) instead of, as in orthodox Christianity, a sort of prison farm which one's soul didn't own but was forced by nature to rent. It is only with Descartes that modern skepticism starts wondering just what sort of knowledge of, control over,

---

[3] Simon Schama, *The Embarrassment of Riches* (New York: Knopf, 1987), pp. 375–480.

housekeeping skills and responsibilities for—indeed, even what sort of possession of—its bodily home consciousness may be said to have. And indeed, the cessation of prolonged but temporary pain, partial paralysis, or muscular dysfunction makes us feel as if we had been somehow displaced in our bodies, to which now we had returned home.[4]

This range of concentricities is interestingly marked in German by the range of senses of the word for "home," *Heim,* from the widened boundaries of *Heimat* to the extremely constricted notion of secrecy, let alone mere privacy, in the extended form *Geheim.* The feeling that one's home is itself really the center of a series of radiating circles of hominess becomes most apparent when we consider how one returns to a slightly different sense of "home" from the one which one ventures forth from. The Greek word *nostos,* meaning a homeward journey, probably derives from an Indo-European base that means only "a safe return"; it survives on loan to English only through the interestingly distorted "nostalgia." This word originated in a Swiss medical treatise of 1688 as a translation of the Swiss-German *Heimweh,* considered as a mode of something like melancholia.[5] We designate by it not literal "homesickness" but a strange and perhaps not quite legitimate extension thereof, a longing for a time and not for a place, and perhaps a time that one knows like E. A. Robinson's Miniver Cheevy (who "loved the Medici, / Albeit he had never seen one; / He would have sinned incessantly / Could he have

---

[4] But to push this one step further and suggest that one cannot be at home in one's mind, goes past the point of functional agency here. I think that one must be oneself in order to feel at—be at—home, where safety, privacy, etc. are characteristic of the ambience. In other words, I have only been talking about relatively sane persons throughout.

[5] Johannes Hofer, *Dissertatio de Nostalgia oder Heimweh* (Basel, 1688). There is a good discussion of some of these feelings about exile, enforced or elected, in Alan D. McKillop, "Local Attachment and Cosmopolitanism—The Eighteenth-Century Pattern," in *From Sensibility to Romanticism,* ed. Frederick W. Hilles and Harold Bloom (New York: Oxford University Press, 1965), pp. 191–200.

been one"[6]) from literary or historical hearsay. But in the *Odyssey*, the *nostos*, the journey toward and arrival at home, almost becomes an end in itself, and we find Odysseus on Calypso's pleasure isle wanting "to reach my house and to see the day of my return" (*oikade t'elthemenai kai nostimon hêmar idesthi*, 5.219–220). Elsewhere, too (5.115), "to reach his high-roofed house [*oikon es hypsorophon*] and his native land [*patrida gaian*]" we feel that to translate *oikos*, "house," as "home" might be almost allegorizing. (To feel how this can be true, one should imagine the word "homecoming" as if it meant what it does to us, but without there being any English word "home" at all, and that its first syllable designated nothing.)

Of our own word "home" we are led to observe here that the sense of *nostos* as a return to a point of origin inheres in some of our modern derived uses of our word, whether in the homely baseball designation of a home base which one contrives, even strives, to leave only in order to complete a *nostos*, or in the further extended sense of a goal or *telos* or target of activity, whether in the instance of an arrow or a rhetorical point "hitting home" or, as early as 1625, in Bacon's epistle dedicatory to his *Essays*, where he remarks that now that his newer and revised essays have been published, thereby "as it seemed they came home to Mens Business, and Bosomes."

The necessity for revising or redifining the locus of one's own home is important in many central heroic stories we have told about our origins. We are all the children of Adam and Eve, who were at home everywhere there was for them; it was only by losing this privileged human place forever that they entered a world in which they would have to internalize, and go on successively internalizing, the place-of-being-at-home, as it were. At first, this is literally a matter of technology, for which there was no more need in the Edenic environment than a

[6] Edwin Arlington Robinson, "Miniver Cheevy," from *The Town Down the River* (1910).

fetus *in utero* "needs" a prosthesis. It is only after the Fall from perfection into nature that "being-at-home" could ever be localized in something like a house. What Joseph Rykwert has so revealingly written about "Adam's house in Paradise"[7] applies to the visions and desires of fallen, natural human consciousness. Even the crucial distinction inside/outside had not become so invested with human hopes and fears, and the consequent dialectic of walling-in and -out I alluded to earlier; it remained in Paradise no more than a possible option of pleasant pattern and playful design. From the Edenic standpoint, Adam and Eve had no house because they were so purely at home.

Milton in *Paradise Lost* (book 9) implies that the very first bit of technology to ward off homelessness occurs even within Eden: with the first flush of sexual guilt and of feeling not at home in their bodies, Adam and Eve "with what skill they had" (line 1112) housed their shame in fig-leaved dress. Even more remarkably, Milton seems to sketch out the entire subsequent history of the conceptualization of home, from a concrete locus in a hut of some kind, built "with what skill" the historical moment had, to a fully metaphoric transformation. Just before the expulsion, Adam is told that ultimately he will "possess / A paradise within thee, happier far" (12.586–587; and note that "possess" means, all too literally, to contain); and Eve reciprocally redefines home not as a sheltered or contained place, but as the presence of the only other person: "In mee is no delay; with thee to go / Is to stay here; without thee here to stay, / Is to go hence unwilling," she says to Adam as they are about to set forth, with the world "all before them," into natural history. It is almost as if, for Milton, the essence of the original, paradigmatic condition of being-and-feeling-at-home consisted in the unfallen matrimonial domicile, that the relation between two persons generated a space and an

---

[7] Joseph Rykwert, *On Adam's House in Paradise: The Idea of the Primitive Hut in Architectural History,* 2d ed. (Cambridge, Mass.: MIT Press, 1981).

enclosure which superseded literal emplacement. They leave
their lost Paradise bearing the invisible germ of at-homeness
which will flower when they have by hard labor wrenched,
urged, twisted a place of dwelling out of the earth.

In another sort of heroic tale of departure from home,
Abram leaves the northern land of Hur to find and make a
new home that will be (and for this he is renamed *Av-raham*,
"father of multitudes") a future *Heimat* but only after long
years of being not at home. The outward journey of Exodus is
neither a *nostos* of return, nor a circular, continuing nomadic
motion; it is rather a directed wandering, a quest for a single
ultimate home by a people who had long since forgotten their
original tribal one. Virgil's Aeneas bears his father on his back
out of the burning ruins of their old home of (not so much
"in") Troy to find and found a new Troy in Italy, dispossessing
its older inhabitants by conquest. Even as his precursor
Odysseus eschews a number of wonderfully comfy or elegant
or exciting places of sojourn for his true royal home of Ithaca,
so Aeneas moves on ruthlessly past the various attractions of
What Might Have Been. In his recent study of the ways in
which Old English literature constituted its culture's history,
Nicholas Howe has explored the relevance of Exodus to the
stories told by the Anglo-Saxons of how they "were a chosen
people to whom a promised land had been entrusted by virtue
of their migration."[8] But from the picaresque tale through the
nineteenth-century *Bildungsroman* to major modern romances
like *Moby-Dick, Huckleberry Finn, Kim,* and countless others, the
contingent heroes of bourgeois modernity have left the homes
that they felt were no longer truly theirs to wander in search of
a home not for a future nation of multitudes but for their own
multitudinous selves. Our stories, then, tell us that we have all
been Bedouin at some point; it is as if the abstract "home" we
carried with us in our wanderings—the way Aeneas was said to

[8] Nicholas Howe, *Migration and Mythmaking in Anglo-England* (New Haven: Yale
University Press, 1989), p. 180.

have carried his original Penates or household gods[9] out of Troy with him—then could possess and inhere in the actual houses we built, as if they were thereby somehow ensouled.

I wish to consider now another aspect of the problem of "what you mean by home," that is, what our English word "home" really means. It is possible that the very agenda of this entire conference could not be framed in anything but English, German, Dutch, or another Germanic language. The relation between "house" and "home" has become complicated in contemporary usage by a number of ironic reversals of original meaning. The common—and, unlike many common expressions, vulgar—use of "home" as a euphemism for "house" is by and large the linguistic waste product of the American real-estate industry. Literate people can be reminded of how continually we repress our disgust at this particular vulgarity as when, for example, a student of mine recalls a Chinese emigré academic who had taught her in college reading aloud in disbelief an ordinary sign: "*Homes for Sale?* How can you buy or sell a home? Home is [and he groped for the formulation] . . . memories."

There were probably two pressures at work on the replacement of "house" by "home" in the real-estate business. One is simply hyperbolic and more benign: as early as 1835 the celebrated versifier Felicia Hemans's immediately and subsequently famous lines about "The stately homes of England! How beautiful they stand" still referred to ancestral houses, but easily shifted its ambience to bourgeois aspirations. And thus, an account in *Harper's Magazine* of 1882 refers to "a lovely drive . . . bordered with homes, many of which make pretensions to much more than comfort," while seven years later a real-estate advertisement in the *Kansas City Times and*

---

[9] Their name derives from *penus*, or "storehouse," and in the most ancient times had been, according to Michael Grant in *Roman Myths* (New York: Scribner's, 1971), p. 79, "the principal objects of the cult maintained by every Roman household, in which they represented the forces or powers that each family honoured to make sure it had enough food every day."

Star boasts "For rent, a fine home at 1223 Broadway." On the other hand, the euphemistically shortened form "house" for "whore house" or "house of prostitution" undoubtedly urged the substitution as well.[10] It is perhaps with a sense of this developing substitution that Edgar A. Guest, the popular homely versifier of the *Detroit Free Press,* had even before World War I been able to proclaim that "It takes a heap o'livin' in a house to make it home."

Needless to say, ordinary users of "home" = "house" are today unaware of how strange the equation might seem—I remember myself, as a child of Manhattan, referring without question or wonder to my parents' or a friend's parents' apartment as "my (or Billy's) house," but only in the sense of, say, "*chez moi (ou Billy).*" One may nonetheless observe how the multiple resonances of the word "home" may possibly confuse purely practical argument, for example, the debate among various reformers as to whether homelessness is simply houselessness or something more abstract—institutionally or spiritually. If a "home" is something you can buy, then that appears to be all there is to it. In any event, there is no word so loaded as "home" in the Romance languages, and English (or German, etc.) sentences containing the word are always variously translated.

It is particularly interesting in this regard to observe the role of the Latin word *focus,* meaning "hearth" or "fireplace," which even in classical times serves as a metonymy for "household" or "family." In Romance languages, the *focolare domestico, le foyer familial, el hogar,* perhaps the Portuguese *lar,* all retain this sense.[11] But certainly the hearth as the center or focus of the

[10] In ironic contrast with this is the early instance of "home," in the 1830s, apparently referring to a barroom or tavern or public house, probably to avoid a tavern tax on entities so named.

[11] The modern uses of "focus" in English, involving a center of attention, a sort of internal cynosure or, indeed, what has been "homed in on," all seem to derive from Kepler's first use of it in geometric senses in 1604, although he may have been influenced by an earlier use of it in connection with a parabolic mirror, whose "focus" is at its hottest point (and thus the connection with fire).

home is notable in literature; from Athena's remark to Zeus at the beginning of the *Odyssey* (1.58–59) that Odysseus longs "to behold if only the smoke springing up from his land" (*kapnon apothrôskonta noêsai hês gaias*) through its recollection by the Renaissance poet Joachim Du Bellay in a canonical locus of nostalgia,[12] "Quand revoiray-je, hélas, de mon petit village / Fumer la cheminée: et en quelle saison, / Revoiray-je le clos de ma pauvre maison / Qui m'est un province, et beaucoup d'avantage." (Although this mode of preferring one's Local to the culture's Central gets short shrift from Robert Burton, in his *Anatomy of Melancholy,* who declares that " 'Tis a childish humour to hone after home, to be discontent at that which others seek. . . .") In many of our representations of our lives, home is where the hearth is, just as the other element of Du Bellay's longing, the homeliness and lowliness of home contrasted with the grandeur of, in his case, Rome, shows up continually in our literature, the central American text probably being the aria from Sir Henry Rowley Bishop's opera of 1839, *Clari, or the Maid of Milan,* which begins " 'Mid pleasures and palaces tho' we may roam / Be it ever so humble, there's no place like home." (Only in English, it will be noted, does "home" not only rhyme with "Rome" and "roam," but lurks in the name of the eternal domicile of origin of all our literature, Homer.)

We know that words are used without regard to their own origins save by pedants and sometimes poets, but it is instructive when considering linguistic and social constructions of "home" to consider the etymologies of some common words that touch on it. From the (hypothetical) Indo-European base *weik*, designating a clan, a social unit above that of the household, we get not only the Greek word for "house," *oikos*, but the Latin *villa*, a country house or farm, and *vicus*, meaning a quarter or neighborhood in a city, whereas the familiar *domus*

---

[12] The famous sonnet from his *Regrets*, beginning "Heureux qui, comme Ulysse, a fait un beau voyage."

possesses and generates all those meanings of house and household that become even more independently manifest in Romance languages, and on loan in English from "domicile" and "domestic" to "dominate," "dame," and "domain"—in modern Western languages, both dominion and economics begin at home.[13]

Our resonant Germanic word "home" (*Heim, ham, heem,* etc.) seems to derive from an original Indo-European **kei,* implying lying down, a bed or couch, and something dear or beloved, which also yields "haunt" and even "cemetery" (from Greek *koiman,* "to put to sleep"). The metaphorical implication of the semantic change is that home is a place to lay your head. And yet the Anglo-Saxon *ham* that is the ancestor of our word designates a village or town, an estate or possession. It is rather the word "house" which has always had the sense of "home" embedded in it. "House" (with its cognates) itself is strange in that it has no base in Indo-European, but belongs to that group of Germanic words of no known origin and that have always apparently meant exactly what they now mean—words like "arm" and "sea," for example. A house was always a building for human habitation, and most often the dwelling place of a family; all of the subsequent extensions of the term to cover various sorts of public building arise, not unsurprisingly, in the fourteenth century and after.

The semantic energy of the English word "home" has been charged particularly in the last three centuries by the interanimation of the various instances of "what you mean by home." That extended sense of the legal "domicile of origin,"

---

[13] The trace of a sense of **weik* in one extended use of our very different word "house" can be seen in the English phrase "house of X," meaning patrilineal line, whether of kingship, lordship, or bourgeois possession of a business. The Russian *rodia* (= mother- or father- or birth-land, ancestral land, etc.) deriving from *rod* (= kin, kind) is opposed to *dom* (= house) and is even more strongly differentiated from *priut* (= asylum, shelter). In these brief observations, I have not been able to touch on anything beyond Indo-European, but it might be noted that these derivations move in various directions: I am told that the modern Turkish *yurt* (= tent) contracts down from the wider reaches of the Old Turkic word for "country" or "fatherland."

of home as the end as well as the beginning of all journeys, resounds through the phrase from Ecclesiastes mentioned earlier, "and man goeth to his long home." This translates the Hebrew for "eternal dwelling" (*beit olamo: bayit,* designating a house or housing, sheltering structure, generally gets extended to mean various sorts of private or public buildings but, in another direction, to mean a household or a family). And as is frequently the case with the poetic texture of the King James Version, an inadvertent ghost metaphor arises from the modern reader's misconstruing of the earlier English. "Long" thus becomes dimensional rather than durational, and "long home" the final, horizontal dwelling of the grave, the place of dust returned to, the place that really was our home all along.

On the other hand, we may remember Wordsworth's skylark, in his sonnet, who flies so high that the poet first wonders whether its "heart and eye" are with some ultimate vanishing point or with its nest on the ground; but he then concludes that the bird, as an emblem of wisdom—but we might rather say of fully self-conceived life—confounds the question, in being "Type of the wise who soar, but never roam, / True to the kindred points of Heaven and Home."[14] The implication that a home, and an inconceivably distant point toward which imaginative energies and enterprise aspire, are somehow kindred suggests an important parable of modernity: the journey out is as much part of the heroic *nostos* as the journey back. This formulation may be more interesting than the mere Neoplatonic reversal of the "Heaven, which is our home" (that is, the soul's: the body's remains, as it were, "Dust, which is our home") of Wordsworth's earlier great "Immortality" ode.

An individual's idea of his or her home can embrace so many of the different senses touched on above. At the same time, any one of them may seem on one occasion or another to be more essential: is home the place where you lay your head, eat

[14] William Wordsworth, "To a Skylark" (1825).

your supper, do your work, ignore your work, make love, experience being greeted, if only exuberantly by one's dog, problematically by one's cat, or even more mutely by one's possessions, feel safe, feel well, instruct one's children? For Georg Simmel, making a home is a unique piece of women's work, bringing into being something concrete and institutional both, rather like a work of art: "The home is an aspect of life and at the same time a special way of forming, reflecting, and interrelating the totality of life."[15] It will also be remembered how a specific local home may cease to be a place one feels at home in; this may entail reinterpreting it as a mere "domicile of origination," and then making one's own private version of a biblical or Virgilian quest for a new, or true, one.

The world of nature does not necessarily owe one a home; we must in fact construct them, even if only by—in that other sense of the word—construing some bit of naturally afforded shelter as our home. In this, I suppose, cats are our great domestic teachers. Whereas our dogs inhabit our lives, our cats inhabit our dwellings, and are constantly making themselves at home in all sorts of regions and spaces, conforming and causing to conform in ever-renewing instances. But we moderns talk as if we feel that the world of other people does indeed owe everyone a home, or at least some material object to house a home in. And it may be that being a person entails being able to be, and having to be, at home, in the world at large and, by extension, in a successively narrowing set of loci.[16]

[15] Georg Simmel, "Female Culture" (1911), in *Georg Simmel: On Women, Sexuality and Love,* tr. and ed. Guy Oakes (New Haven: Yale University Press, 1984), pp. 93–94. Here also he observes more generally, "At least within the more advanced culture of Europe, there is no interest, no gain or loss of either an internal or an external sort, and no domain affected by individuals that does not, together with all other interests, merge into the unique synthesis of the home."

[16] I wonder here, though, at the implications of William James's observation, of which Richard Poirier reminds me, that "All 'homes' are in finite experience; finite experience as such is homeless" ("Pragmatism and Humanism," in *Pragmatism* [Cambridge, Mass.: Harvard University Press, 1978], p. 125.)

In this regard, it might be observed that another important characteristic of home is that "Home is the place where when you have to go there / The way they talk is yours." The matter of language cannot be overlooked, and 'here again the outwardly radiating circles of enclosure of different spheres of homeliness move out from the idiolect of the household—its private nuanced version of the most local language, which would include both the allusive modes and the allusive materials of its forms of talk—to the dialect of the tribe, as it were. But being at home in, and with, a language is a most complex matter: it may be that there are certain modes of periodic estrangement from certain aspects of one's native speech that can occasion poetry in it, for example. The whole question of language in, and as, home is one whose importance can only be acknowledged, rather than detailed, here.

"Home" can perhaps be construed even as the site, and the seat, of civilization itself. Plato, who seems to want the citizen to be at home only in his *polis,* and who prescribes in the *Laws* (8.848) that every inhabitant of his Just City have a country house and a town house, would not want to associate our Germanic sense of "home" with its withdrawals into the safe-houses of our dwellings or, even further, of our post-Cartesian bodies with the houses, which are more for him counters in a game of just allocation.

This brief exploration of some of "what you mean by home" might conclude with home as the very place of such explorations, the thinker's and writer's home. The cloister and the cell as home places of meditation and work are reflected in secular modernity by the idea of the writer's home, character-ized by Montaigne as that *arrière-boutique* or storeroom to which one retires from the outside world of family, bed, and board of the rest of his house. The young European or American bourgeoise might be said to retire in sequence from the household to her room to the pages of her dear dairy. Ultimately, we can see what looks like a conscious revision both of this and of Montaigne's notion in T. W. Adorno's

implication that the ultimate home or study of the deracinated
modern writer and thinker is not only on the pages of his text
itself but in the matter inscribed there:

> In his text, the writer sets up house. Just as he trundles papers,
> books, pencils, documents untidily from room to room, he
> creates the same disorder in his thoughts. They become pieces
> of furniture that he sinks into, content or irritable. He strokes
> them affectionately, wears them out, mixes them up, re-
> arranges, ruins them. For a man who no longer has a homeland,
> writing becomes a place to live. In it he inevitably produces, as
> his family once did, refuse and lumber. But now he lacks a
> store-room, and it is hard in any case to part from left-overs. So
> he pushes them along in front of him, in danger finally of his
> filling his pages with them.[17]

But we might conclude with the high household of
philosopher-nobles that we might all be, in Emerson's
wonderful appraisal of the economy of material and function
and how it runs out of hand. This great passage from his essay
"Nature" also constitutes one of the best comments I know on
the complex relations between the means and ends of material
"house" and more transcendent "home." It propounds thereby
a fitting cautionary parable for our very proceedings in these
discussions, that have required a place to house them, but must
escape the bondage to materials, constructions, and artifacts
that those requisites all too easily afford—we do need to hire a
hall, but we had damned well better say something worthwhile
there:

> This palace of brick and stone, these servants, this kitchen, these
> stables, horses and equipage, this bank-stock, and file of
> mortgages; trade to all the world, country house and cottage by
> the waterside, all for a little conversation, high, clear and
> spiritual! Could it not be had as well by beggars on the highway?
> No, all these things came from successive efforts of these

---

[17] T. W. Adorno, *Minima Moralia*, tr. E. F. N. Jephcott (London: NLB, 1974), p. 87.
But also see Adorno's remark earlier, p. 39, to the effect that "It is a part of morality
not to be at home in one's home," and cf. the observations of George Kateb elsewhere
in this issue.

beggars to remove friction from the wheels of life, and give opportunity. Conversation, character, were the avowed ends; wealth was good as it appeased the animal cravings, cured the smoky chimney, silenced the creaking door, brought friends together in a warm and quiet room, and kept the children and the dinner-table in a different apartment. Thought, virtue, beauty were the ends; but it was known that men of thought and virtue sometimes had the head-ache, or wet feet, or could lose good time whilst the room was getting warm in winter days. Unluckily, in the exertions necessary to remove these inconveniences, the main attention has been diverted to this object; the old aims have been lost sight of, and to remove friction has come to be the end. . . .[18]

Emerson implicitly reminds us of how humanly insubstantial our constructions of localization may be, and that placing, locating, housing are by no means necessarily homing.

[18] Ralph Waldo Emerson, "Nature" (1844), in *Essays and Lectures* (New York: Library of America, 1983), p. 552.

House and Home

BY JOSEPH RYKWERT

Home is where one starts from. That much is obvious. A home is not the same as a house, which is why we need two different words. Does a home need to be anything built at all, any fabric? I think not. Home could just be a hearth, a fire on the bare ground by any human lair. That may well be the one thing that nobody can quite do without: a fireplace, some focus. After all, if a home had no focus, you could not start from it.

Home is at the center. For many of us, a hearth marks that focus from which we start. Its fire need not necessarily burn in the fireplace of the living room or the hall, since even where it is not needed for warmth, fire can shelter from terrors of the encroaching night. Predators fear it. As human beings seem unable to subsist on raw food alone for long, cooking is also essential. In the hottest desert or tropical swamp, you may have to make a fire in order to eat. Eating is usually done close to it, so that eating and sleeping together have come to define the household: the old English marriage service speaks of a common bed and board as the summary of the life of the nuclear family. For many of us the focus may be a kitchen range.

Taming fire is *the* origin of culture, the token of control over environment. Fire is also the mark of settlement. Hearths and middens, kitchen-refuse heaps, are some of the earliest traces of human habitation—the very notion of home seems to have grown round the hearth. It follows that a notion so deeply rooted in human experience should have its appropriate term in every language: yet translators have always complained about the difficulty of finding an exact equivalent for it—particularly in Romance languages.

Take French. "His home" is usually rendered by *chez lui*, and "my home" is *chez moi*. Although *chez* is a preposition, not a noun like "home," it is a corruption of the Latin noun *casa*, a hut or cottage, something humble. Where we use "house" the Romans said *domus*; which could also mean domesticity, household effects, homeliness—even peace—and is as close to "home" as you will get in Latin. And yet Latin also provides two other words for the house: as a thing built, *aedes*, and as a place of rest—which home so emphatically is—*mansio*, from *maneo*, I remain or abide, and it is from that word that the French get their *maison*, which in turn translates into our "house."[1]

The Greeks called the house *domos*, which sounds almost the same as the Latin: yet the Greek home was *oikos*, a word from which we get a whole range of concepts, such as economy. The business of building a fabric, of sheltering the home, as it were, was *oikodomein*: the words were run together to emphasize their separate meaning.

The very similar words arrived in classical languages by different routes. The Romans got their *domus* from the Old Indo-European root *dem*, family; while the Greeks derived it from exactly the same-sounding root, meaning to build. That the two different words moved so close together, linguists now tell us, was a coincidence, but it seems to me to indicate an affinity which is not just accidental.

Or to move outside Europe: the Chinese dealt with such matters quite differently when they inscribed the character for "fire," *huô*, under the thatched radical for "roof" or "hut," *miǎn*, so that the result was *zai*, "disaster." On the other hand, if they inscribed "pig," *shì*, beneath that same radical, they suggested well-being or—at any rate—easy

---

[1] See Emile Benveniste, *Indo-European Language and Society* (Coral Gables, Fla., 1973), pp. 241ff.

circumstance; the-pig-in-the-house, *jia,* which the character drew, read "home"—as well as "family."[2]

German might seem to provide the closest and the easiest translation into English: *Heim* is, after all, almost a homonym of "home"—yet the grammatically neuter *Heim* has a feminine *Heimat,* for which the English word is not really the "mother country," "motherland" which the dictionaries offer but the now more common "fatherland," which has a romantic and quite unarchaic sound; so that the familiar word acquires an alien association. Indeed, it was German-speaking Swiss mercenary soldiers who first suffered *Heimweh* in the fifteenth century, and it took the English another three centuries to name the unfamiliar sentiment "homesickness." Of course, the Germans, like the English, distinguish *Haus und Heim,* by which they signify not only all their possessions but their very citizenship of a place, to which the English equivalent would be "hearth and home."

Both English words, "house" and "home," are in turn heavily colored by a notion embedded in case law that the great Jacobean judge, Sir Edward Coke, enshrined in the dictum: "The house of everyman is to him as his castle and fortresse, as well as his defence against injury and violence, as for his repose."[3] A nineteenth-century legal historian cheapened it into "the Englishman's house is his castle,"[4] and this was adopted instantly as a slogan for all that is implied by the notion of a home. Almost imperceptibly the householder's legal rights were stamped on the land beyond—they moved from house to home.

---

[2] Edoardo Fazzioli, *Chinese Calligraphy: From Pictograph to Ideogram* (New York, 1987), p. 155. This is an archaic usage, however; the same word, *zai,* is now written as water-and-fire. Character spellings I have given here—following Fazzioli—are all archaic. Unfortunately, Chinese characters cannot be reproduced here.

[3] Sir Edward Coke, *Reports, 1600–1615* (London, 1738), V, 91b. He was, in fact, translating the Anglo-Norman adage of Sir William Stanford, *Les Plees del Coron: Divisees in plusiours Titles & Common Lieux* (London, 1567), p. 14 b.

[4] Edward A. Freeman, *The History of the Norman Conquest of England* (Oxford, 1873), 2: 82.

Without that move, I suspect the development of the suburbs in Anglo-Saxon countries could not have been possible.

Some distinction between home, the situation—with its implication of well-being, stability, ownership—as against a rather more inert notion of the house, persists in most languages, persists through very powerful cultural shifts and over vast distances. Its variation may be an indicator of differing mentalities, as well as of radical social innovation. Yet almost always *home* is at the centrifugal hearth, the fire burning at the center of my awareness, as its light once spread like a stain in the hostile night.

It is the family.

"House" means shelter, and implies edges, walls, doors, and roofs—and the whole repertory of the fabric.

"Home" does not require any building, even if a house always does. You can make a home anywhere: a little tinder, even some waste paper, a few matches, or a cigarette lighter is all you need. In our technically advanced civilization, it can be secured with less trouble (but a great deal of equipment) by a VCR tape, which will make flames leap up on your television screen at the push of a button.

But a house must be brick and timber, mortar and trowels, carpentry and masonry, foundations and topping off: and it requires taking thought.

Taking thought about building is one of several useful definitions of architecture—which is where I come in, I suppose; particularly as a common accusation against architects is that they fail to do just that. On the other hand, too much taking thought by architects is not considered entirely desirable either. Only too often in the last twenty years or so, they have been hectored about how wrong they had been to take on themselves the role of social thinkers and reformers; they should instead have got on with what has been called "packaging a life-style"; and should have done so in the most expeditious and agreeable way they might.

A "life-style," after all, is thrown up by the people: through it they instinctually and mutely declare their will and aspirations. Like the market, this popular "style" has its internal, imperious laws of life and growth which cannot be defied.

Without wishing to digress, I would like to remind you of a very popular slim book, full of beautiful images, published some years ago, which was called *Architecture Without Architects,* as if such a thing were not a contradiction in terms. It suggested that the shelters of monkeys and the dams of beavers were analogous to those of "untutored builders in space and time,"[5] nomads, peasants and suchlike, whose houses had evolved from those of the animals without any need for deliberation—like the animals, they worked by instinct.

A century earlier, the Reverend George Wood, who was a very prolific scientific popularizer, called an analogous, much bulkier book more accurately *Homes Without Hands,* and discussed animal dwellings only. The Viennese architect and wit Bernard Rudofsky, the author of my first book, admired the buildings of primitive people for their intuitive rightness, the way they seemed to "fit in" with nature. He echoed a belief common among historians of architecture that there was an unarticulated, immediate harmony between the primitive builder and his environment which had been lost by the overly reflective, brain-bound modern designer. School-trained architects, who take too much—or perhaps the wrong kind of—thought, not only go against the nature of place but also against that of the society in which they work.

Now, I suspect that if one were to investigate any of the human dwellings illustrated in Rudofsky's book, however "instinctual" they may appear, one would soon find that many were produced by specialist craftsmen who could be very articulate indeed about what they were doing. Their notions may have been framed in terms of legend, but their accounts of them would often contain the word "because."

Even when they merely followed a rule of thumb, and built

[5] Bernard Rudofky, *Architecture Without Architects* (New York, 1964), p. 16.

according to habit, the rule of thumb still had to be taught to be transmitted from generation to generation; and often such teaching had the character of initiation. It teaches by cross-reference between techniques of building and cosmogonies, or between stories about the origins of the tribe and the builder's skills. At their simplest, such references were often enshrined in the work songs in which people celebrated their efforts and the trouble to which the population of a settlement was put when building was a communal rather than a specialized activity; at their best, such songs could even turn the act of building, with its repeated rhythmic action, into a game and a festival.

Unlike even the most elaborate animal construction, human building involves decision and choice, always and inevitably; it therefore involves a project. A project may demand only a close adherence to a traditional type—but a type can almost always be specified in words: whether it is the Mongol *yurts* of skin and embroidered felt stretched over a wooden frame, or Eskimo igloos built up of blocks of ice, or the mere propped mats of Andaman Islanders or even the leaf shelters of pygmies in Central Africa—all these types can not only be "specified" by their builders and by their inhabitants, as I said, but also "justified," glossed in mythical terms, and given some specific legendary weight. However atrophied and ritualized that life-style may seem to us, building for them is never the "packaging of a life-style."

Moreover, "primitive" or "traditional" buildings always presuppose neighbors. An isolated nuclear family in such dwellings is not thinkable. Indeed, our word "home," like the German *Heim,* is sometimes thought to derive from the Indo-European root *kei,* "to lie or settle"—from which came the Greek *khomi,* which means a settlement, a village (as against a town), a rustic place and rustic festivals that extended into dances and play acting, which the Greeks (and therefore also we, following them) called "comedy," so that "home" becomes also a communal and neighborly manner of dwelling. A hermit may make a home for himself in isolation, of course—but for all that, human dwellings are always more or less communal.

However shabby and casual it may look, a rustic dwelling depends on being part of an articulated (I am even tempted to say an organic) layout; often a layout which was understood as a body with head and members into which the homesteads were "integrated."

I would argue further that a house, whether it is rural or urban, can be a true home only in such neighborly circumstances. While the lonely hearth will not quite make a home, therefore, yet the erection of the home-house into a castle which defies its neighbors, and may be seen as quite separate from the public realm, makes it much less of a home. Or, in other words, an individual can have many houses, but only a person can make a home.

In the villages of preindustrial Europe, and to some extent also in the towns there, even in the early settlements of the New World, neighborliness was a normal condition. It was taken for granted as long as the body continued to be the metaphor for the body politic. However, about 1800 the new science of biology taught that the human body was just one kind of organic tissue among many. The notion of an *organic* substance—meaning any tissue containing protoplasmic carbon compounds—displaced that of the *organon*, the body as an instrument of a will or mind. By then the Industrial Revolution was already in full swing in the United States and in Great Britain, and the organizing of energy for production was seen as the overriding social good from which all other benefits would flow.

Industrialism was to bring vast benefits. Meanwhile, it would also involve much suffering: the version of social Darwinism which inspired many of the great industrialists of the nineteenth century—and therefore presided over the building and the rebuilding of cities—taught that progress was an organic process, that society developed following internal and inexorable laws, like those which governed the growth of plants; and that (by inference) the ills of the environment were the mere detritus of the great onward march—which one popular writer of the time called *The Martyrdom of Man.*[6]

Older images of a corporate city faded into an increasingly stiff and remote irrelevance before the imperatives of production. In the two principal English-speaking countries, the form and extent of cities grew in a way that had no precedent. Business was increasingly packed at the center; the perfecting of metal structure and the first safe elevators made ever-greater heights possible, and promoted the speculation in land values. In consequence, the main and usually older institutional buildings—town halls, government offices, law courts, churches—were soon dwarfed by the increasingly high monuments to enterprise. Those who profited most by these buildings (and what went on inside them) soon moved out of the darkening city centers; they built their castles and palaces in the surrounding countryside. They were followed by their most successful employees, and so on down the scale, until the dormitory suburb, where everyman's house truly was his castle, extended all round the tall urban core.

There was nothing new about the suburb, the *faubourg,* of course; even while city walls offered the only available security, areas outside the city gates were populated by those who, for one reason or another, were brave enough to escape city regulations and city taxes. When that security became something of an irrelevance, magnates who wanted to benefit from large landholdings within easy reach of the centers of power joined the riffraff. St. Honoré and St. Germain in Paris, Piccadilly and Bloomsbury in London, were crowded with palatial mansions from the sixteenth until the nineteenth century.

But the new industrial suburbs were quite different. Since they were not within walking distance of the city, they required transport. The upper crust of commerce and the middle

---

[6] William Winwood Reade, *The Martyrdom of Man* (London, 1872). There were many subsequent editions.

classes had taken over the land of the magnates who simultaneously moved to town houses and country ones, having parceled out their suburban palaces at vast profit. The riffraff had for the most part moved back into the city centers, since a concentration of urban workers was easier to batten on than the diffuse suburbanites. By the third quarter of the nineteenth century, the notion of the hearth-on-the-ground as the center of the house had been firmly grafted onto that of the house as everyman's castle. Put the essential hearth into everyman's castle, and you have the powerful commonplace of the suburban house. Such houses cannot be piled up, one on top of the other—the hearth has to be on the ground.

Building in height was forced on the older cities by their immoderate nineteenth-century growth. In Europe, the various *ensanches*—a term coined in Barcelona, like the very word *urbanism*, and by the same man, Idelfonso Cerdà[7]—were additions to (or rings around) older cities, so that historic centers continued to play the institutional role for the enlarged areas and populations, while in the New World very few towns had such points of reference.

Where (as in Washington) such reference was deliberately created on the scale of new and much larger cities but in a quasi-rural environment, it was to produce its own problems. The great majority of towns built in the New (as in the Old) World during the nineteenth century were gridded and undifferentiated tissues into which the new proletariat was herded, usually with disastrous results, and they in turn produced horrid new linguistic usages: housing reforms, housing questions, and housing schemes.

By the middle of the nineteenth century, housing became a word which signified doing good to the poor by providing them, institutionally, with houses in which they could make

[7] Idelfonso Cerdà's *Teoria general de la urbanización y aplicación de sus principes y doctrinas a la reforma y ensanche de Barcelona* was published in Madrid in 1867. Cerdà's plan was originally drawn up in 1859.

some kind of home. Some of these do-gooders were philanthropists, others (of whom Ebenezer Howard may have been the most interesting and the most successful) were planners and utopians. A few of them did see that the provision of places to live had in some way to be related to a physical structure which would in turn correspond to the articulated organization of older towns. Still, none foresaw the world population catastrophe that has overtaken our cities in the last quarter of this century, and through which we are still working and living.

Housing reforms and schemes spawned questions, ministries, administrations. Soon all this became more ambitious: "Homes for Heroes" was the program of the British housing administration after 1918; it was not an unqualified success, but it was echoed and amplified in the great rebuilding of war-ravaged countries after 1945. Architects went at it with a will. The notion of the *Existenzminimum*, which had been launched in the 1920s in Germany, had an enormous success in the '50s and '60s.

Architects tried to fit everything that went on in a "typical" household into a closely packed shell. It was as if they saw their business not as the provision of houses but the enclosure of Home, over which Frank Taylor and his motion-study was patron. They forgot the important moral which Karl Kraus once tried to instill in them, when he said that he expected of the city to provide him with water, gas, electricity, and working roads: *die Gemütlichkeit besorge ich* — I will supply the homeliness, he added.

Obsessed with the detailed working of the home where every movement was planned, where a bed would never stand under a window, and baby carriages could be stored away under the stairs, they forgot that their business was with house and not with home. It is, moreover, with house in context, whether in the town or in the country. For all their concern with the exact layout of the home, the assumption was somehow made by many of those concerned with planning and building that the point or the slab block would provide the answer to all the bulk problems of urban housing. A number of factors have brought disappointment to the planners. The most important is the deterioration of the social structure, for which they cannot be held responsible; which has been attributed to the loss of faith, the two-income family, or television—or a combination of all three. But almost equally weighty is the poor performance of the physical fabric of many of those buildings, their all-too-rapid decay.

I must therefore plead with my contemporaries to reassess the conjunction between house and home. Let the professionals recognize that their business is with the house, not with home; with structure, with physical fabric, with limits, with context.

Look at the real-estate advertising in New York papers with this in mind. If a home is offered you on the sixty-ninth floor of a pencil-sharp skyscraper, know for sure that the sidewalks and indeed the surroundings of the building will be the purlieus (if not the home) of the dispossessed, however many the varieties of marble which line its walls, or photo-eyes blink from its cornices.

The apartment in the New York point block is, in its luxurious and alienating way, no more welcoming or safer than quarters in municipal-housing slab blocks in the immediate postwar period, of which Pruitt-Igoe in St. Louis, dynamited by the authority that had paid for its erection twenty years earlier, has become the most infamous. In spite of that clamorous destruction, entire cities of slab-block housing have been built since—in Eastern Europe, in some African countries, and in South America. In the West, private developers have replaced the regimented slab with a chaos of points, which are sometimes decked out with fancy "classical" detailing, as if cosmetics of that kind had anything to do with the case. Others have tried to focus attention on the possible adaptation of the quasi-public spaces left over between skyscrapers; it is essential first-aid action, but in conceptual terms, it is like applying Band-Aid to a cut jugular vein.

The truth is that planners, developers, architects need to recognize again that they are not the creatures, nor yet the servants, of inexorable natural forces, but are in the business of taking thought about building. Architects may not be entitled to impose their utopian ideas on their clients—and yet, all those concerned with building must recognize that every foundation laid is always and inevitably a political act. The damage they can inflict is more grievous than that of a bungling surgeon or a physician. I would therefore like to see developers and housing directors liable in law for professional malpractice: not for the collapse of a building (for which the architect and engineer are almost always blamed anyway), but for putting up buildings which should be blown up—because they are so ugly, or because they damage the texture of urban life. The constraints of market forces or the alienating, capitalist conditions of labor are not an extenuating circumstance for our sins of commission.

The trouble is to find a suitable judge and jury. To exercise judgment, such a court would need to learn again, as we all need to, that the city is what we will it to be; it is our common act—not a piece of organic tissue growing at the behest of inflexible and barely comprehensible forces. This is a lesson which it will take many years to articulate and to apply. Perhaps in any case it is too late, our cities are no longer salvageable. I think it is worth trying. And the sooner we begin, the better.

EXILE: A KEYNOTE ADDRESS

Home moves us most powerfully as absence or negation. Homelessness and exile are among the worst of conditions, alienation and estrangement, the feelings of greatest despair.

Introduction

New York, the city of the homeless, is a good place to think about home, the simplest definition of which, I suppose, is "a roof over one's head." New York, a city of immigrants, is a good place in which to reflect on the concept of home, which is essentially not the destiny of our journeys but the place from which we set out and to which we return, at least in spirit. And the New School, or at least that part of it which was once known as the University in Exile, indeed of exiles, is an obvious place to talk about the exile's perception of home, as Breyten Breytenbach is about to do.

New York must be fuller than any other city I know of people who remember some other place from which they once came. Migration is not necessarily exile, though there is no sharp line that separates the economic migrant, even the one who eventually stays, from the exile who cannot go back but wants to. Both remain linked to the old country by the strongest bonds, the immigrants from the Dominican Republic who remitted $242 million per annum in the mid-1980s to their kin as much as the South African political exiles. Both, we may think, would have preferred not to leave their country if things had been different. Both talk about it and dream about it. Nostalgia is no longer the killing disease it once was when it was diagnosed as such by medical men among the Swiss peasant soldiers who hired themselves out abroad. New York proves how humanity has learned to live far from its roots, even under some of the least attractive conditions. But nostalgia, *Heimweh, mal du pays* still moves us.

But what exactly is it that moves us? Let me, as someone who has in his time moved from country to country, and is even now living that extraordinary life that has only been made possible by jet travel, direct-dial international phones, and fax, namely, to live almost simultaneously in two widely separated countries, reflect for a moment on this experience of looking back. From England to the Austria of my childhood, the Berlin of my early teens, from America to Europe: for it is still true that crossing the North Atlantic is, for most Europeans irrespective of their native country, a culturally more unsettling experience than crossing each other's borders.

Nostalgia means, or at least in my experience it has meant, two quite different things. Childhood experience is that of the home in the concrete sense of household, family, face-to-face relations. When I returned to the Vienna I had left at the age of 14 after almost thirty years, I found myself almost automatically looking for exactly those things: the houses or apartments where we had lived, the street down which I had walked to school, the station one got off to visit grandmother, and the route one went along from there to her apartment, past the café where grandfather used to go in the evening to play Tarock, and which bore the Homeric name Café Ilion. And I felt a sort of childhood joy when I discovered that nothing had changed, except for seeming just a little bit smaller than it had once been, and a childhood disappointment when it turned out that the Café Ilion was no longer where it had been and where it should have stayed. And even now Vienna still evokes home in this literal sense: *Heim*, not *Heimat*, in the German vocabulary. As I pass them, I look up at the window behind which I slept when I was woken one morning with the news that my father had died, I look down at the park by the Danube canal, where I was taken to play, and wonder what happened to the two steamers, the *Orel* and the *Sokol*, which used to pass along the canal from time to time.

But this is not so for adults who think of home. I am sure that for emigrants and exiles who come from the sort of communities where there is no sharp distinction between house, neighborhood, and town, the line between *Heim* and *Heimat* is fuzzy. That, after all, is still the attraction of Lake

Wobegon for those of us who have never lived in cities of less than a million inhabitants, except as students. But when most adults in exile remember where they came from, they remember *Heimat* and not the domestic hearth which defined the family home, at least until the era of central-heating boilers in the cellar. In the army, when people were asked where they came from—and this is the first question by which adults seek to situate each other among strangers—they named a city, a country, a province, not a house or a neighborhood. Emigrants formed and no doubt still form what in Yiddish is called *Landsmannschaften*, societies of people from the same *land*. That "land" may be small by modern standards—it may be no more than a middling city and its environment—but it is conceived of as a public universe. When expatriate Englishmen—colonial administrators in the past, or businessmen today—talk of going home or taking home leave, they do not mean to their domicile, which, if they have had good tax lawyers, they have been careful to give up, but England.

Here lies the ambiguity of the word which gives our conference its name. Or rather the contradiction inherent in it. For home in the literal sense, *Heim, chez soi*, is essentially private. Home in the wider sense, *Heimat*, is essentially public. It is almost always a social construction rather than a real memory, for the *Bialystoker landslayt* include not just the people who have come from that place but all manner of emigrants from villages and *shtetl* in the region who wouldn't have seen themselves as Bialystoker at home. As a French historian has said: the emigrants from the various villages of the Creuse department don't discover themselves as "Creusois" until they are in Paris. At the limit, as when we look back across oceans or generations not to a concrete *Heimat* such as that in the well-known German TV series, but to a *Heimatland* (which easily slips into being a *Vaterland* or fatherland), it becomes an imagined community.

When did home divide into *Heim* and *Heimat*? When did it come to include both the complementary and the opposite concept? I don't know. Perhaps this conference will throw light on the question.

Heim belongs to me and mine and nobody else. Anyone who has been burglarized knows the feeling of intrusion, of a private space violated. *Heimat* is by definition collective. It cannot belong to us as individuals. We belong to it because we don't want to be alone. Moreover, it doesn't need us. It goes on quite well without us, which is the tragedy of political exile.

However, unlike those who are permanently uprooted like descendants of African slaves in the New World; unlike diaspora people who have nowhere to go "back" to; unlike even third-generation Americans for whom the country of their ancestors isn't "home" but "roots," political exiles are people who can go back, who hope one day to go back, but whose relation to their homeland is particularly complex, because "home" for them is not just the "old country" but, if they are to return to it, must become in some sense a new country.

Breyten Breytenbach, poet, painter, political activist, and prisoner, has packed a multiple experience of exile into his fifty-one years: exile as an artist, as a white South African married to a Vietnamese wife in a society which made interracial marriage a crime, as a stranger in his own country, as a prisoner in solitary confinement in South Africa. He is perhaps the finest living poet in his language, Afrikaans. His *True Confessions of an Albino Terrorist* is one of the most powerful and moving books about political imprisonment produced in a country which has, unfortunately, been the occasion for much literature on this subject. He belongs to South Africa, as very few whites do; his family have been there for centuries. What does "home" mean for such a man, and in such a life? Breyten Breytenbach will, I hope, give our conference a dimension which it would not, it could not, have without his participation.

The Long March from Hearth to Heart

BY BREYTEN BREYTENBACH

> O toi qui vas à Gao:
> fais un détour par Tombouctou
> murmure mon nom à mes amis
> et porte-leur le salut parfumé
> de l'exilé qui soupire après
> le sol où résident ses amis,
> sa famille, ses voisins.

THESE WORDS were written by Ahmad Baba, a scholar of Islamic law, born 1556 in Timbuktu and died there in 1627. During his lifetime the Moroccans laid siege to the town and conquered it, thus destroying the last Songhay empire. Ahmad Baba was accused of fomenting a rebellion against the new rulers, captured, and taken in chains across the Sahara to Marrakesh, his place of exile. At the time Timbuktu was famous for its University of Sankore and scores of other schools. Today the learning and the creation and the institutions have been swallowed by the desert, more so still by sands of neglect and indifference. From the air the town resembles a few paltry crusts of bread floating in a vast bowl of milk. Dunes silently stalk the streets and cover the walls, which have taken on the color of dead roses. A big yellow bulldozer pushes the sand from the thoroughfares in an attempt to stall oblivion. The mosque looks like the mud-drippings from a giant hand. Not far from there UNESCO subsidizes a small documentation center where one can leaf through books such as Mahmud Kati's *Tarrikh al-Fattash* (Chronicle of the Seeker after Knowledge) and Abd al-Rahman as-Sadi's *Tarrikh as-Sudan* (Chronicle of the Sudan). The oldest book dates from

1204. These volumes are kept in the open air—perhaps the fiery desert tongue preserves them naturally. An approximate translation of Ahmad Baba's words, framed in the entrance to the documentation center, would be: "O you who go to Gao, do so by way of Timbuktu and murmur my name to my friends. Give them the fragrant greetings of an exile who sighs after the soil where his friends, his family and his neighbors reside."

I have started at the above point because the place and its history, and the loss of its history as memory itself is sanded over, seem to illustrate one of the traits of my theme. It is not so much a rending to be separated from your own, to be rendered ineffective as it were; no, the pain is in being disconnected from normalcy and eventually to become the living experience of the fact that exiled memory is the slow art of forgetting the color of fire.

The theme I've been asked to talk around—it is as old as a desert map—is exile. I do so most reluctantly: I dislike the manner in which the subject has been romanticized, with the exiled ones pitied and slobbered over by vicarious voyeurs. I abhor feeding the stereotyped expectations of exile as consisting of suffering and deprivation. Those who claim to be exiles themselves only too often purvey and reinforce the hackneyed perceptions. "Do feel sorry for us," they seem to say. "Blame us on history. Take on the responsibility for our survival." And for too many refugees this suspended state becomes an easy sentimental beat. They wallow in self-pity. All experience becomes frozen. On auspicious occasions they bring forth the relics and sing the cracked songs and end up arguing like parakeets about what "back home" was really like. They are dead survivors waiting for postcards from the realm of the living. The clock has stopped once and for all, the cuckoo suffocated on some unintelligible Swiss sound, and they will continue forever in terms of an absence which, naturally, is now embalmed and imbued with rosy dreams. They lose the language but refuse to integrate the loss, and accordingly will think less, with fewer words and only morbid references to suspend their thoughts from. They still assume it is possible to hold back the shifting dunes of time. In the meantime the condition of exile becomes a privileged status from which to morally and emotionally blackmail the world with special pleading. It becomes an excuse for defeat. It is a meal ticket. And yet—isn't it true as well that exile is a chance, a break, an escape, a challenge?

I'm not suggesting that I know more or better. The fact is that I've been skirting the issue—partly because of embarrassment at the false histrionics (and I distrust my own penchant for exploiting and manipulating the situation, I too am attached to the familiarity of the field, as to a known insecurity), partly because it obliges me to an uncomfortable self-analysis. Sometimes, quite often, it is better not to know. It would be disingenuous, however, to pretend to have no thoughts on the matter. But again, I cannot lay claim to any original contribution, or to a coherent analysis. I'm neither scholar nor theorist: what I have gleaned on the subject I can only express in elliptical or allusive terms, and often by platitude. One also becomes what is expected of you!

One way in which I've tried to approach the problem was to equate exile with writing, more precisely the creative act. Because it might as well be painting. By *writing* I mean the act of using shared matter—a convention, a texture, a set of references encapsulating the codes of communication—to define or invent a history, to secrete or enshrine a viewpoint or a conduit (call it the I), and to determine a future. Different media of painting partake, for me, of different languages. The matter, or language, could after all be more or less acquired, artificial, or spontaneous. Thus I always draw in Afrikaans, my mother tongue, which, because it is my mother tongue, is prerational. The only skill needed to draw is to sharpen the pencil. Maybe that is the only nonconditioned thinking man is capable of. I think in images and metaphors, which must complicate communication.

The individual creative act is certainly an attempt to make consciousness. This implies drawing upon memory. Memory, whether apocryphal or not, provides the feeding ground or the requisite space allowing for the outlining of imagination. Imagination is a biological necessity for inventing a future. The process is hazardous—but considerations such as free will, intentionality, escapism come into it, so that it can never be totally haphazard. Above all, the creative act aims to be narrative. The narrative is a feint in trying to come to grips with chaos. Sometimes the only pointer is the telling. If nothing else, I am telling the telling.

From the beginning everything is. Consciously creating or "discovering"—uncovering by chance or on purpose—implies structuring. Writing is a process and therefore a discipline. It is the discipline of using illusion by way of capturing the real. There comes a point, of course, where true reality is an illusion. You could then call it the illusion of understanding. In due time the two may merge. There will then be no more dichotomy, no dialectic, and finally one has death. Or one has become death. This doesn't mean that the writing ceases. On the contrary, one accedes to the homeland of perpetual movement. In life you may be hovering on the lip of silence; in death—which is but a matter of misjudging the distance—the silence is given lips.

By the way, I recently read somewhere that Appius had expressed the wish that the letter z be banned from the alphabet, "since, in pronouncing it, one is imitating the teeth of a dead person." Similarly, that the proofreader's sign for "to delete" is a bastardized version of the Greek thêta, the first letter of thanatos, which emperors were in the habit of scribbling in the margin opposite the names of those sentenced to death.

I should perhaps have entitled my paper: From the Unconscious via the Subconscious to the Conscious, and from There to the Unconscious—and all of the above over the killing fields of reality.

I have suggested that writing is a structure for shaping experience past and present and future. It is to my mind also a means of sharpening the awareness of the interaction between the observer, or the I, and the work of the environment. Let me propose a few preliminary statements pointing at the contradictory redundancy and fertility of the state of exile: To be in exile is to be free to imagine or to dream a past and the future of that past. To be an exile is to be written.

It is hard to let go of this line of reasoning. The exile, after all, is also marked by the obsession of playing out his or her own guts. Jean Genet is his last book, published after his death (*Un Captif Amoureux*), has some remarkable passages on writing, and furthermore links that reflection to a social reality. I am translating freely and adding my own annotations: "The blacks in white America," Genet says, "are the signs writing history; on the white page they are the ink giving it meaning." And later: "Translucence and whiteness [of the page] have a stronger reality than the signs which disfigure them. . . . Whiteness remains the support [backing? environment?] of writing, and it constitutes its margins, but the poem is composed of the absent blacks—*you may say the deads if you wish*—anonymous, the articulation of which will make up the poem whose sense will elude me, but not its realness." Thus one may compare the written page to a white ground with black skeletons.

Roland Barthes writes: "Life is but language." Then he continues, rather ambiguously: "La mort c'est l'évènement qui sort du langage." I understand this to mean: Death is the happening—or enunciation—which flows from the language, its inevitable conclusion; or: Death is the event outside and beyond language, and thus unspeakable.

All of the foregoing, you may have noticed, is posited on the notion of contradictions. It has been my purpose to try and reconcile the contradictions which I have experienced, to go beyond them, to dissolve them. Using exile as a *pense-bête*, I have endeavored to make of that condition a survival technique. In

other words, to wipe out the self. One contradiction which refuses to go away is obviously that the exile cannot think himself
loose from the process of alienation: he cannot ascertain whether
what he has become is the natural result of aging, whether it
was exile which gave his tongue this bitter taste, or whether he
used and abused this station to become a foreigner, a *Luftmensch*,
in my instance a hypothetical *homo sud-africanus*. How would I
have been different if it hadn't been for expatriation?

Many platitudes can be employed to describe the sharpened
sense of loss and the increased awareness of gain—and I have
used most of them at one time or another. To be away from
your natural environment is to be deprived of ever again
functioning completely and fitting in instinctively. No other
surroundings can replace the shared and unquestioned and
thereby indigenous feeling of belonging made up of smells,
sounds, gestures, and natural mimicry.

In the beginning there is the hearth, the ancestral fire, and
you are a native of the flames. You belong there and therefore
it belongs to you. Then comes exile, the break, the destitution,
the initiation, the maiming which—I think—gives access to a
deeper sight, provides a path into consciousness through the
imitation of thinking. Now you can never again entirely relax
the belly muscles. You learn, if you're lucky, the chameleon art
of adaptation, and how to modulate your laughter. You learn
to use your lips properly. Henceforth you are at home
nowhere, and by that token everywhere. You learn to live with
the flies, and how to slide from death into dream. You learn
about creation—because you must compensate—and thus
transformation and metamorphosis, although you also come to
realize that everything is since all time.

So you begin to understand the feel of harmony, if only
because it has become a conscious construct from which you
are excluded. Therefore you acquire a knowledge of the
tension between the jump or the break, and harmony, and how
the one is in fact the other.

You husband your weaknesses: these are the souvenirs of

your native land. You make sure that you are tougher than "they" are, or you damn well learn how to pretend to. You never quite master the mysteries of financial transactions. When you are down and out, or when your clothes are not presentable, you keep out of sight. You demand to be treated respectfully—your edges are sharper and your paranoia more acute—in fact, your evaluation of dignity becomes a taut string. You are invited to New York for a conference? Insist upon being put up in a good hotel!

You end up speaking all languages with an accent, even the distant one of your youth, the one which you kept for love and anger. You have acquired the knack of fitting in pretty much with any society, it can be said that you are a good impersonation of the cosmopolitan, but you probably never really penetrate beneath the surface of concerns of those around you. You are engaged with an elsewhere that cannot be reached: isn't it the defining characteristic of exile?

Guard against the scratches becoming sores, the mounting tide of bitterness, the fear of losing control, the constant danger of succumbing to the shadows you see flapping their gowns at you from the corner of your eye. Remind yourself that policemen and politicians are also human.

In the book from which I have already quoted, Genet writes: "My life was thus a composition of gestures without consequence, subtly swollen into acts of audacity. When I realized this much, that my life is written in the hollows (*engraved in counterpoint, counter acts*), this crease became as terrifying as an abyss."

The exiled person is probably marked by a loss that he or she doesn't want to let go of, especially when occasioned by a political situation. But it goes without saying that one can replace, to all intents and purposes, the word "exile" by refugee, misfit, outcast, outsider, expatriate, squatter, foreigner, clandestine, heretic, stranger, renegade, drifter, a displaced person, marginal one, the new poor, the economically weak, drop-out. The irony is that if we were to add up all these individuals we'd probably find ourselves constituting a new silent majority!

If I may at this point enter a plea for exiles at the risk of contradicting my opening paragraphs, I'd say they are often enough admirable people. The courage and the perseverance, the futile quest for survival of these stowaways, wetbacks, throwbacks and other illegal humans, always astonish me: Tamuls sneaking with false passports over the border, Angolans surfacing in Berlin from some "underground railway," Ghanaians passing themselves off for citizens from Zaire or the Ivory Coast, whole families making it to the "capital" to be crammed into one room, boat people working like beavers to build dams for a future generation. And nearly always they are starving themselves to help provide for more unfortunate relatives back home.

How resilient they are! See them come to terms with the writ of the rat. See how quickly they pick up the art of negotiating the labyrinths and warrens of Administration and Order, how rapidly they snick their tongues around the foreign language, how keen they are to learn! Along the beaches of Europe, on the squares of its cities, you come across the young men from Mali—distant descendants of Ahmad Baba—tirelessly unrolling their bundles of African knickknacks, made in Hong Kong, the bangles and the beads and the imitation effigies. They peddle the instantly discardable. They squint at the gray skies and wind up plastic doves which they throw in the air to flutter and fall. Somehow they survive. Have you noticed the pride and joy when these people manage to afford that first new dress or leather jacket?

History has produced many forgeries, but here—in the seams and folds of adaptation, where history is meandering along more obscure paths into deeper dimensions—the new nomadic man of the future is being forged. To be exiled is to weave in and out of history the way a Bird Parker or a Sonny Rollins gives a solo edge to a body of sound.

Still, the personal compensation of survival and existential enrichment can never justify the willful destruction of hearth and habit, the forced removal of population groups or the expulsion of individuals. Will Romania ever recover from the mindless destruction of the peasant villages? Can South Africa knit into a serviceable national cloth the torn fibers caused by apartheid? How will the Touaregs, driven to give up their nomadic existence and herded into the shallows of Western civilization, survive as flyswatters in shantytowns? And how can one ever explain—let alone understand or condone—the crimes perpetrated by Israel when they wall up and dynamite the homes of suspect Palestinians?

My personal Declaration of Human Rights could be resumed in four brief points: 1. Every human being has the birthright to struggle for justice and equality. 2. Every human being has the right to a home. 3. Every human being has the survivor's right to the preservation of our planet with all its life. 4. Every human being has the right to die with his or her dignity intact.

"For our purposes, it matters little what strange thoughts occur to people in Albania or Burkina Faso." This phrase from Francis Fukuyama's arrogant and fatally shortsighted article, "The End of History?," may for now seem to be apposite. Likewise Milan Kundera, in his *The Unbearable Lightness of Being*, may have been right when he chose a war in Africa during the fourteenth century as an example of the most meaningless event in human history.[1] In proposing that any event that happens only once is meaningless, he suggests a life that disappears once and for all, that does not return, is like a shadow, without weight, dead in advance, dead by procuration and procreation; and whether it was horrible, beautiful, or sublime, its horror, sublimity, and beauty mean nothing. He wrote: "We need take no more note of it than of a war between two African kingdoms in the fourteenth century, a war that alters nothing in the destiny of the world, even if a hundred

---

[1] I'm quoting from an article written by Richard Dowden in *The Independent*, Aug. 28, 1990.

thousand blacks perished in excruciating torment." Indeed, one is tempted to ask: Why bother to look back that far? How about now?

On the continent with which I identify, whose cause— however weak—will always be mine, there are at present an estimated thirteen wars being fought: in Angola and Ethiopia and Liberia and Mali and Mauritania and Mozambique and Uganda and Rwanda and the Western Sahara and Senegal and Somalia and the Sudan and Chad. (South Africa is not in a war situation; we just have ongoing large-scale slaughtering.) Who cares?

True, for now the rich countries or the developed world or the North—call it what you wish—evidently decided, unilaterally and disdainfully, that developments in the poor countries can have no incidence on the course of history (by "developments" I mean stages of stagnation and deterioration). But this *real moral* is a-historical, it brings with it a shrinking of public ethics in the rich world too. Recent events, and events to come, will show—I am sure—that it is foolhardy for the West or the North to close its eyes and close off its heart behind the pretentious bulwarks of a "new world order." It was Althusser who said: "The future lasts a long time." History may no longer be deterministic or predictable, and it certainly does not progress, but it is never completed. It vomits at unexpected moments. I agree with Gertrude Himmelfarb in her reading of Hegel: "The synthesis of the preceding stage is the thesis of the present, thus setting in motion an endless dialectical cycle— and thus preserving the drama of history."

In telescoping many contradictions and opposites, exile has provided me with a panoply of lessons. I have said that it showed me, like a flasher, the mechanisms of survival. It made my mother tongue into a "homeland," a movable feast, indeed a dancing of the bones—as with the Famadihana ceremony of Madagascar when the remains of the deceased are brought up once a year for a festive family meal and a waltz. It gave a *taste* to words. It altered my perceptions of space and time. Time, I learned, can be stilled, warped, colored, preserved, killed, suddenly speeded up, and sometines it can become immaterial. Space, I found out, can be provisional or hostile or vibrant and textured and tactile. Exile gave me the motifs for my work: silence, death, transformation, shadows, ink, games, the void, dreams, immobility, interchangeability, essense, breaks . . .

It has shown me that you can become a master of dreams—since you had to recreate loss and articulate the void. I now understand that to reflect on the act of writing is to follow the courses of consciousness and not to be discoursing on the nature of the real, that it is in fact not possible to reconstruct the real as the very process of re-memberment becomes reality. I know that dreams have a meaning because their field of reference is the charted area of experience— however warped the mirror—but also that the order, the hierarchy, the linking create other references. I have learned that you can become hooked on the inner logic of dreams— and that you always become what you have mastered. I have learned that the dream constitutes a necessary make-believe, an outside border, a means of *dépassement*—and from the moment of its inception and enunciation it is a given which will modify expectations and behavior to become a constiuent element of reality. I think it has taught me something about tolerance, and that to dream, in a social sense, is an affirmation of generosity. Exile has stimulated my obsession with *métissage*, transformation, metamorphosis. Perhaps it has made me superstitious, so that I now perceive the interaction between expression or projection, and becoming or destiny. I have experienced that alienation allows one to go to the essential, the existential.

Exile has brought it home to me that I'm African. If I live in Europe most of the time, it is not as a participant but an observer, an underground activist for Africa. When I'm asked what nationality I am, I say—depending on my judgment of the perceptiveness of those asking me—Brazilian, or Arab, or some impossible cross-over or quirk of displacement. Nowadays I sometimes say Canadian. I've never been to Canada. Canadian sounds nice and faceless, all accent and no master text. If I were to say French or South African I would have trouble getting the worms back into the can. It is better not to drag your roots with you so as not to attract undue attention by the dust which you will raise. Roots are edible things in Africa. So is the placenta. Maybe, because of the African customs of burying the umbilical cord and eating the roots, one is in danger of becoming what you were!

Yes, exile is a difficult craft, as Nazim Hikmet intimated—climbing up and down strange staircases. One hopes that it is also a useful one, that you may be a producer of awareness, even if marginally so. To contribute what? It is another contradiction that exile should be a pointed experience and yet, in a world of specialization, be promoting lateral vision and parallel thinking. You do have to think yourself out of a hole.

Indeed, the experiences and products of exile could be a dissolvant of border consciousness. It could be a way of reconnoitering, shifting and extending the limits. You may return with scars—as Rimbaud warned—but also with precious gifts: the dip and veer of swallows at nightfall over the Niger river, the depth of the seeing without judging in an old man's eyes, the fly-embroidered smile of a child, the mushy woman-smell of the loquat flower. Exile teaches you about individual fate with universal implications—because it is eternal and has always been with us: we are all dimly aware of our incompleteness, of the thick veils of illusion in which we are draped.

Recently I went back to where the bones lie buried, and I was a stranger. My wife and I spent a night in a small-town hotel; I handed the receptionist my passport and chewed the fat with him. He congratulared me, a "foreigner," on my ability to speak his language, Afrikaans, so well—albeit, he added patronizingly, with an accent. I answered that it was surely the least a visitor could do in trying to respect the customs of a strange country.

An exile never returns. "Before" does not exist for "them," the "others," those who stayed behind. For "them" it was all continuity; for you it was a fugue of disruptions. The thread is lost. The telling has shaped the story. You made your own history at the cost of not sharing theirs. The eyes, having seen too many different things, now see differently.

But the return released me from exile! The crystallized shadow was cut from me. I haven't staunched the bleeding yet, but there's hope, through mourning, of a cure. Exile became a *thing* outside me, which could be discarded. I wound it up and threw it in the sky to fly. I put it to earth with the navel string, the roots and the bones.

Gilles Deleuze, the French philosopher, says in a letter written to a critic (reprinted in his recent volume, *Pourparlers*): "Nietzsche gives you a perverse taste—that neither Marx nor Freud ever could, quite to the contrary: the desire for everybody and anybody to say simple things in his or her own name, to speak by means of emotions, intensities, experiences, experimentations. To say something in your own name is very strange, because it is not at all at the moment of taking yourself for some special I, a person or a subject, that you speak in your own voice. Rather, an individual only properly acquires his own name after a severe exercise in depersonalization, when he or she lays himself or herself open to the multiplicities and the intensities which may run through him or her. The name as instantaneous appropriation of such an intensive multiplicity, is at the opposite of the depersonalization effected by the history of philosophy—it is the depersonalization of love and not of submission. One speaks from the bottom of what you don't know, from the cellars of your own under-development. One becomes—has become—a collection of singularities cut loose, of names and pronouns and fingernails and things and animals and small happenings: the opposite of a star or an expert or a preacher."

And so I shall finish where I started—with sand and with fire. One of the pillars of Hou-neng's teaching as the sixth Zen patriarch (as if there could be pillars in the void!), was the concept of *wou-nien*. *Wou*, in Chinese terminology, is said to mean "not to exist" or "not to have." The ideogram doesn't indicate "heart' however, but literally stands for "fire." *Nien* signifies "to think of," "to remember." Better still: "present or actual thought." *Wou-nien* is thus rendered as "nonattachment." I particularly like in that word-picture the sign of "fire-thought." How does a flame think of itself? How does a thought burn? As the fiery heart?

By *wou-nien* is the Unconscious penetrated. And where do you get the Unconscious? It is to see all things as they are and not to be attached to any of them . . . it is only maintaining the perfect freedom to come and to go.

Hou-neng also consoled us with the following thought: "You should know that, as far as the Buddha nature is concerned, there is no difference between the enlightened and the ignorant person. The only difference is that the one realizes it and the other ignores it." Do we have a choice? Quick! Quick!

the heart of the country

we pray each day to give thanks for the sand
where we walk and sleep and which we scoop
to wash the bodies for worship—
when a prince of the capital comes to the wasteland
we prepare over the coals in the firepit a camel
crammed with a goat stuffed with a pheasant
farced with a desert dove stopped with two eggs
and present the steaming fragrant caravel carcass
as if crouched for praying on the festive table—
high against the fingertips of the towers of convocation
two ostrich eggs are built into heaven
to catch and hold the full moon's light,
nothing ever decays in this burning away of time—
then we show to our guest in the holy writings

how these arabesques of the revelation of faults
like so many consonant insects of God
are silently mounted by the shifting dunes
of a timeless dream of oblivion,
and our words become sand

HOMELESSNESS PAST

Both the problem of homelessness and its remedies have a long history. What does the past tell us about our present situation? Does the condition of being homeless in a democratic society have distinguishing features?

Introduction BY ALEXANDER KEYSSAR

THE SUBJECT of this evening's session is the history of a problem, or phenomenon, that is a very visible and unfortunate feature of present-day life in the United States: the existence, plight, and condition of people who do not have homes. The homeless are men, women, and children who—to deploy the language of this conference—do not have "a place in the world" or whose place in the world is not their own and not secure; if they have a place in the world at all, it is often located in public rather than private space.

The problem, or phenomenon, of homelessness seemed to leap into public consciousness—most vividly, but not exclusively, here in New York—in the 1970s. Since that time awareness of the problem, as well as the problem itself, has spread through much of the nation. Homeless families and individuals can now be found not only in New York, Boston, and Chicago but up and down the West Coast and in the relatively small cities of southern states such as North Carolina. Nearly everywhere, the phenomenon has been greeted, and perceived, not only as tragic and threatening, but also as *new*—as a new addition to the catalogue of urban ills, as a newly visible expression of poverty, inequality, and social disorder.

Yet, as people who lived through the Great Depression certainly remember, the phenomenon of homelessness is not new—not, at least, in its most obvious features. Indeed, images of the homeless in the 1930s constitute an important element in our visual memory of the Depression. Two such images are particularly common. One is of the homeless individual man, the hobo, riding the rails and living in impromptu camps near the railroad tracks. The second is of families, in urban centers, being evicted from their homes for nonpayment of rent, their belongings stacked on the sidewalks. (This memory is often linked to the political protests that sometimes ensued, as activists tried to prevent evictions by carrying people's belongings back into the buildings that had been their homes.) Both of these images, of course, have contemporary analogues (they correspond to distinct subpopulations of today's homeless), yet, curiously perhaps, they are infrequently invoked in contemporary discussion.

Research in social history, moreover—much of it carried out in the 1970s and the 1980s—has made clear that homelessness was an important phenomenon in Europe and in the United States long before the Great Depression. The characterization of homelessness as a distinctive social problem took place in the United States at least as early as the beginning of the twentieth century: by 1913, for example, the Boston Provident Society, aided by the Associated Charities, maintained a "department for homeless men."[1] And decades earlier, beginning in the 1870s, a great deal of public attention was focused on an important precursor to the modern phenomenon, the "tramp problem." Tramps, in the parlance of the late nineteenth century, were unemployed, homeless (or away-from-home) men who were traveling either in search of work or to avoid work—depending upon whose definition and characterization one chose to believe. In either case, these men (women were exceedingly rare) journeyed through communities in which they had no roots or connections, and they lacked the resources to pay for a hotel or "respectable" lodging. Tramps appeared in the Northeast and the Midwest with the rise of industrial capitalism; their numbers increased dramatically during the severe, and prolonged, depressions of the 1870s and 1890s.[2]

---

[1] Associated Charities of Boston, *Thirty-fifth Annual Report* (Boston, 1914), p. 29.
[2] This discussion of tramps is based largely on material from my book *Out of Work: The First Century of Unemployment in Massachusetts* (New York, 1986), pp. 130–142.

Indeed, the "tramp problem" of the late nineteenth century offers a number of suggestive parallels to the "homelessness" of the late twentieth century. Tramps also seemed to be a new phenomenon in the 1870s, and most communities responded to them with a mixture of compassion and fear, of material support and suspicion. Individual citizens and political leaders expressed a willingness to help "legitimately" unemployed workers who may have been traveling in search of jobs, but they were convinced that the tramp population also contained large numbers of wily, slothful impostors who constituted a public nuisance (by begging and cluttering the streets) and were immorally trying to live off charity while avoiding work. Consequently, many communities tried to offer some food and shelter to tramps while simultaneously supporting laws— passed in the 1870s, 1880s, and 1890s—that made it illegal to be a tramp. One important policy or law-enforcement problem accompanying this ambivalence was that it was extremely difficult for anyone to distinguish a "legitimate wayfarer" in search of a job from a "wily tramp" who was too "lazy" to work.

Communities often thus vacillated between periods of tolerance for homeless, unemployed men and periods of strict enforcement of the laws. One place where this occurred was the town of Sharon, Massachusetts, in the 1890s: the town's "tramp officer" later described his attitudes and practices to a state commission whose records constitute an extraordinary collection of documents bearing on the history of homelessness.[3]

> Finally I told the selectmen that I could drive tramps out of the town if they would like to have me go ahead, which they agreed to. In the early part of December, I began to take tramps over to Stoughton, and during that month put fifteen out of eighteen

[3] The Massachusetts Board to Investigate the Subject of the Unemployed, 1894–5, transcripts of hearings and collected documents, Archives of the Commonwealth, Boston, Massachusetts. Some of the board's findings were published in the *Report of the Massachusetts Board to Investigate the Subject of the Unemployed, House Document 50* (Boston, 1895).

through for vagrancy. . . . There are no more than three or four honest men out of a hundred of them. The three that got off, in my opinion, were not honest men more than those that were convicted though they had their dues paid up in a trade union. This, I am very certain of, is merely a means of getting an easier living off the public, because it ensures them against conviction for vagrancy. Another trick is to have a kit of tools, which would seem to be evidence that the owner is in search of work. He really uses it simply as a blind to obtain money and food under false presences.

This extraordinarily suspicious—the term "paranoid" does not seem excessive—town official also explained that he was able to obtain convictions of homeless men by taking advantage of a detail in the tramp laws that made it illegal for anyone to receive public lodging for more than a few nights in a row.

The way I worked the conviction was, as soon as the tramps were locked up at night, I would tell them that a number of thefts and robberies had been committed recently, and that they must give a good account of themselves as to where they had been for the previous three weeks. Almost invariably then, they would pull out a little book and show me just where they had lodged for, perhaps, three weeks' time. These lodgings would usually be a list of police stations and poorhouses in as many different towns. I would copy this down and the next day I would turn it in as evidence that the fellows were tramps. Naturally they could not say anything in refutation of this statement, and conviction was certain.[4]

It should be noted that—in one of those extraordinary twists of history that link the present to the past with symbols too obvious for novelists to use—the name of this mean-spirited tramp officer was Nixson.

Documentary anecdotes such as these surely suggest that it would be mistaken for us, in the late twentieth century, to presume that our homelessness problem is new or unique. But beyond that suggestion, individual anecdotes serve more to raise questions than to offer answers. Were the causes of the

---

[4] Board to Investigate the Subject of the Unemployed, *Hearings*, pp. 1694–96.

"tramp problem" really similar to the causes of today's "homelessness"? Or has the phenomenon itself, as well as key dimensions of society's response to it, changed significantly over the years? Pushing back even further in time: Was the plight of the homeless poor in preindustrial Europe (the problem of homelessness was certainly not born in the nineteenth century) similar to that of "tramps" or the "homeless" in the modern era? How can we explain the apparent cycles in the visibility of the problem and in the attention given to it? Does the historical persistence of the problem suggest that it is not a social accident or error but rather the cyclically visible tip of a poverty iceberg that we cannot or will not eradicate? Have responses to the homeless always been shaped at least as much by fear as by compassion?

These, presumably, are among the issues that the study of homelessness in the past can address. Yet remarkable as it may seem in an era when the field of social history has flourished and the problem of homelessness has been in the newspapers year in and year out, relatively little has been written about the history of the homeless in the United States or elsewhere. As historians and as citizens, we know far less than we ought to about the evolution of a compelling social problem whose presence appears to be both unacceptable and durable. The two essays that follow are therefore especially welcome as pioneering investigations of a somber and significant terrain.

Homelessness and Dickens

BY STEVEN MARCUS

Homelessness in Victorian England was, as it is today, a component of the problem of poverty, particularly though not exclusively urban poverty. There are many resemblances as well as points of difference between social phenomena of that period and our own. Although we cannot on this occasion inquire into the social contexts in which Dickens's writing is embedded, one thing can be noticed. The problems of both poverty and homelessness in London were given continual play and coverage in the press and elsewhere throughout the era. As in New York today, those problems were immense (London was then the largest city in the world) and proved at the time, and on its own terms, to be inaccessible to solution. We can also say that poverty, poor relief, pauperism, and homelessness were inseparably intertwined and were thought of throughout the period as central and indeed symbolic matters, that they were always surrounded with controversy, and that they were regarded regularly, but with fluctuating degrees of urgency, as leading phenomena in what was at the time considered the most wealthy society in the modern world.

The great creative English writer to deal with such matters was of course Dickens, and Dickens's dealings with them began in his own childhood when he actually experienced what it was like to be homeless. When Dickens was twelve years old, his father was imprisoned for debt. The father was joined in debtors prison by his wife and younger children, but Dickens was left on the outside to shift for himself. He worked for more than half a year in a blacking warehouse or factory, and lived for a considerable part of that period on his own. He felt abandoned, bereaved, cast away, homeless, unsupported and unprotected in the world. He spent a good deal of time on the streets and was frequently hungry. As he wrote, much later on:

> I know that I lounged about the streets, insufficiently and unsatisfactorily fed. I know that, but for the mercy of God, I might easily have been, for any care that was taken of me, a little robber or a little vagabond.

He was to become neither, but this experience was without doubt the most important event in Dickens's life. In it the most intense emotions of poverty, loss, betrayal, loneliness, desolation, and estrangement are to be found. And these are combined with ungovernable feelings about social displacement, family ruin, shame and loss of respectability and self-respect. He never stopped feeling these things, and he never stopped writing about them: they are inscribed and encoded in countless ways in every one of his novels. The child who suffered in the blacking warehouse and whose family was in the Marshalsea prison was reborn again and again in the victimized children and their families of his fiction; and he was reborn as well in the novelist who (keeping his childhood experience a permanent secret even from his own wife and children) represented as no one else ever did the world in which such things were of habitual occurrence.

But Dickens did not only write about the homeless in his novels. He wrote about them in his voluminous journalism as well—he was a regular visitor to and observer of workhouses and prisons, ragged schools and other places of refuge and relief. And he actually worked with the homeless as well. For about twelve years, from 1846 onward, he planned, set into motion, supervised, and in an almost literal sense virtually ran from day to day a Home for Homeless Women. He did so with money supplied by Angela Burdett Coutts, an immensely wealthy heiress with evangelical and reforming passions; and the chief documents of his activities in this connection are the more than five hundred surviving letters that Dickens wrote to

Miss Coutts, most of them dealing with the details of this project. They reveal Dickens to be extremely practical, realistic, knowing, and shrewd, as well as decent-minded and fair in his dealings with a variety of homeless young women who came into his charge. He knew about poverty and homelessness from a variety of either first-hand or very closely focused perspectives.

But it is Dickens the novelist who claims our largest interest, and it is to him that I want to turn.

There is no novel by Dickens in which poverty and homelessness are not represented as central dramatic presences. From *Pickwick Papers*, in which Sam Weller recalls how he spent part of his childhood sleeping under the arches, and in its scenes in the Fleet prison and its tales of starvation and indigence, to *Oliver Twist*, which has homelessness itself as the essential and existential condition of its child hero, all the way through to *Our Mutual Friend*, and even the unfinished *Edwin Drood*, the injuries of homelessness and destitution are never very distant from the forefront of Dickens's engrossing preoccupations. In none of his works, however, are such representations of more salient bearing than they are in *Bleak House*, the first novel of his later period. It may be said that the narrative of this novel is in some odd sense itself homeless, or at least decentered, since it has no settled or stable single narrative perspective, but moves back and forth, without a word of comment or explanation, between two narrators: one, an omniscient, third-person voice that speaks unforgettably in various modalities of the present; the other, a first-person, retrospective narrative, composed by Esther Summerson, the orphaned, illegitimate, and formally homeless (as she is altogether ignorant of her parents and has no known family) heroine of the story. The novel, moreover, trains its attention on the principal site of the homeless: it begins with a one word sentence—"London," followed by a full stop. It is, as far as I know, the first novel to begin this way, with, as it were, a dateline—suggesting Dickens's mature purpose of combining extreme complexity and inclusiveness of scope with his sense of the urgency and currency of his materials and themes.

Bleak House sometimes appears to be about virtually everything. It is, as almost everyone knows, also about a great law suit that involves all the major characters and that has led in the past and leads many of them now in the present of the novel to be trapped and ensnared in the deadly grip or *mortmain* of the Court of Chancery and its obsolete and cancerously consuming procedures, being macerated morsel by morsel into ruin. It is also about homelessness in its larger and more subtler senses and variations, since it includes a whole series of representations of middle-class families whose existences and homes are destroyed by a variety of ravaging derelictions—personal, ideological, legal, and social—that seize hold of those responsible for keeping and maintaining homes and families together. And as part of this wider inclusiveness, it contains as well dramatizations of certain kinds of intact middle-class domesticity and home-endorsing doctrines, sentiments, and behaviors that are both destructive in themselves and serve as pretextual disguises for the exploitation of others.

But our immediate locus of concern here is with the homelessness of the poor and destitute, and such representations occupy a primary matrix of interest in *Bleak House* as well. For example, on her first morning in London, Esther goes out for an early walk into the already bustling streets and observes there, as the shops are beginning to open, "extraordinary creatures in rags, secretly groping among the swept-out rubbish for pins and other refuse" (ch. 5). These rags lead us directly (and within a page) to Krook's "Rag and Bottle Warehouse," a second-hand or junk shop in the legal quarter (in which most of the novel's action occurs); this enclosed accumulation of refuse specializes in "waste paper," rags, blacking bottles, law books, and other trash and garbage, and is run by a half-crazy old villain named Krook, who has taken in two pieces of human flotsam as casual lodgers. One of them is an old lady named Miss Flite, a genteel and harmless creature who has been driven into both penury and madness by her case that has, like so many others, been deadlocked in the Court of Chancery for most of her lifetime. The other is an impoverished and homeless law-writer or copyist who calls himself Nemo; this reduced remnant of a man is in fact Esther's illegitimate and unknown father, the long-lost lover of Lady Dedlock, and the repository of several mysteries of identity and detection that constitute at the same time filaments that go into making up the novel's extraordinary weblike structure. He makes his sole appearances in the novel as a dead body, and here is how he is discovered:

> It is a small room, nearly black with soot, and grease, and dirt. In the rusty skeleton of a grate, pinched at the middle as if Poverty had gripped it, a red coke fire burns low. In the corner by the chimney, stand a deal table and a broken desk; a wilderness marked with a rain of ink. In another corner, a ragged old portmanteau on one of the two chairs, serves for a cabinet or wardrobe; no larger one is needed, for it collapses like the cheeks of a starved man. The floor is bare; except that one old mat, trodden to shreds of rope-yarn, lies perishing upon the hearth. No curtain veils the darkness of the night, but the discoloured shutters are drawn together; and through the two gaunt holes pierced in them, famine might be staring in—the Banshee of the man upon the bed.
>
> For, on a low bed opposite the fire, a confusion of dirty patch-work, lean-ribbed ticking, and coarse sacking . . . [is] a man. He lies there, dressed in shirt and trousers, with bare feet. He has a yellow look in the spectral darkness of a candle that has guttered down, until the whole length of its wick (still burning) has doubled over, and left a tower of winding-sheet above it. His hair is ragged, mingling with his whiskers and his beard—the latter ragged too, and grown, like the scum and mist around him, in neglect . . . foul and filthy as the air is, it is not easy to perceive what fumes those are which most oppress the senses in it; but through the general sickliness and faintness, and the odour of stale tobacco, there comes . . . the bitter, vapid taste of opium. (Ch. 10)

There is, we need hardly to be reminded, nothing new about the association together of immiseration, homelessness, and drugs.

A nearby medical man is summoned, who states that he has been supplying Nemo with the narcotic for some time and that he is certainly dead "of an over-dose of opium," but whether he took so much deliberately or not is impossible to say. Although a number of other people in the immediate neighborhood are acquainted with him by sight, no one knows a thing about him. He is six weeks behind in his rent, moneyless, propertyless, relationless, and nameless, and lies there, Dickens writes with pointed irony, a pauper corpse, "with no more track behind him, that any one can trace, than a deserted infant." Such circumstances require as a matter of course a Coroner's Inquest, which Dickens does up in appropriately scathing and compressed high sardonic style.

Like other half-deranged human wrecks, Nemo had learned to run away from people who approached him and had been "sometimes hooted and pursued about the streets." The only person to whom in his isolation he is known to have spoken is another member of the homeless, a boy who sweeps a nearby street crossing. This boy is summoned by the Coroner and "put through a few preliminary paces."

> Name, Jo. Nothing else that he knows on. Don't know that everybody has two names. Never heerd of sich a think. Don't know that Jo is short for a longer name. Thinks it long enough for *him*. *He* don't find no fault with it. Spell it? No. *He* can't spell it. No father, no mother, no friends. Never been to school. *What's home?* [emphasis added] Knows a broom's a broom, and knows it's wicked to tell a lie. Don't recollect who told him about the broom, or about the lie, but knows both. (Ch. 11)

Because of the "terrible depravity" of his heathen ignorance of the truth, Jo is rejected as a legally competent witness. The inquest concludes, and Nemo is borne off to be buried in a "pestiferous and obscene" paupers' graveyard in the city itself.

> With houses looking on, on every side, save where a reeking little tunnel of a court gives access to the iron gate—with every villainy of life in action close on death, and every poisonous

element of death in action close on life—here, they lower our dear brother down a foot or two: here, sow him in corruption, to be raised in corruption: an avenging ghost at many a sick bedside: a shameful testimony to future ages, how civilisation and barbarism walked this boastful island together. (Ch. 11)

There follows a Shakespearian abjuration for night to fall and cover this iniquity, and at night, in darkness, along comes Jo, "slouching" up through the tunnel and to the gate to look at the burial mound; he sweeps the step and archway passage clean, as a matter of gratitude and simple human solidarity, and then departs.

But not for long. Because he is known to have been spoken to and perhaps befriended by Nemo, he is entoiled in the immense life of the plot of the novel and, like some bedraggled leitmotif, keeps being brought back for incremental, recurrent appearances as the novel develops. Jo stays alive by sweeping the mud, mire, and horse-droppings from a London street crossing that he has chosen as his own "turf"; when stray pedestrians come by, he in his bare feet crosses with them and begs for pennies—a rather more useful functional equivalent of New York's windshield cleaners of recent years. His most frequently uttered response to almost any kind of question is "*I* don't know nothink," and at one point the narrator tries to get inside of him and follow him as he sets out to get through another day.

It must be a strange state to be like Jo! To shuffle through the streets, unfamiliar with the shapes, in utter darkness as to the meaning, of those mysterious symbols, so abundant over the shops, and at the corners of streets, and on the doors, and in the windows! To see people read, and to see people write, and to see the postmen deliver letters, and not to have the least idea of all that language—to be, to every scrap of it, stone blind and dumb! It must be very puzzling to see the good company going to the churches on Sundays, with their books in their hands, and to think (for perhaps Jo *does* think, at odd times) what does it all mean, and if it means anything to anybody, how comes it that it means nothing to me? To be hustled, and jostled, and moved on; and really to feel that it would appear to be perfectly true that I have no business, here, or there, or anywhere; and yet to be perplexed by the consideration that I *am* here somehow, too, and everybody overlooked me until I became the creature that I am! It must be a strange state, not merely to be told that I am scarcely human (as in the case of my offering myself for a witness), but to feel it of my own knowledge all my life! . . .

Jo comes out of Tom-all-Alone's, meeting the tardy morning which is always a bit late in getting down there, and munches his dirty bit of bread as he comes along. His way lying through many streets, and the houses not yet being open, he sits down to breakfast on the door-step of the Society for the Propagation of the Gospel in Foreign Parts, and gives it a brush when he has finished, as an acknowledgment of the accommodation. He admires the size of the edifice, and wonders what it's all about. He has no idea, poor wretch, of the spiritual destitution of a coral reef in the Pacific. . . .

He goes to his crossing, and begins to lay it out for the day. The town awakes; the great tee-totum is set up for its daily spin and whirl; all that unaccountable reading and writing, which has been suspended for a few hours, recommences. Jo, and the other lower animals, get on in the unintelligible mess as they can. It is market-day. The blinded oxen, over-goaded, over-driven, never guided, run into wrong places and are beaten out; and plunge, red-eyed and foaming, at stone walls; and often sorely hurt the innocent, and often sorely hurt themselves. Very like Jo and his order. . . . (Ch. 16)

Tom-all-Alone's, where Jo spends his nights, is a piece of inner-city real estate that is involved in the interminable law suit of Jarndyce and Jarndyce and has consequently been eaten up in costs and deteriorated into a slum, indeed into a rookery. It is, says Mr. Jarndyce, who avoids the place as both an eyesore and a heartsore,

"a street of perishing blind houses, with their eyes stoned out; without a pane of glass, without so much as a window-frame, with the bare blank shutters tumbling from their hinges and falling asunder; the iron rails peeling away in flakes of rust; the chimneys sinking in; the stone steps to every door (and every door might be Death's Door) turning stagnant green; the very crutches on which the ruins are propped, decaying." (Ch. 8)

Later on, it is represented in still further, though condensed, detail:

Jo lives—that is to say, Jo has not yet died—in a ruinous place, known to the like of him by the name of Tom-all-Alone's. It is a black, dilapidated street, avoided by all decent people; where the crazy houses were seized upon, when their decay was far advanced, by some bold vagrants, who, after establishing their own possession, took to letting them out in lodgings. Now, these tumbling tenements contain, by night, a swarm of misery. As, on the ruined human wretch, vermin parasites appear, so these ruined shelters have bred a crowd of foul existence that crawls in and out of gaps in walls and boards; and coils itself to sleep, in maggot numbers, where the rain drips in; and comes and goes, fetching and carrying fever, and sowing . . . evil in its every footprint. . . .

Twice, lately, there has been a crash and a cloud of dust, like the springing of a mine . . . and, each time, a house has fallen. These accidents have made a paragraph in the newspapers, and have filled a bed or two in the nearest hospital. The gaps remain, and there are not unpopular lodgings among the rubbish. As several more houses are nearly ready to go, the next crash in Tom-all-Alone's may be expected to be a good one. (Ch. 16)

Nevertheless, Jo is not permitted to continue to pursue, without interruption, his miserable, exiguous street existence. According to the Metropolitan Police Acts of 1829 and 1839, such livers-off and workers upon the streets could be considered as loitering and in violation of the law, and Jo turns up next in the grip of a police constable.

"This boy," says the constable, "although he's repeatedly told to, won't move on—"

"I'm always a-moving on, sir," cries the boy, wiping away his grimy tears with his arm. "I've always been a-moving and a-moving on, ever since I was born. Where can I possible move to, sir, more nor I do move!"

"He won't move on," says the constable, calmly, with a slight professional hitch of his neck involving its better settlement in his stiff stock, "although he has been repeatedly cautioned, and therefore I am obliged to take him into custody. He's as stubborn a young gonoph as I know. He WON'T move on."

"O my eye! Where can I move to!" cries the boy, clutching quite desperately at his hair, and beating his bare feet upon the floor. . . .

"Don't you come none of that, or I shall make blessed short work of you!" says the constable, giving him a passionless shake. "My instructions are, that you are to move on. I have told you so five hundred times."

"But where?" cries the boy.

"Well! Really, constable, you know," . . . [interposes a friendly bystander] coughing behind his hand . . . [a] cough of great perplexity and doubt; "really that does seem a question. Where, you know?"

"My instructions don't go to that," replies the constable. "My instructions are that this boy is to move on." (Ch. 19)

Jo is then sermonized over by an evangelical preacher who actually calls him a glorious human boy

"O running stream of sparkling joy
To be a soaring human boy!"

He retreats in fear and bewilderment to his hovel in Tom-all-Alone's where he has been bilked and robbed of the few bits of money that he has gotten for telling a disguised Lady Dedlock about the dead Nemo; he is further pursued to his hiding place there by a detective and other information-seeking characters, grilled about what he has done, threatened about making further disclosures, and then sermonized over again before an audience of others by the evangelical speaker.

"We have here among us, my friends," says Mr. Chadband, "a Gentile and a Heathen, a dweller in the tents of Tom-all-Alone's and a mover-on upon the face of the earth. We have here among us my friends," . . . [says] Mr. Chadband, untwisting the point with his dirty thumbnail . . . "a brother and a boy. Devoid of parent, devoid of relations, devoid of flocks and herds, devoid of gold and silver, and of precious stones. Now, my friends, why do I say he is devoid of these possession? Why? Why is he?" (Ch. 25)

Badgered on all sides, frightened, battered at, this "friendless outcast" runs away from London, goes on the tramp and is next found wandering about by some vagrant and semihomeless brickmakers near Bleak House itself. He is now burning up with "a very bad sort of fever"—either typhus or small pox or some third kind of contagious ailment—and one of the brickmakers' women tries—with unsurprising results—to get the resourceless boy some institutional help. She

> had been here and there, and had been played about from hand to hand, and had come back as she went. At first it was too early for the boy to be received into the proper refuge, and at last it was too late. One official sent her to another, and the other sent her back again to the first, and so backward and forward; until it appeared to me [this is Esther narrating] as if both must have been appointed for their skill in evading their duties, instead of performing them. (Ch. 31)

In the event, Jo is given refuge and shelter in Bleak House by Esther and her friends; he stays there just long enough to infect Esther and her maid with the dangerous disease— Esther's looks are permanently ruined by it—and is then, for a variety of reasons, turned out again in the middle of the night by the pursuing detective, who is aided by a venal and slightly disreputable friend of Mr. Jarndyce. Sent off on a destination- less journey to nowhere, dying of everything, the homeless boy makes his hopeless, semiconscious way back to the London slum that is first and last his den, lair, and place of hiding. He unexpectedly comes across and is cornered by the friendly medical man whom he first saw at the Coroner's Inquest, to whom he weakly confesses,

> "I don't know how to do nothink, and I can't get nothink to do. I'm . . . poor and ill, and I thought I'd come back here when there warn't nobody about, and lay down and hide somewheres as I knows on till arter dark, and then go and beg a trifle. . . ." (Ch. 46)

The young physician now feels responsible for Jo. He gets him something to eat, but Jo is too far gone to have any appetite. But what is the physician to do with his new and helpless charge? "It surely is a strange fact," he thinks to himself, "that in the heart of a civilized world this creature in human form should be more difficult to dispose of than an unowned dog" (ch. 47). Even more, he goes on:

> "I am unwilling to procure him immediate admission, because I foresee that he would not stay there many hours, if he could be so much as got there. The same objection applies to a workhouse; supposing I had the patience to be evaded and shirked, and handed about from post to pillar in trying to get him into one—which is a system that I don't take kindly to." (Ch. 47)

He finally decides to take Jo to a combination shooting gallery, gymnasium, and fencing practice room, run by two homeless, vagabond discharged soldiers—something like a pair of maladapted Victorian Vietnam veterans, if that makes any sense. The place has become a refuge for other harried outcasts. Jo is brought in and at the same time silently and implicitly ushered forward once again as a kind of specimen, at which point the narrator rises to mordant and inflamed utterance:

> Jo is brought in. He is not one of Mrs. Pardiggle's Tockahoopo Indians; he is not one of Mrs. Jellyby's lambs; being wholly unconnected with Borrioboola-Gha [on the banks of the Niger]; he is not softened by distance and unfamiliarity; he is not a genuine foreign-grown savage; he is the ordinary home-made article. Dirty, ugly, disagreeable to all the senses, in body a common creature of the common streets, only in soul a heathen. Homely filth begrimes him, homely parasites devour him, homely sores are in him, homely rags are on him: native ignorance, the growth of English soil and climate, sinks his immortal nature lower than the beasts that perish. Stand forth, Jo, in uncompromising colours! From the sole of thy foot to the crown of thy head, there is nothing interesting about thee.
> He shuffles slowly into Mr. George's gallery, and stands huddled together in a bundle, looking all about the floor. He seems to know that they have an inclination to shrink from him, partly for what he is, and partly for what he has caused. He, too, shrinks from them. He is not of the same order of things, not of the same place in creation. He is of no order and no place; neither of the beasts, nor of humanity. (Ch. 47)

Jo is a piece of native, home-made human waste and degradation; he seems virtually not of the same species as we, or part of the same order of nature, let along society. He belongs to nothing and no one. And yet he is at the same time in his radical isolation deeply connected—with us, with the social world of the narrative, with the social world that the narrative refers to and that yet resonates with the social world today, a century and a half later. This simultaneous existence at both the extreme periphery and the symbolic social center is characteristic of such a distinctive and radical yet common circumstance as homelessness—it signifies without ending.

Jo soon succumbs and dies, of the fever and of his entire life—the scene is intensely moving and famous, and I am not going to read it, or its terrible indicting last paragraph, here today. Instead I want to take us back to an earlier scene. When Jo has been first picked up by the police constable, he is brought to the home of a friendly law-stationer who is acquainted with him, in order to be identified; it is there that he is checked over by several people and preached over by Mr. Chadband. He is given some scraps of food and a penny, and with the constable's injunction to "move on," shuffles off into the heat of a London summer evening. And here is how the narrator takes his temporary farewell of him:

> Jo moves on, through the long vacation, down to Blackfriars Bridge, where he finds a baking stony corner, wherein to settle to his repast.
> And there he sits, munching and gnawing, and looking up at the great Cross on the summit of St. Paul's Cathedral, glittering above a red and violet-tinted cloud of smoke. From the boy's face one might suppose that sacred emblem to be, in his eyes, the crowning confusion of the great, confused city; so golden, so high up, so far out of reach. There he sits, the sun going down, the river running fast, the crowd flowing by him in two streams—everything moving on to some purpose and to one end—until he is stirred up, and told to "move on" too. (Ch. 20)

In this great passage, Dickens is at once referring back to his own childhood memories of poverty in Camden Town (remembering himself looking at the cupola of the cathedral "looming through the smoke") and to an apocalypse of obscuration, muddlement, and disarray in the present. The golden cross at the top of St. Paul's is itself an emblem of a civilization that is both Christian and capitalist/modern and dealing with the strains and contradictions that are entailed in being the two at once inadequately. There is no doubt here about Jo belonging to us; we are all moving on toward the same end under the same perplexed circumstances. It is very much to the point that Dickens, unlike many of his contemporaries, does not regard Jo as a primary embodiment of the "dangerous" classes—that he represents by foreboding neither revolution nor mass death through fatal contagion. Some contagion, yes; he does not, however, have to prove his brotherhood to us by killing us with infectious disease. Our denial of his common species-hood with us, our denial of his brotherhood, is for Dickens proof itself of the obverse and of the damage done by it. The homeless are, among much else, a nuisance, an eyesore, an offense, a bother, and an expense; it is next to impossible not to respond with ambivalence to them; but what Dickens reminded his readers, in this small but expressive section of *Bleak House*, is that they are also an inseparable part of us and that, however mixed and ill-assorted and imperfectly controlled our feelings and responses may be, we are responsible for them. And I think that one of the things that rises afresh from this examination is that even though we are no longer a Christian society in anything like the sense that Victorian England was, these matters still bear with comparable force on us and these contentions still hold true.

1. Studio Portrait of the Schnaper Family at a Seder Table, New York, 1924, 15½ × 19¾ in.; Collection of the family of Samuel and Rebecca Schnaper, Brooklyn, New York. Courtesy of Sylvia Rubin.

This and the following three photographs are taken from *Getting Comfortable in New York: The American Jewish Home, 1880–1950,* Susan L. Braunstein and Jenna Weissman Joselit, eds., New York: The Jewish Museum, 1990 (catalog for an exhibition at the Jewish Museum, September 16–November 15, 1990, associated with "The Home Project").

2. Model Tenement Kitchen, Young Women's Hebrew Association, New York, ca. 1917. Courtesy of the Archives of the 92nd Street YM-YWHA, New York.

3. Tenement Kitchen Interior, New York, early 20th century; Courtesy of United States History, Local History and Genealogy Division, The New York Public Library, Astor, Lenox and Tilden Foundations.

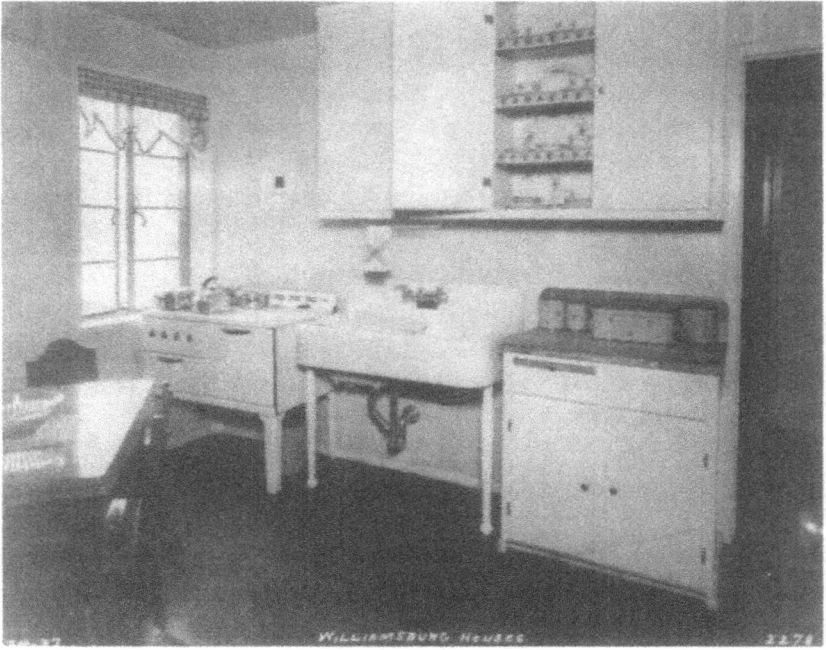

4. Modern Kitchen of the Interwar Years, ca. 1937; the Fiorello H. LaGuardia Archives, LaGuardia Community College, City University of New York.

A Poor Apart: The Distancing of Homeless Men in New York's History*

BY KIM HOPPER

> . . . a curse to themselves and a menace and
> injury to the city.
> —Conference of Charities of the City of
> New York, 1894

SEVEN MONTHS AGO, the front page of the *Los Angeles Times* (Sept. 2, 1990) carried a rather unusual article purporting to chart the subterranean lifeways of a group of homeless "mole people" living in the vast reticulate system of New York's underground rail and subway tunnels. Wizened, pale, mottled in appearance, near blind, and nearly invisible in the darkened tunnels they inhabit, they number between 5,000 and 25,000, according to unnamed sources. Of late, it seems, the hapless denizens of this new underworld have become something of a problem to the Transit Authority. They steal tools, prey on maintenance workers, and, most disruptive of all, occasionally roll onto the tracks, causing trains to derail. Attempts to displace them have proven unsuccessful. Outreach efforts are a laughingstock: such people can rarely be found, let alone convinced to vacate their premises. Nor do more aggressive efforts work: displaced from one redoubt, they simply relocate into a deeper, more inaccessible space. Police dogs sent down to roust them fail to return; rumor has it that the dogs are caught and eaten—no mean feat, it might be noted, for a weakened and all but sightless group of hunters. A local sociologist who attempted a census of such people two years ago is quoted as saying that the "eerie" stories surfacing could be seen as part of "an emerging homeless subculture."

I would like to suggest that this preposterous concoction—for that is what it is—may be read as part of an enduring theme in the history of homelessness in New York: an affirmation of the "otherness" of the homeless poor, even to the point of casting them in the mold of the grotesque.

In what follows, I review roughly a half-century of this history (the formative years from the 1890s through the Great Depression), and examine a succession of three constructs of homelessness, each of which serves to locate the figure of the homeless man in a kind of cultural limbo. I then ask how this distancing maneuver has informed the official response to homelessness and how, alternatively, popular practice may be seen to have parted company with it. Briefly, I argue that this rhetoric of disdain and the accompanying practice of institutional isolation may be read as ways of staving off a recognition of this society's complicity in the making of "unaccommodated men." The unarticulated and, for the most part, unrecognized counterpoint to official policy is provided by certain traditions of popular practice. Among these practices are the unanticipated uses to which the institution of relief may be put, and the ordinary, taken-for-granted inclusiveness of kin and friends. And while the first of these (unorthodox patterns of use) has been the bane of successive generations of almshouse and shelter administrators, the second (informal support) has proven indispensable to the relative success of any regime of relief bent on deterring all but the truly desperate.

Such notions are not new, but drawing their implications, if any, for contemporary practice is still a hazardous undertaking. I venture a few, taking courage from the example of some contemporary commentators, while mindful of the fact that such dilemmas have defeated far finer minds.

A Suspect Confederacy—Varieties of Disgrace in the Annals of Vagrancy

> "Perhaps nature made these people to be tramps."[1]

Poverty in the Old World may have been a permanent feature of the landscape, as enduring as the seasons, but it was not without its ambiguities. Ecclesiastical inquiry into the desserts of the poor, the obligations of the rich and of the church, and the logic of almsgiving dates from late antiquity. Varieties of need were reckoned with, degrees of urgency delineated, and poverty's spiritual advantage honored in the abstract. Practice did rival high ambition in the tradition of the *imitatio Christi* that espoused voluntary poverty—here the figure of Francis of Assisi, "God's fool" living among those he would assist, is emblematic. But though the place of the poor was "sublimated" in the registers of the church, too often this was a distinction that made no difference in everyday life. Even when his position in the social order was fixed, preordained, and his station in the "economy of salvation" secure (as a means to redemption for the better-off), the pauper—and especially the visible, insistent beggar—remained an object of fear and repugnance. Indeed, it could be argued that his spiritual value was enhanced by virtue of his loathsomeness; after all, it was not simply the amount of the gift but the arduousness, even the pain, occasioned by the giving that ennobled and redeemed.[2]

---

[1] Erasmus, in M. Mollat, *The Poor in the Middle Ages*, tr. A. Goldhammer (New Haven: Yale University Press, 1986), p. 298.

[2] *Ibid.*, passim, but esp. pp. 70, 113. For a more contemporary discussion of this point as it pertains to rescue missions, see J. F. Rooney, "Organizational Success Through Program Failure: Skid Row Rescue Missions," *Social Forces* 58 (March 1980): 905–924; A. L. Mauss, "Salvation and Survival on Skid Row: A Comment on Rooney," *Social Forces* 60 (March 1982): 898–904; and Rooney's "Reply," in the same issue, pp. 905–907. Anthropological analysis of the gift relationship is also relevant, but to date has been little applied. For exceptions, see G. Stedman Jones, *Outcast London* (London:

Revulsion was one thing, fear quite another. Matters took a sharply repressive turn when laws to suppress begging[3] were enacted throughout Europe in the aftermath of the Black Death. The desperately poor had always suffered when their numbers multiplied, as they did with unerring regularity in the wake of war, famine, and social dislocations. But the chronic destitution that haunted the late feudal period meant that they were now a source of constant trouble. The new logic of secular "relief" that succeeded medieval "mercy" and swept Western Europe in the early sixteenth century was aimed as much at protecting civil society as it was at relieving widespread distress. With it, "policing" the poor took clear precedence over feeding and sheltering them. Forced work and closed hostels, licenses for begging, pass laws and penalties, replaced the rough accommodations and uneven redistributions of an earlier age.[4]

Frightful measures (ranging from banishment to branding) were instituted to curb the wanderings of the rootless poor.[5] To be without ties—"masterless" and mobile at a time when the able poor were supposed to have masters and stay put[6]—was to be permanently suspect, a threat to the standing social order, an outrage to convention. Here is the historical nucleus of what sociologists would come to call the "disreputable poor"[7]: people literally beyond the pale, agents (witting or not) of disorder and immorality, satires upon common decency.

Oxford University Press, 1971) and Michael Ignatieff, *The Needs of Strangers* (New York: Viking, 1984).

[3] Literally, to "reduce beggars and vagabonds to obedience" (cited in Mollat, *Poor in the Middle Ages*, p. 290).

[4] N. Z. Davis, "Poor Relief, Humanism, and Heresy: The Case of Lyon," *Studies in Medieval and Renaissance History* 5 (1968): 217–275; J. A. Garraty, *Unemployment in History* (New York: Harper, 1978); Mollat, *Poor in the Middle Ages,* esp. pp. 290–293.

[5] C. J. Ribton-Turner, *A History of Vagrants and Vagrancy and Beggars and Begging* (London: Chapman & Hall, 1887); S. Webb and B. Webb, *English Poor Law History*, Part I, *The Old Poor Law* (Hamden, Conn.: Archon, 1927).

[6] A. Beier, *Masterless Men: The Vagrancy Problem in England, 1560–1640* (New York: Methuen, 1985).

[7] D. Matza, "The Disreputable Poor," in R. Bendix and S. M. Lipset, eds., *Class, Status, and Power*, 2d ed. (New York: Basic Books, 1966), pp. 289–302.

If the pauper had remained troublesome even when his worldly and otherworldly credentials were in order, how much more problematic his status when neither condition was met. Colonial poor laws were harsh and dismissive of "vagrants." No value was attached to the lodging of strangers (neighbors were another matter altogether) and virtually none to almsgiving. Huge sums were spent on relocating those with no claim of residence. Little thought was given to the forces driving such mobility and uprootedness; it was enough that such people didn't "belong."

New York City was a case in point.

Versions of the Imagined "Other" in New York's History

> Homeless, unemployed, and with little apparent commitment to family or community, the tramp and beggar seemed to be the very negation of the reformers' prescription for the good society.[8]

By the 1840s, the new metropolis was already a city of extremes: unmatched as a node of commerce in the New World, it was also unrivaled for the depths of misery to be found there. Like many port cities, New York had long served as a gathering point for rootless wanderers, casual laborers, runaway slaves, mendicants, and others who eked out livings in the interstices of a market society. It was a city founded and flourishing on a commercial ethic of unusual intensity, one that brooked little governmental interference and was, for the most, unleavened by strong traditions of paternalism, religious affiliation, or benevolent societies.[9] The appearance of order

---

[8] K. Kusmer, "The Underclass in Historical Perspective: Tramps and Vagrants in Urban America, 1870–1930," in R. Beard, ed., *On Being Homeless: Historical Perspectives* (New York: Museum of the City of New York, 1987), pp. 20–31.

[9] Not entirely so: See M. J. Henle, "Humanitarianism in the Early Republic: The Moral Reformers of New York, 1776–1825," *Journal of American Studies* 2 (1968):

was of great concern, however, and outbreaks of common
street "beggary" especially vexing.[10]

A Suspect Poor. Poverty itself—especially the visible kind that
stretches out its hand and looks passersby in the eye—was a
nettlesome anomaly, an embarrassment, a misplaced survival
of bygone days. Not that it was a sudden or recent arrival; far
from it.[11] It simply wasn't supposed to happen here, not in this
land of boundless opportunity. The deep divisions of class and
inherited privilege were supposed to have been done away
with by the American experiment. Victims of disease, injury,
old age, or widowhood—the worthy poor—belonged in
institutions, not parading their afflictions on the street and
terrorizing decent folk with their importunings.[12] The only
excuse for street poverty was the perversity or laziness of the
poor themselves (or, worse, their "impostors"), and for that the
police ("mendicancy officers") were needed, not charity. In a
word, the street poor were dangerous. Not only did they form
"debased," outcast "societies of their own" but, like garbage
everywhere, they exuded a dangerous "miasma" that corrupted others. In this case, the debility was moral—
pauperism—rather than a physical disease.[13]

161–175, and C. S. Rosenberg, *Religion and the Rise of the American City* (Ithaca: Cornell
University Press, 1971) for discussions of "tract societies."

[10] L. Brandt, *Glimpses of New York in Previous Depressions* (New York: Welfare
Council, 1933); E. K. Spann, *The New Metropolis* (New York: Columbia University
Press, 1983).

[11] As the tolls from epidemics repeatedly showed.

[12] As early as 1810, the Commissioners of the Almshouse wrote that "it is a
lamentable fact that our Streets swarm with beggars, and would lead to the conclusion,
especially with Strangers, that the poor are but illy provided for; whereas it is a truth,
within our knowledge, that many have been regularly supplied at the Alms House
[and elsewhere] with Food, Fuel and other necessaries. . . ." Therefore, the
Commissioners concluded that "these paupers should be discountenanced"—a request
the Common Council complied with (Brandt, *Glimpses of New York*, p. 34).

[13] D. Rothman, *The Discovery of the Asylum* (Boston: Little, Brown, 1973); Spann, *New
Metropolis*, pp. 35–41, 82ff; K. Jackson, "The Capital of Capitalism: The New York
Metropolitan Region, 1890–1940," in A. Sutcliffe, ed., *Metropolis: 1890–1940* (London:
Alexandrine Press, 1984), pp. 319–353; "The Bowery: From Residential Street to Skid

From the outset, then, the ranks of the visible poor were suspect and official commentary was unsparing in its depiction of these "offenses to the good order of society."[14] Running through the various constructions set out by government agencies, professional reformers, and scientific charity[15] is the notion that the homeless man[16] is not like the rest of us, being made of ruder, less durable stuff. The distinctive species of "otherness" ascribed to such men was typically underscored by seeing them as standing outside of, or apart from, *our* history. They occupied, as it were, a time warp of their own and, sometimes at least, of their own making as well. Whether he was construed as civilization's exile, its nemesis, or as evidence of its failure, the homeless man was denied recognition as part of the present of the observer—a practice Johannes Fabian has termed the "denial of coevalness"[17] by which anthropology temporally distances the objects of its study. Understand "coevalness" as designating "shared time" and, by extension, equality of stature in occupying that time. Accordingly, Fabian argues forcefully that any

> discourse employing terms such as primitive, savage (but also tribal, traditional, Third World, or whatever euphemism is

Row," in Beard, *On Being Homeless*, pp. 68–79; P. Boyer, *Urban Masses and Moral Order in America, 1820–1920* (Cambridge: Harvard University Press, 1978), pp. 89–90.

[14] T. A. Ingram, "Vagrancy," *Encyclopedia Britannica*, 11th ed. (1910–11), 27:837.

[15] I cover from the mid-nineteenth century onward and ignore some notable exceptions.

[16] The paucity of documentation on the homeless woman owes in no small measure to the fact that her situation was typically ascribed to her deviant trade—prostitution—rather than to her poverty, as Stephanie Goldin's work (in progress) should show. (Mollat's work on medieval poverty suggests in a number of places that women prostitutes were linked with male vagabonds among the most degraded of the poor in the Old World as well.) Women were not unknown, but neither were they common, among the "tramp" population. Until the very recent modern period, they were seen as relatively rare, appearing only in the wake of widespread social unrest and turmoil (T. Caplow et al., "Homelessness," *International Encyclopedia of Social Sciences* [1968], 6:494–499). The treatment of homeless families as a distinctive subgroup of the poor is almost entirely an artifact of welfare and housing policies from the 1970s onward.

[17] J. Fabian, *Time and the Other* (New York: Columbia University Press, 1983).

current) does not think, observe, or critically study, the "primitive;" it thinks, observes, studies *in terms* of the primitive.[18]

Further, to speak of "past" vs. "present," "tradition" vs. "modernity," etc. is simply bad

> metaphorical talk. What are opposed, in conflict, in fact, locked in antagonistic struggle, are not the same societies at different stages of development, but different societies facing each other at the same Time.[19]

My argument here is simply that the practice has its domestic field of application as well. But this will come as no surprise to an audience that has witnessed the decision of the *New York Times* to update its readership on the varieties of contemporary street homelessness in New York through a series of editorials entitled "The New Calcutta."

Preview. Three versions of official discourse on homeless men in New York City will be covered here: (1) the tramp as primitive in the late nineteenth century; (2) the vagrant as genetically deficient in the Progressive Era; and (3) the lost culture of "shelterized" men in the thirties (a theme that has reemerged of late[20]). Each of these distances and disavows the homeless man as a social product; he is recast instead as, variously, a vestige of prehistory, an error of evolution, or as a

---

[18] *Ibid.*, pp. 17–18.

[19] *Ibid.*, p. 155. See also E. Wolf, *Europe and the People Without History* (Berkeley: University of California Press, 1982) and W. Roseberry, *Anthropologies and Histories* (New Brunswick: Rutgers University Press, 1989) for exemplary alternatives within anthropology.

[20] See J. Grunberg and P. Eagle, "Shelterization: How the Homeless Adapt to Shelter Living," *Hospital and Community Psychiatry* 41 (May 1990): 521–525; D. Goleman, "Shelter Life: Why It's Hard to Get Out," *New York Times*, May 24, 1990, p. B14; and the exchange of letters in *Hospital and Community Psychiatry*, December 1990. The term has entered popular discourse as well: if squatting families are sent to city shelters, a home-care nurse worries, "They'll be a bunch of zombies. There's a depression people get in shelters. They become very dependent, they don't believe in themselves. They become shelterized" (*Village Voice*, Oct. 9, 1990, p. 44).

token of an alien (possibly irreclaimable) mentality. All three are variations on the theme from Erasmus cited above: that it is nature, not culture,[21] at fault.

The same theme was later elaborated along two distinctive paths which I will not have time to elaborate upon here, but which deserve mention: (4) the postwar sociology of the skid-row man as "undersocialized" (culture's missed recruit) or "disaffiliated" (society's exile, sometimes described as inhabiting a Rousseauian landscape of prehuman forms); (5) contemporary attempts to pathologize homelessness as the simple expression of psychiatric disorder—as one journalist put it, just a new "code word for mental illness."[22]

The Campaign to Eliminate the Tramp.[23] "[A] barbarian, openly at war with society" was how social worker and reformer Mary Richmond described the figure of the tramp in the late nineteenth century. (Her particular concern was deserting fathers, who left potentially homeless families behind.) And, to be fair, hers was a rather moderate version of a rhetoric of contempt and exclusion that could reach near-hysterical proportions.[24] The tramp took on almost mythic dimensions at times, a living icon who figured prominently in both popular symbolisms of evil and theories of contagion.[25] The *New York Times*[26] saw fit to situate him in mythology rather than history: Cain, the brother of dutiful Abel, was the first tramp, according to the *Times* (and murder, it will be recalled, is thus the occasion of his appearance). He was, as one historian has

[21] Not the dominant or "mainstream" culture, at any rate.

[22] J. Franklin, remarks at the Annual Meeting of the American Library Association, session on "Patrons in Crisis," New York, June 26, 1986.

[23] Or, tellingly, "the tramp evil" (*Nation*, Jan. 24, 1878).

[24] As one example, here is Francis Wayland's definition of the tramp of twenty years earlier: ". . . a lazy, shiftless, sauntering, swaggering, ill-conditioned, irreclaimable, incorrigible, cowardly, utterly depraved savage" ("Tramps," *Papers on Outdoor Relief and Tramps* [New Haven: Hoggson & Robinson, 1877], p. 10).

[25] E.g., W. H. Dawson, *The Vagrancy Problem* (London: P. S. King, 1910).

[26] Aug. 8, 1875, p. 9.

summarized it, "a creature midway between the vegetable and animal world."[27] "Leech" and "parasite" were other favored terms.

Popular and official denunciations were echoed, in part, by scholarly pronouncements. James McCook, in what is considered the first "scientific" study of a sample of tramps, invoked the tenuous sway of civilization over its reluctant charges. Like those "converted aborigines" recruited to work on Australian sheep stations, who happily quit their jobs when the "festive" seasons of their "savage life" come round, so too the tramp becomes tuned to the rhythms of a prehistoric time. He discovers "that living and labor are not interchangeable terms" and reverts to a primitive state.[28]

Ironically, what was dangerous about the tramp was not his "otherness" but his familiarity (*our* repressed otherness, as it were). He embodied some of the strongest yearnings, regrets, or misgivings—however one wants to characterize a deeply felt skepticism—of a working populace only newly and imperfectly harnessed to the wheel of the factory. The point implicit in McCook's analysis (and explicit in more anxious commentators) is that we are all latent tramps by inclination and heritage, and it is an essential part of the work of culture to hold that impulse in check.[29]

For although most "tramps" were, in reality, "wandering workers with homes only part of the time," who for the most part retained mainstream values,[30] there was an element of

[27] K. L. Kusmer, "The Underclass in Historical Perspective: Tramps and Vagrants in American Society, 1875–1930," Ph.D. dissertation, University of Chicago, 1980, pp. 64–66.

[28] "The Tramp Problem: What It Is and What to Do With It," *Proceedings of the National Conference on Charities and Corrections,* 1895, pp. 293, 295.

[29] This may also be interpreted as part of the late nineteenth century's version of "manufacturing consent" (M. Burawoy, *Manufacturing Consent* [Chicago: University of Chicago Press, 1979]).

[30] E. H. Monkkonen, *Police in Urban America, 1860–1920* (New York: Cambridge University Press, 1981), p. 88. Compare E. Liebow's *Tally's Corner* (Boston: Little, Brown, 1967) on the persistence of shadow values among unemployed black men in Washington three-quarters of a century later.

dissent—or, better, a cohort of dissenters—in their ranks. Some of these were men who had acquired "a special feeling for life on the tramp . . . who worked to live on the road" and who rejected conventional responsibilities.[31] There were others who, for a time at least, had simply had enough of subsisting at the pleasure of the industrial machine—some sought higher wages or more skilled work, others rebelled against "the demands of the time clock and the bell tower," still others saw the road as the last rite of untrammeled adolescence before the claims of adulthood set in. However it was played out, it was clear that among the working class were many who joined the ranks of tramps "temporarily, for varying periods, because they wished to."[32]

There was, then, truth to the reformers' and professional charities' suspicions that the tramp was a creature from another time, but it was a recent, not prehistoric one. There was something compelling, even seditious, about his refusal to accept the terms and conditions of modern labor. Living proof that a livelihood might be had without being earned, his example might well be considered "demoralizing." His refusal to conform symbolized what was still for many a faint but living memory of a different kind of work; closer to home, his mobility also signified the precarious employment situation of many urban dwellers. The denunciation of the tramp is thus one of those cultural moments in which a distance is enacted because something near and feared (or remembered and prized?) must be disavowed. It was against this backdrop of deep ambivalence—the hostility of organized benevolence coupled with the connivance, even open support, of the populace at large—that formal institutions of shelter for the homeless would take shape.

The idea that the tramp was the living vestige of an undisci-

---

[31] J. Schneider, "Tramping Workers, 1890–1920: A Subcultural View," in E. H. Monkkonen, ed., *Walking to Work: Tramps in America, 1790–1935* (Lincoln: University of Nebraska Press, 1984), p. 212.

[32] Kusmer, "Underclass in Historical Perspective," pp. 14–15.

plined age gave way only gradually to a view that recognized the sway of larger forces. Recurrent economic depressions were needed before the notion took hold that vagrancy might be the result of unemployment rather than the other way around.[33] But by then, new intellectual fads were in the air.

Eugenics in the Progressive Era. The conviction that we are up against something implacable in the nature of the tramp receives a rather different expression in the early decades of the twentieth century. Here it is not so much as a representative of primitive culture or mythic time that the homeless man is perceived; rather, he is seen, in evolutionary terms, as a regression.

Disturbed by a number of personality characteristics he found in the course of interviewing homeless men in the Municipal Lodging House, the author of a dissertation submitted to Columbia's Political Science Faculty concluded that until such time as "eugenics" offered the means for eliminating "anti-social traits," there will be men unfit for work in a competitive market and bound for dependency at the state's expense.[34] This fond hope took a bizarre, utterly unexpected turn in the work of Charles Barnes. It is a classic instance of a mind, to steal a phrase from Eliot, "violated by an idea." In the process was scuttled the closest thing to an ethnography of homeless men the Progressive Era would produce.

Barnes was a young researcher engaged by the Russell Sage Foundation to examine the operations of the Municipal Lodging House (that period's public shelter). He proved prodigal in his use of sources: frequenting the haunts of homeless men, visiting the institutions serving them, interviewing their staffs, observing

[33] P. T. Ringenbach, *Tramps and Reformers, 1873–1916* (Westport, Conn.: Greenwood Press, 1973).

[34] F. C. Laubach, "Why There Are Vagrants," Ph.D. dissertation, Columbia University, 1916. Laubach had in mind such things as low mental skills, low ideals, and attitudes he described as "treacherous," "eccentric," "exasperating," "untidy." A fifth of the men he interviewed were classified as "uninteresting" (pp. 19–64).

their work, devising questionnaires to uncover attitudes. He himself posed as homeless on occasion, visited other cities for comparative purposes, and passed many a night with the desk clerks at lodging houses. Out of extended interviews, he fashioned "life histories." It was the first disciplined effort to see this life "from the native's point of view."[35]

Against the rank, uninformed moralism of his contemporaries, Barnes set a closely documented account of men struggling, not always successfully and not with the finest of tools, to cope with an economy of scarcity. Among the men whose company he kept, the problem was less the attenuation of the work ethic than its tenacity in men with no means of exercising it. The invisible hand of the market has no memory and honors no debts: but how, Barnes wondered, do you explain that to an elderly man who refuses to go to the almshouse because he cannot let go of the notion that there ought to be something useful for him to do?

Barnes's reckoning is so informed and incisive, his commitment to grasping the truth of these discredited lives so evident, and his analysis is so well-tempered and nuanced, that it comes as something of a shock to read the concluding chapter of his report. The argument here is unadorned social Darwinism: the brute fact overriding all else about these men, he declares, is that "from 50–60 percent, if not more, are morons." He means this quite literally, scientifically in fact: "feeble-mindedness," an uncorrectable "structural abnormality" of the brain, is what explains the recurrent unemployment of apparently capable men and their inability ever to manage self-sufficiently.[36]

In a word: the homeless man was a piece of nature's mischief, not culture's product.[37]

---

[35] C. Barnes, "A Night in the Municipal Lodging House," unpublished paper, 1912; C. Barnes, "The Homeless Man," 2 vols., unpublished ms., Russell Sage Foundation, 1914.

[36] Barnes, "Homeless Man," pp. 167–175.

[37] At this time, two years after the publication of Goddard's *The Kallikak Family: A Study in the Heredity of Feeble-Mindedness*, eugenics had reached the dimensions of an

The Lost Culture of Shelterized Men in the Thirties. The process by which a tramp is made (or the traces of culture removed) was a common concern of early analysts, most of whom concluded that the forcing house of vagrancy—the company of other initiates, the carefree life of the road, the lowering effects of life in lodging houses—could undo in short order much of civilization's handiwork. Mobility, refusal to stay put and be counted as reliable, was key to this disculturation process. The same idea acquired the veneer of respectability in the thirties with the formulation of the "shelterization" thesis by two Chicago sociologists.[38] Briefly, the notion was that after an initial period of disorientation, the newly homeless man settles into the regimen of the shelter and begins to adapt to a life without work in the company of men who have made their peace with that absence. As he completes his novitiate and "acquires the customs and traditions of the shelters," he tends

> to lose all sense of responsibility for getting out of the shelter; to become insensible to the element of time; to lose ambition, pride, self-respect, and confidence . . . to identify himself with the shelter group.[39]

We have here, of course, the embryonic form of the later "culture of poverty" thesis, and the only partially degraded vestige of the earlier "pauperization" thesis.

---

intellectual "fad" and its consequences would be felt for years to come (R. Hofstadter, *Social Darwinism in American Thought*, rev. ed. [Boston: Beacon, 1955]). A further irony is apparent here: Barnes would get his wish and later that decade systematic testing of an even larger sample of men would indeed reveal that half fell into the "feeble-minded" range. But these were not homeless men; they were Army recruits called up during World War I. If the test results were valid (and they were endorsed, not without a good deal of distress at their implications, by some of the leading figures in American psychometrics of the day), this meant that "we are a nation of nearly half morons" (S. J. Gould, *The Mismeasure of Man* [New York: W. W. Norton, 1981], pp. 196–197).

[38] E. H. Sutherland and H. J. Locke, *Twenty Thousand Homeless Men* (Chicago: J. P. Lippincott, 1936). I include this work here because it continues and codifies earlier observations made by Solenberger in Chicago (1910) and by Barnes in New York, and shared by many others, including (see above, note 9) some of our own contemporaries.

[39] *Ibid.,* p. 142.

Again, a logic of displacement and distancing may be discerned. Social work and social research at that time were preoccupied with the "demoralization" of unemployed workers and their families, a problem that the ministrations of unorganized relief were thought to compound. Even so, it was recognized by some that, as E. Wight Bakke wrote: "The real danger of a permanent relief population is not that the men will lose the desire to work, but that such a desire will make no difference."[40] What had begun as a lively debate about the structural roots of unemployment among reformers and academics, another observer remarked, had devolved to a concern with the social and psychological needs of "special populations" of the unemployed.[41] "Shelterized" men were one such group.

The problem with the "shelterization" thesis is less its accuracy—the observation was too common then and is too often repeated today for it to be seen as sheer sociological fiction—than its incompleteness. It surely pertained to some. But there are indications (fragmentary, to be sure) that many destitute men made use of a variety of arrangements to enable them to get by, including occasional resort to public shelters. They never really "left" mainstream culture so much as supplemented its informal resources with formal assistance. Nor, for a process that was thought to culminate in the depths of "defeatism," did shelterization's effects prove all that difficult to undo. When the American war economy was cranked up in the early forties, the ranks of skid row were depleted of all but the elderly and severely disabled. Shelterized men apparently had no trouble acquitting themselves as soldiers or factory hands.

Reprise—Images of Distance and Disgrace. When Howard Bahr (director of the Columbia Bowery Project in the 1960s) sat

---

[40] "Fifth Winter of Unemployment Relief," *Yale Review* 24 (1934): 268.

[41] M. van Kléeck, "Our Illusions Concerning Government," *Survey* 70 (1934): 190–193.

down to encapsulate public attitudes toward "skid row" (that most degraded form of recognized "homelessness") in the postwar era, he settled upon a formulation that will serve to sum up the prior century as well. It was "his perceived defectiveness as a human being" that most distinguished the skid row man.[42] Here was the premise underlying such common epithets as "degenerate" and "derelict." Here, too, is the reason for Bahr's mentioning "pollution" and the feeding and clothing of "lepers"[43] in connection with public policy toward skid row. In the annals of stigma—negatively valued difference[44]—apparently, few groups rival vagrants in the intensity of the public response occasioned by their presence.

True, alternative understandings of "dependency" (especially those played out in informal networks of support) cannot be ignored. Cultures need not be coherent wholes for their parts and pathways to be charted; but neither should our charts yield coherence as mere artifact.[45] In paying homage to the role of custom and kinship I do not mean to accord them equivalent weight in the setting of municipal policy, even if (as will become clear) these contrary tendencies are centrally ingredient to the feasibility of official policy. Rather, it is to call attention to dominant images, the ones created and propounded by those to whose "custody"[46] official accounts of the poor have been entrusted. For those are the images we find embodied in the institutions and practices that have been devised to deal with the problem of the homeless poor.

[42] H. Bahr, *Skid Row: An Introduction to Disaffiliation* (New York: Oxford University Press, 1973), p. 120.
[43] *Ibid.*, pp. 62, 86.
[44] S. Estroff, *Making It Crazy* (Berkeley: University of California Press, 1981), pp. 220–239.
[45] R. M. Keesing, "Anthropology as Interpretive Quest," *Current Anthropology* 28 (April 1987): 161–175.
[46] G. Bateson, *Naven*, 2d ed. (Stanford: Stanford University Press, 1958), p. 227; as cited in *ibid.*, p. 164.

The Legacy of Public Shelter: Zone of Discard/Zone of Refuge[47]

Ethnographers read history not only to situate their own inquiries within proper bounds and force fields, but the better to be able to "take the back traces" (as one of Le Carré's characters put it)—to ask how and with what consequences the past continues to inform the present, insidious though that shaping may be. The exercise is bracing, imparting a kind of low-voltage culture shock, upsetting habits of seeing that normally escape notice and scrutiny; it is especially useful, I would suggest, in examining issues of public policy, where the questions *not* asked, the practical alternatives *not* debated, and ways of framing the problem considered *un*thinkable to contemporary common sense, may offer clues to the nature of the cultural reality at stake.

Three themes will serve to limn the history of New York's attempts to deal with the homeless poor.

Nature of the Problem. Persistent efforts have been made to reduce the problem of homelessness to the problems of the homeless poor themselves—variously construed as defects, vices, or ailments. The three constructions reviewed above are representative of such efforts. Typically, they appear to have had only limited success with the populace at large. The more vicious images have also tended to give way during periods of unusual hardship to an acknowledgment of the role of larger, "structural" factors.[48] Studies of homeless men (also usually mounted in times of widespread distress) have, with few exceptions, identified the crucial role played by the labor market in determining their fate, whatever their personal

[47] "Zone of discard" is a phrase used by the urban geographers R. E. Murphy et al., "Internal Structure of the CBD," *Economic Geography* 31 (1955): 21–46; "zone of refuge" is from C. Cohen and J. Sokolovsky, *Old Men of the Bowery* (New York: Guilford Press, 1989). Both refer to skid-row areas.

[48] Cf. E. Wolf, "Distinguished Lecture: Facing Power—Old Insights, New Questions," *American Anthropologist* 92 (1990): 586–596.

quirks or quiddities may be. Indeed, throughout most of his history, the present being the exception, the homeless man was defined primarily in terms of the work he did not (or could not) do, rather than the home he did not (or could not) make.

The strong ambivalence toward dependency that was the colonial heritage of the English Poor Laws is apparent as well, manifest chiefly as a suspicion of those who apply for aid (whatever the causes of their distress) and a "penitential" attitude toward those who accept it. This is contested, periodically and sometimes aggressively, by vernacular expressions of assistance which tend to be far less judgmental or punitive.

Terms and Locus of Assistance. Officially, a premium has been placed on isolated, marginal settings as the appropriate site for public shelters. This use of out-of-the-way sites was intended to help deter all but the truly needy (to adopt an unfortunate but fitting anachronism). The forbidding character of the place became part of the "means test" that applicants were expected not only to pass as a condition of entry but to endure as a token of worth for the duration of their stay.[49] These marginal sites—off the shores, in unused or surplus properties, at the boundaries of polite society—amount to public shelter as a form of domestic exile. They were exercises in quarantine designed to keep at bay species of "demoralization" or "insubordination" or simple dependency that were viewed as potentially threatening or troublesome (by virtue of the burden of support they imposed). Thus the institutional space of refuge both contained and reproduced the social status of those who were its proper occupants.[50] If such inmates are to

---

[49] Thus the site chosen for the consolidation of the institutional response to the poor in the mid-nineteenth century was Blackwell's (now Roosevelt) Island in the East River. Piers and ferry boats were considered the logical resources for handling the overflow of the Municipal Lodging House. In 1979, when a court order forced the opening of the first public shelter in forty years, the location was once again an island.

[50] As, in another place and time, Steven Marcus has argued, forms of shadow

be considered "disaffiliated"[51]—the leitmotif of postwar studies of the homeless man—it is because that is a condition of
their assistance, not an expression of their characters.

More generally, while the principle of "less eligibility"[52] may
have been the axiom of poor relief, it was one that proved
damnably difficult to realize in practice. Brave plans for an
architecture of deterrence and rehabilitation foundered
repeatedly, checked by the sheer scale of need and the wiles of
"an intractable and slippery poor" whom want had left both
desperate and canny.[53] On the one hand, institutional "terror"
(discipline, forced work, and isolation) found it difficult to
compete with the everyday squalor and degraded conditions in
the tenements and cellar dwellings available to the indigent. To
the chronic frustration of official visitors, residents of the
almshouse and workhouse[54] were often found to prefer that
setting (at least in winter) to others available to them. On the
other, on those repeated occasions when need was widespread,
organized protest (or the threat of it) may well have boosted
minimal standards of decency in the shelter provided.[55]

We have, then, the makings of an institution whose actual
practice will both embody a social attitude of containment and
concealment and yet can be made to accommodate the needs

---

work—collecting the garbage and offal from the streets—have done (*Engels, Manchester
and the Working Class* [New York: Vintage, 1974], pp. 196ff). In that regard, too, it
might be remarked that the mode of subsistence on the streets today—eking out an
existence from the discarded refuse of a society of abundance—reproduces in
spontaneous fashion the social status of the street homeless as redundant,
unproductive, and "surplus" populations.

[51] An inability to form, or refusal to abide by, the ties that bind us together as
members of a common society. Cf. Bahr, *Skid Row*, passim.

[52] That the situation of the assisted pauper was to be less attractive (or "eligible")
than that of the most menial laborer, so as to keep sharp the spur of necessity and
preserve the incentive to work.

[53] S. A. Klips, "Institutionalizing the Poor: The New York City Almshouse,
1825–1860," Ph.D. dissertation, City University of New York, 1980, p. 346

[54] Even the prison: as one exasperated city alderman found, for all its horrors, some
inmates "instead of looking to prison as a terror, they look forward to it as an abode of
care, as asylum from wretchedness" (*ibid.*, p. 340).

[55] A function served primarily by public-interest litigation in our own time.

of a poor well drilled in the arts of turning official design to
contrary utilities.

Institutional Deterence/Popular Makeshifts. Much as had been the
case with reformist campaigns against street begging in the
nineteenth century, popular practice seems to have been badly
out of joint with official policy on the matter of "less eligibility."
Professional charity and social workers would rail time and
again against "indiscriminate almsgiving" as a counterproduc-
tive, "pauperizing" practice. Common folks just as predictably
found it awkward and demeaning to try to divide "deserving"
from "undeserving," and organized drives to distribute food,
fuel, and clothing during times of acute need. More pervasive
still were the varieties of unobtrusive aid, the everyday
practices of sharing and support which ordinary people
resorted to as routine matters. These things were done quietly,
out of sight, without any public declaration of need or
intention to relieve, and thus for the most part have eluded the
social scientist's prying gaze. But they are worth stressing, if for
nothing else than because they constitute the invisible and
enabling complement to institutional deterrence.[56]

Men who found their way to the shelters represented only a
small fraction of the population which was out of work and,
temporarily at least, without fallback resources. Most of them
managed to cope most of the time without ever calling
attention to themselves by a formal application for relief. The
ingenuity and improvisations of the families of the unemployed that would so impress researchers in the 1930s were
already well-established traditions among the urban poor by
the turn of the century—not as exceptional measures instituted

---

[56] Or so, at any rate, I have argued in "Public Shelter as 'a Hybrid Institution',"
Journal of Social Issues, forthcoming. I draw here on Alex Keyssar, *Out of Work: The First
Century of Unemployment in Massachusetts* (New York: Cambridge University Press, 1986)
on adaptations to unemployment in late nineteenth-century Massachusetts as well as,
in the longer view, Olwen Hufton, *The Poor in Eighteenth Century France, 1750–1789*
(Oxford: Clarendon, 1974).

in response to a transient crisis, but as commonplace means of getting by, "indistinguishable from the larger and more permanent task of coping with being poor."[57] Routine hardship, acute misfortune, and spells of real scarcity were familiar presences in these households, and the decision to seek out institutional aid—especially when that meant enduring the humiliation of the almshouse or the seedy, anonymous democracy of police station-house lodgings—was one of uncommon desperation. For the most art, such folks resorted to kinship and custom (traditional family supports), not the state; and when those failed, single men took to tramping in order to alleviate the burden at home.[58]

Reprise—Varieties of Institutional Use. For all practical purposes, then, the undifferentiated poorhouse never really disappeared. If it "began with few accomplishments and confused designs,"[59] the same may be said for the way in which it has endured. Indeed, I would argue that any distinction between the almshouse and the municipal lodging house (public shelter)—other than the old age and decrepitude that characterized the former's inmates after the turn of the century—is finally an artificial one. Actual patterns of use, whatever may have been intended by their architects, appear to have been shaped to a significant degree by the pragmatic, deliberate action of the men (mainly) these institutions lodged and the shadow support of their friends and family.

The logic of official discourse is something else altogether. Repeatedly, the language of pathology and images of the grotesque have been resorted to in order to explain distressed circumstances. At times, as with Charles Barnes, the maneuver is frankly gratuitous, even bizarre—and perhaps the more telling for that.[60] The issue isn't the premise of such arguments

---

[57] Keyssar, *Out of Work*, p. 156.
[58] E. H. Monkkonen, "Afterword," in Monkkonen, *Walking to Work*, pp. 240, 242.
[59] Rothman, *Discovery of the Asylum*, p. 287.
[60] For a contemporary version of a similarly telling slip: in an otherwise closely

but their tenacity, the regularity with which they crop up whenever sustained attention is paid to a group whose ordinary *modus vivendi* is to avoid detection.[61]

There is, however, an instructive exception to the rule: beginning in the Progressive Era, administrators of public-shelter programs recognized that in times of industrial depression their burgeoning clientele was made up of "two populations."[62] The one, in desperate need of rehabilitation or custody, was rooted in individual deficiencies; the other, in desperate need of a job, was rooted in structural defects in the labor market. The trick was somehow to keep the first from infecting ("demoralizing") the ranks of the second, and thus converting temporary setback into vagrant career. Selective inoculation, in pursuit of some moral "herd immunity," would never prove effective, given the scale of need.[63] In the end, the crisis was weathered, not resolved; serious confrontation with the forces of dispossession common to both groups was avoided.

But the suppressed premise is clear. Fears of pollution attest to underlying identity as well as avowed difference. A proposal that would have yoked shelter and labor needs together was unthinkable because it would have challenged the basic

---

reasoned work, two economists have recently argued that "it appears that there are two distinct populations, *each with its own pathology*," among the homeless and go on to identify one as the economically marginal—that is, those who are "sensitive to fluctuations in economic conditions such as housing and labor markets or to policy variables such as the level of income or housing assistance" (R. K. Filer and M. Honig, *Policy Issues in Homelessness: Current Understanding and Directions for Research* [New York: Manhattan Institute, 1990], p. 14; emphasis added).

[61] The premise is itself questionable: that the distinctive shape of a social niche is best explained by examining (or fabricating) the traits of its occupants. To begin with, this confounds two distinct notions of function, present state and historical origin.

[62] S. A. Rice, "The Homeless," *Annals of the American Academy of Political and Social Science* 77 (1918): 140–153, and "The Failure of the Municipal Lodging House," *National Municipal Review* 11 (1922): 358–362.

[63] "Targeted" programs (special shelters, for example) designed for a "better class" of homeless men (M. Josephson, "The Other Nation," *New Republic*, May 17, 1933, p. 15) were puny in size and served mainly to perpetuate status distinctions within the lower depths.

distinctions relief programs were set up to protect. It would have meant seeing recurring homelessness and unemployment—not as "accidents" of nature or deviant by-products of an otherwise well-functioning system—but as part of what it means for such a system to "work." That never happened. Instead, public shelter hobbled along its way, a vast, congregate "hybrid institution" that managed, not without a great deal of anxiety and criticism, to do a disservice to both groups of clients.

Writing much later, a public-health historian took note of the horrible toll of morbidity and morality that was the lot of the Victorian poor in terms that will serve us well here. Forget about all the talk of vicious habits and self-destructive practices, George Rosen urged; even the studies of that era made it "abundantly clear [that] what was the matter with the poor was their poverty."[64] Look not to the grotesque, but to the ordinary . . .

Which brings me full circle.

Conclusion

> . . . for human communication to occur
> co-evalness has to be *created*.[65]

Like "the heath" in Shakespeare's time,[66] "the street" in our own has come to signify a kind of close repository of things evil and alien, and that is a badly damaging misrepresentation.[67]

---

[64] G. Rosen, "Disease, Debility and Death," in H. J. Dyos and M. Wolf, eds., *The Victorian City: Images and Realities* (New York: Methuen, 1973), 2: 651.

[65] Fabian, *Time and the Other*, pp. 30–31.

[66] Ignatieff, *Needs of Strangers*, pp. 40–41.

[67] E.g., M. Magnet, "Homeless: Craziness, Dope and Danger," *New York Times*, Jan. 26, 1990, p. A31; J. Toth, "N.Y.'s 'Mole People' Shun Society in Transit Tunnels," *Los Angeles Times*, Sept. 2, 1990, p. A1. On the dark side of society, the street shares with the penal colony, madhouse, theater of horror the distinction of being a dreaded cultural entity, but one that contains performances that have traditionally exerted a certain fascination all their own (R. D. Abrahams, "Ordinary and Extraordinary

For every hapless sidewalk Lear (that reckless, ruined king) for whom the street is a public stage for grappling with private demons, there are dozens of others for whom it means a rather complicated way of extracting a livelihood from the waste spaces and resources of the city. That, it seems to me, is both the lesson of history and the yield of contemporary ethnography. It is not, however, the image of homelessness that prevails in public discourse or neighborhood disputes on the siting of new facilities.

In part, no doubt, the animus toward the homeless poor has to do with the sheer arithmetic of need: when the number of the visibly suffering gets large enough, distinctions get drawn, rank orders of need and acceptability are established. Lifeboats, at least of the sort we are content to let float nearby, can accommodate only so many of certain kinds.

In part, too, as Peter Marin has nicely argued,[68] it has to do with the still vague, but unmistakably unsettling, bundle of anxieties set off by these standing affronts to notions of bourgeois order.[69] The sensibilities of culture may be invented but they are no less real or insistent for that. Those who violate our sense of order are especially ill placed to prompt in us some aboriginal sense of a lost "contract," some pact whereby it is made clear that no "casualty of the free-market system" should have to *earn* the elemental goods of survival.

The real alternative to homelessness, then,[70] is not shelter but solidarity. That, I take it, is at least in part what Peter

Experience," in V. W. Turner and E. M. Bruner, eds., *The Anthropology of Experience* ([Chicago: University of Illinois Press, 1986], p. 88).

[68] P. Marin, "Helping and Hating the Homeless," *Harper's Magazine*, January 1987, pp. 39–49.

[69] Nor are such sentiments restricted to the well off, as is apparent in the sometimes bitter opposition to shelter programs in poor and working-class neighborhoods. The wellsprings of such opposition, however—whether, for example, it has more to do with perceived loss of local control than with the stigma attached to the incoming groups—have yet to be closely studied.

[70] Necessary, if not sufficient. And here I follow Ignatieff, *Needs of Strangers*; J. Berger, *And Our Faces, My Heart, Brief as Photos* (New York: Pantheon, 1984), p. 67; and Marin, "Helping and Hating the Homeless," at least as I read them.

Conrad is driving at in his adamant *refusal* to distance the street homeless, his insistence instead on making them *our* interlocutors:

> The homeless are never without a home. Their appalling pathos, which makes me shiver with *recognition* as I pass them, lies in the way they fantasticate houses for themselves, conjuring them magically out of air or assembling them from cartons, wagon-trains of shopping trolleys, screens made from garment racks. . . . On the pavement or windswept parks, they deploy all the arts whereby we live, and convince ourselves that we are at home in the world. They solemnly trust their flimsy barricades and tottering ramparts, yet at the same time—*with an honesty the rest of us can't afford*—they admit they are inhabiting an illusion.[71]

That is a kind of coevalness, or at least a step in its direction, and it isn't an easy achievement. But neither is it clear how Conrad knows this is what they feel about their constructions, or what difference it makes to the homeless poor themselves to be newly vested with the role of playing sidewalk Fool to our blind complacencies. The writer still walks by, inwardly shaken perhaps; the street poor still brave the elements with less cover than a hunter-gatherer band would deem respectable. Aren't there echoes here of the spiritually "sublimated," but practically inconsequential, status of the medieval poor? Does it really matter that they *signify* differently?

Still, the alternative to thinking along these lines and, especially, of being open to the lessons likely to emerge from the ranks of the homeless poor themselves, is grim. If history is the least bit reliable as a guide, the alternative is to await the next round of sweeps and confinement, confident (or so we will try to convince ourselves) that whatever measures are undertaken, no matter how repressive or alienating, they will be instituted "in the best interests of the poor."

Recall the description of homeless people I chose as a text for this talk—"a curse to themselves and a menace and injury

---

[71] P. Conrad, *Where I Fell to Earth* (New York: Poseidon Press, 1990), p. 203; emphasis added.

to the city." It comes not from some broadside in the "campaign to eliminate the tramp" as might well be supposed, not from an attack on street begging and the misguided citizens who conspire in its perpetuation. No, the phrase comes from an informational pamphlet distributed by the Conference of Charities of the City of New York in 1894, and entitled "How to Help Homeless People."

* For helpful comments on an earlier draft, I would like to thank Mary Brosnahan and Alex Keyssar.

EXILE, ALIENATION, AND ESTRANGEMENT

What does it mean to "belong"? There is a painful condition of being which is not tied to having a home or homeland in any ordinary sense. This is the condition of alienation or estrangement.

Introduction

THE TITLE of our panel, "Exile, Alienation, and Estrangement," indicates that we take up again some of the themes discussed in the first panel on "The Idea of Home." Orlando Patterson's paper is a meditation on the uprootedness of slavery and the way in which slaves can give birth to a new idea of freedom. David Bromwich deals with the way in which the presence of an old, poor, homeless, and wandering man can give birth, in those who see him, to a new idea of belonging. Sanford Budick treats of the stubborn and dreamy relation of womb and home. All three papers thus weave connections between the two main emphases of this conference: home as a physical place and space, and being at home as a mental or spiritual condition.

I would like to begin by offering a few remarks on being at home as a mental or spiritual condition. I mean, casually and briefly, to defend an idea that is not commonly defended. (It is not clear to me that any of our three panelists or, indeed, any of the participants in our conference would defend it, even though all of them thrive because of their unstated faith in it.) The idea is that alienation or estrangement is good, and hence that wanting to be at home mentally or spiritually is questionable and ought to be questioned.

I approach this matter by asking, What is the best way of being at home in the sense of living in one's own place? One answer, but not a frequent one, is to try to become alienated (or estranged) mentally or spiritually—perhaps I should add, to some degree. Another word for alienation in some of its meanings is distance. Each one of us needs a little distance, needs to learn to see as from a distance. That, in turn, can mean, in Nietzsche's sense, to see as from a height. But in a

democracy—the only culture of individual distance as distinct
from group distance—distance should not mean height,
because height means disdain or even insolence. These latter
sentiments poison democracy. Rather, democratic distance is
part of what Emerson calls self-reliance. To be alienated, to
some appreciable degree, then, is to be on the way to
self-reliance. Self-reliance is thinking one's own thoughts, and
thinking one's own thoughts through. Self-reliance is a
process; it is arduous, intermittent, expressed in and defeated
by moods. Self-reliance is actually, in Emerson's conception,
self-recovery.

A great example, in literature, of self-recovery is Socrates,
who at the start of his *Apology* says that his accusers have
almost made him forget who he is—almost, but not quite, not
at all. This self-examined man could withstand the descriptions
that others made of him. Self-examination sets and keeps one
at a distance. One can develop a self-understanding that is
self-reliant. His accusers do know him, but not well enough,
because they are not self-examined, and hence they are at
home mentally and spiritually (religiously) and he is not.

If Socrates is noble, it is then noble to praise alienation. On
the other hand, it is pathetic, sad, to praise the condition of
being at home in the mental or spiritual sense. The best praise
of alienation comes from those who use being at home (in the
familiar sense) to aspire to alienation. They do not accept it
with gladness; rather they see it as indispensable to self-
reliance. The most understandable praise of being at home
mentally or spiritually comes from those who are in exile, and
who may therefore be disoriented and hence in a condition
unfavorable to the right kind of distance, which is mental or
spiritual. Socrates refused to travel out of Athens; he went
away "less than the lame and the blind and the crippled": he
knew that he would lose distance if he were physically distant;
he would lose the thread if he left; just as Thoreau acted as if
he could travel widely in Concord. Socrates knew that to be
alienated properly, he had literally to be at home. Gratitude

for one's place is shown by mental or spiritual distance. Democracy builds its connectedness partly out of mutually respected distance, the distance that grows out of the self-examination that Socrates (and then Emerson, Thoreau, and Whitman) thought that a democracy exists to encourage, and that is intrinsic to the process of self-reliance. So, what is *not* praiseworthy, I would say, is praise of being at home in the mental or spiritual sense by those who have a home. All they are—these spiritually homesick ones, the ones to whom Stanley Cavell referred in his opening remarks—is unhappy. They want more home; they will not grow up and try to become self-reliant.

At home, they want more home. They are homesick, even though they are home. What is their desire? They crave that the self be made of answerable questions. They want no real self-process. They want an identity, a self-same self. They want to be defined, known, and understood by those around them. Others are their furnishings. They do not believe in the right of self-trust. All this longing replaces the Delphic command, "Know thyself," which Thoreau renders as "Explore thyself." All this longing replaces the Socratic plea to lead the self-examined life so that we can hope to become, in Emersonian language, self-reliant.

I grant that it may not be much that one discovers if one tries self-examination. Certainly, no true, deep self. That is a fiction as bad as the idea of a self made of socially answerable questions. Perhaps the most that one can learn is who or what one is not; and thus be able to say to those who share one's home, one's world, such phrases as: No, I'm not what you say; I'm more, I'm better; I'm worse, I'm less; I could be different; I could have been different. Thoreau, for one, discovered that, as he says in *Walden*, "I never knew, and never shall know, a worse man than myself." From such negative self-knowledge his charity flowed.

In turn, the identity that results from self-examination may not be more than what is left over when all inadequate characterizations of oneself are discarded, as Socrates discards the picture of him that his accusers draw. Home, in the mental or spiritual sense, is only the collaboration of oneself and others—in "Self-Reliance" Emerson calls it a conspiracy—to accept a false, incomplete, or premature identity, as if the only believable and livable identity had to be false, incomplete, or premature. To reject being at home mentally or spiritually—to praise alienation—is to accept a burden, but it is the same thing as trying to live honestly rather than living a story.

Alienation and Belonging to Humanity

BY DAVID BROMWICH

I WANT TO DISCUSS what it means to be alienated from one's purposes, or dispossessed of one's full human faculties; in the course of doing so, I hope to suggest something unexpected about what the opposite of alienation might be. On the view that is explored here, the opposite of alienation turns out not to be a state of healthy functioning, social usefulness, self-understanding and self-esteem. It may have more to do with one's capacity to participate in a free act of sympathy. But the idea of sympathy itself, in the argument I offer, will come to have a sense that is unfamiliar. It is feeling for another person. But, from the operation of respect and distance, it is feeling of an impersonal sort, and it does not include the possibility of feeling *as* another person. Nor does it include any expectation of reciprocal feeling. Sympathy is my recognition of someone else—a recognition that cannot be altogether private—under the aspect of a common humanity. This recognition is usually followed by, or anyway related to, an action that I perform. The action like the feeling anticipates nothing in return.

Any such idea of sympathy has its source in nineteenth-century thought. One suggestion of the greatest romantic poetry is that we are all of us often at the edge of a dispossession of our full selves. Our humanity, that is, does not derive from a confident sense that the things that are ours belong to us and we belong to them. Property, status, function, the whole train of social and moral relations, which are laid down by prescription or which we come into by an effort of will: between none of these things and ourselves can there be the kind of happy fit that defines a human identity. To be deprived, therefore, of the assurance that there is such a fit is sometimes, perhaps much of the time, a given fact of consciousness. We may call this alienation even though no real poet in English has ever used the word. Wordsworth, for example, in *The Prelude,* describes the sensation of such a moment in these words: "And all the ballast of familiar life, / The present, and the past; hope, fear; all stays, / All laws of acting, thinking, speaking man / Went from me, neither knowing me, nor known." But there is another suggestion in such poetry: that through the sympathy I feel for another person—someone whose claim on me was not to be taken for granted, but took on reality only by vivid interest and recognition—I can come to feel what it is for me to belong to humanity.

This seems to be the only belonging that ever marks a recovery from alienation; and Wordsworth, when he speaks of it, shows that the cure is almost as strange as the disease: it leaves him with a sense of being "turned round / As with the might of waters"; of being turned back upon himself "As if admonished from another world." This happens, Wordsworth implies in *The Prelude* and elsewhere, when one experiences the being of someone else as merely human. It follows that the action of sympathy, or recognition, or acknowledgment, for Wordsworth not only is not associated with the idea of receiving something back, but cannot be expected to yield any result of a calculable sort—the sort of result one might expect from a beneficiary, a fellow sufferer, or whatever. Yet sympathy, on the rare occasions when we feel it outside the bonds of friendship or familiar response, does make an addition to consciousness that can change a life. In this way it assists in defining a community, or home in the widest sense of the word.

Because much of the abstract argument here grew out of

my reading of a poem by Wordsworth, "The Old Cumberland Beggar," it seems more in keeping with the aims of the conference to share the poem with you than to suppose a general acquaintance with it and trace the implications for moral philosophy. The implications, I hope, will emerge from the reading. "The Old Cumberland Beggar" was written in 1797, when Wordsworth was twenty-six, but it does not feel like a young man's poem, and it may indeed come from the kind of experience that can seem to take youth away. I mean an experience of political disenchantment. Wordsworth in his early twenties had been an enthusiast of the French Revolution, and all his life he retained a loyalty to the ideals of individual dignity and human solidarity which the revolution seemed, to him, above all to embody. By the time he wrote this poem, the idea that a single movement of political justice could represent the hopes of all humanity had become for him unreal. Partly, this was an unreality of feeling—prior to, and more important than, any doubts that analysis might raise. From the evidence of his own response, Wordsworth came to think that one could not feel a fraternal connection to all of humanity at once. He still shared with the radicals of 1789 the rooted conviction that any other person was owed the same respect that is always owing to oneself. But, for Wordsworth, this meant potentially anyone, and not actually everyone at once. To feel the common humanity by which he was bound to someone, Wordsworth had to bring another life close to home.

Here, then, is the text of "The Old Cumberland Beggar" (incorporating the poet's later revisions):

The class of Beggars, to which the Old Man here described belongs, will probably soon be extinct. It consisted of poor, and, mostly, old and infirm persons, who confined themselves to a stated round in their neighbourhood, and had certain fixed days, on which, at different houses, they regularly received alms, sometimes in money, but mostly in provisions.

I saw an aged Beggar in my walk;
And he was seated, by the highway side,
On a low structure of rude masonry
Built at the foot of a huge hill, that they
Who lead their horses down the steep rough road
May thence remount at ease. The aged Man
Had placed his staff across the broad smooth stone
That overlays the pile; and, from a bag
All white with flour, the dole of village dames,
He drew his scraps and fragments, one by one;   10
And scanned them with a fixed and serious look
Of idle computation. In the sun,
Upon the second step of that small pile,
Surrounded by those wild unpeopled hills,
He sat, and ate his food in solitude:
And ever, scattered from his palsied hand,
That, still attempting to prevent the waste,
Was baffled still, the crumbs in little showers
Fell on the ground; and the small mountain birds,
Not venturing yet to peck their destined meal,   20
Approached within the length of half his staff.

    Him from my childhood have I known; and then
He was so old, he seems not older now;
He travels on, a solitary Man,
So helpless in appearance, that for him
The sauntering Horseman throws not with a slack
And careless hand his alms upon the ground,
But stops,—that he may safely lodge the coin
Within the old Man's hat; nor quits him so,
But still, when he has given his horse the rein,   30
Watches the aged Beggar with a look
Sidelong, and half-reverted. She who tends
The toll-gate, when in summer at her door
She turns her wheel, if on the road she sees
The aged Beggar coming, quits her work,
And lifts the latch for him that he may pass.
The post-boy, when his rattling wheels o'ertake
The aged Beggar in the woody lane,
Shouts to him from behind; and, if thus warned
The old man does not change his course, the boy   40
Turns with less noisy wheels to the roadside,
And passes gently by, without a curse
Upon his lips, or anger at his heart.

He travels on, a solitary Man;
His age has no companion. On the ground
His eyes are turned, and, as he moves along,
They move along the ground; and, evermore,
Instead of common and habitual sight
Of fields with rural works, of hill and dale,
And the blue sky, one little span of earth   50
Is all his prospect. Thus, from day to day,
Bow-bent, his eyes for ever on the ground,
He plies his weary journey; seeing still,
And seldom knowing that he sees, some straw,
Some scattered leaf, or marks which, in one track,
The nails of cart or chariot-wheel have left
Impressed on the white road,—in the same line,
At distance still the same. Poor Traveller!
His staff trails with him; scarcely do his feet
Disturb the summer dust; he is so still   60
In look and motion, that the cottage curs,
Ere he has passed the door, will turn away,
Weary of barking at him. Boys and girls,
The vacant and the busy, maids and youths,
And urchins newly breeched—all pass him by:
Him even the slow-paced waggon leaves behind.

But deem not this Man useless.—Statesmen! Ye
Who are so restless in your wisdom, ye
Who have a broom still ready in your hands
To rid the world of nuisances; ye proud,   70
Heart-swoln, while in your pride ye contemplate
Your talents, power, or wisdom, deem him not
A burthen of the earth! 'Tis Nature's law
That none, the meanest of created things,
Of forms created the most vile and brute,
The dullest or most noxious, should exist
Divorced from good—a spirit and pulse of good,
A life and soul, to every mode of being
Inseparably linked. Then be assured
That least of all can aught—that ever owned   80
The heaven-regarding eye and front sublime
Which man is born to—sink, howe'er depressed,
So low as to be scorned without a sin;
Without offense to God cast out of view;
Like the dry remnant of a garden-flower
Whose seeds are shed, or as an implement
Worn out and worthless. While from door to door,

This old Man creeps, the villagers in him
Behold a record which together binds
Past deeds and offices of charity,   90
Else unremembered, and so keeps alive
The kindly mood in hearts which lapse of years,
And that half-wisdom half-experience gives,
Make slow to feel, and by sure steps resign
To selfishness and cold oblivious cares.
Among the farms and solitary huts,
Hamlets and thinly-scattered villages,
Where'er the aged Beggar takes his rounds,
The mild necessity of use compels
To acts of love; and habit does the work   100
Of reason; yet prepares that after-joy
Which reason cherishes. And thus the soul,
By that sweet taste of pleasure unpursued,
Doth find herself insensibly disposed
To virtue and true goodness.

                                 Some there are,
By their good works exalted, lofty minds
And meditative, authors of delight
And happiness, which to the end of time
Will live, and spread, and kindle: even such minds
In childhood, from this solitary Being,   110
Or from like wanderer, haply have received
(A thing more precious far than all that books
Or the solicitudes of love can do!)
That first mild touch of sympathy and thought,
In which they found their kindred with a world
Where want and sorrow were. The easy man
Who sits at his own door,—and, like the pear
That overhangs his head from the green wall,
Feeds in the sunshine; the robust and young,
The prosperous and unthinking, they who live   120
Sheltered, and flourish in a little grove
Of their own kindred;—all behold in him
A silent monitor, which on their minds
Must needs impress a transitory thought
Of self-congratulation, to the heart
Of each recalling his peculiar boons,
His charters and exemptions; and, perchance,
Though he to no one give the fortitude
And circumspection needful to preserve
His present blessings, and to husband up   130

The respite of the season, he, at least,
And 'tis no vulgar service, makes them felt.

    Yet further.—Many, I believe, there are
Who live a life of virtuous decency,
Men who can hear the Decalogue and feel
No self-reproach; who of the moral law
Established in the land where they abide
Are strict observers; and not negligent
In acts of love to those with whom they dwell,
Their kindred, and the children of their blood.   140
Praise be to such, and to their slumbers peace!
—But of the poor man ask, the abject poor;
Go, and demand of him, if there be here
In this cold abstinence from evil deeds,
And these inevitable charities,
Wherewith to satisfy the human soul?
No—man is dear to man; the poorest poor
Long for some moments in a weary life
When they can know and feel that they have been,
Themselves, the fathers and the dealers-out   150
Of some small blessings; have been kind to such
As needed kindness, for this single cause,
That we have all of us one human heart.
—Such pleasure is to one kind Being known,
My neighbour, when with punctual care, each week
Duly as Friday comes, though pressed herself
By her own wants, she from her store of meal
Takes one unsparing handful for the scrip
Of this old Mendicant, and, from her door
Returning with exhilarated heart,   160
Sits by her fire, and builds her hope in heaven.

    Then let him pass, a blessing on his head!
And while in that vast solitude to which
The tide of things has borne him, he appears
To breathe and live but for himself alone,
Unblamed, uninjured, let him bear about
The good which the benignant law of Heaven
Has hung around him: and, while life is his,
Still let him prompt the unlettered villagers
To tender offices and pensive thoughts.   170
—Then let him pass, a blessing on his head!
And, long as he can wander, let him breathe
The freshness of the valleys; let his blood

Struggle with frosty air and winter snows;
And let the chartered wind that sweeps the heath
Beat his grey locks against his withered face.
Reverence the hope whose vital anxiousness
Gives the last human interest to his heart.
May never HOUSE, misnamed of INDUSTRY,
Make him a captive!—for that pent-up din,   180
Those life-consuming sounds that clog the air,
Be his the natural silence of old age!
Let him be free of mountain solitudes;
And have around him, whether heard or not,
The pleasant melody of woodland birds.
Few are his pleasures: if his eyes have now
Been doomed so long to settle upon earth
That not without some effort they behold
The countenance of the horizontal sun,
Rising or setting, let the light at least   190
Find a free entrance to their languid orbs.
And let him, *where* and *when* he will, sit down
Beneath the trees, or on a grassy bank
Of highway side, and with the little birds
Share his chance-gathered meal; and, finally,
As in the eye of Nature he has lived,
So in the eye of Nature let him die!

The old beggar of this poem is pictured at first as an alien object—a ruined piece of nature, something human reduced to an almost animal state. He does not have the protection of a family, or for that matter a place of shelter: "his place knows him not." And yet he belongs, and is felt by others to belong, to a certain neighborhood: a stretch of turnpike road in the county of Cumberland. He is known there as a familiar landmark by the persons who regularly use the road—the postboy, the woman who keeps the tollgate, the villagers who live nearby. They give him modest provisions, which are as much as he needs; and, in a way that mere description cannot capture, they incorporate him in their lives. For them, he is a habit so well worn that it appears to have joined the nature of things. The story of where he came from is lost in a time before the beginning of anyone's memory. Wordsworth, or the narrator through whom Wordsworth speaks and who can stand for any of the villagers, says of him typically: "Him from my childhood have I known; and then / He was so old, he seems not older now." He has endured so much change from the slow processes of time that at last he has come to seem changeless. And for this reason, or because of this unreasoning impression, he evokes, from the small community of those who pass him by, a sense of loyalty to something steady in their way of life. They give him coins or food, they salute him, or ease his way by lifting a latch at a stile. They do not serve him as companions; they do not watch over him. They help to sustain him in the life that he holds.

So far, I have been surveying the beggar from a distance, but that is a mode of treatment far from Wordsworth's own, and I want to look more closely now at the story this poem tells and the argument it suggests. Wordsworth sees the beggar on his walk, and describes him as if for the first time (he is oddly called *an* aged beggar; *the* would be more appropriate if the experience were customary). He approaches the man with this degree of restraint, I think, because he wants to make him as strange to the reader as he is to anyone encountering him for the first time. The old man is drawing scraps of food from his bag, scanning them, Wordsworth says, "with a fixed and serious look / Of idle computation": he would count the scraps, but his mind is beyond the effort of counting; only the look of serious attention remains. There is an impression of enormous care in the poet's gaze too: we learn everything about how the man looks, even which step he was sitting on.

Now comes a significant detail. Some of the food slips through the fingers of his palsied hand, the birds are coming close and later they will pick up the scraps. Why does the poem dwell on this? The beggar's care for himself has carried wide of its aim: a fact in which much pathos might be found, but in which Wordsworth finds none at all. If anything, the detail suggests a chain of human and natural economies. As the villagers feed the man, following a custom they can no longer justify or track to its source, so the man regularly, involuntarily feeds the birds. In both cases the givers do what they do without choice, because of who they are. It is an unconscious process. By contrast, the act of reading a poem, or of reflecting on the justice of a society, must at some point become a conscious process. Wordsworth's purpose is to make his reader see the good of continuing, by an exertion of the will, a way of life that can seem to have been carried forward in the absence of will.

The second verse paragraph describes the acts of mild, but habitual, charity which the beggar creates in those around him. That certain things are done for him seems, in the eyes of others, to define who he is and who they are. With the fresh interest established by this fact, Wordsworth, in a second careful portrait, comes back to the man again, on the road and slowly walking: "He travels on, a solitary man" (line 44). The way his eyes move along the ground, seeing each spot for a moment, brings out the great difference between the old beggar and the people to whom he is a familiar figure. As they see him, he belongs to their place. That is why he matters, to them. But in his own eyes this man can hardly seem to belong anywhere. His eyes are bent upon the ground, as, before, they were bent over his food, in idle computation. He moves from step to step, seeing the earth in glimpses, possessing nothing but the spot of earth he sees. Or, one could say that each of these spaces is his for a moment, but none is more so than another. His "rootedness," to call it that, is an unassimilable sequence of gestures that only looks like a pattern. The man makes no claim for himself, and it would be wrong to see him as signifying, to the poet or these villagers, a claim for any broad associated sentiment like the sanctity of old age or the freedom of the open road. That he is, is his claim.

The bareness of this assertion ought to be puzzling, the more so as Wordsworth will go on to make a direct appeal, *that this man matters*. His incorporation in the lives of other people humanizes the life of a community. In fact, Wordsworth will say more: that there is a right way, and a wrong way, to treat such a man. And more: that the right way has nothing immediately to do with how well he is fed, how well he is sheltered, how well his years are nursed into longer years. These things might all be done on a system, and yet the system might be wicked. I will return in a moment to the likely political emphasis of the poem in its time; let us turn now to Wordsworth's account of why it is right for this man to live as he does. He stands as an example of "A life and soul, to every mode of being / Inseparably linked" (line 78). This can seem a difficult or perhaps an imprecise idea. Wordsworth means something very precise by it. As he interprets it, we see that it is anything but a sentimental idea. The poem describes in almost impersonal terms the good of the moral relations that the Cumberland Beggar brings into being for the villagers: "the villagers in him / Behold a record which together binds / Past deeds and offices of charity / Else unremembered." Each of the villagers, that is, has performed certain acts for the beggar. Each, seeing him, recalls the common link of feeling among these acts—common, in that it binds together the acts of a single person, and shows an affinity among the acts of many persons. In a curious way, the old man bears the substance of their community. This is not a matter of the record that he keeps but, rather, of the record that he is.

"Where'er the aged Beggar takes his rounds," Wordsworth continues, "The mild necessity of use compels / To acts of love; and habit does the work / Of reason, yet prepares that after joy / Which reason cherishes." This seems to me a remarkable thought about the way motives and judgments work together to form a system of moral conduct. But it is so compressed that it warrants some account of the special meaning Wordsworth assigns to each word. By "use," I take it he means the repeated performance of a given action. Such use carries with it a sense of necessity because our having already done a thing many times predisposes us in favor of doing it again. It is a *mild* necessity because no outward compulsion, or coercion, is involved. The shaping of conduct here, in which both the

mind and body participate—the body half-consciously forming, the mind half-consciously approving the action—from the
way it inclines us to fall in with a given stimulus may as well be
called *habit*. And habit, says Wordsworth, "does the work of
reason": a guided, but unreasoning, impulse gives all the
sanction to an act that we could hope to obtain from rational
reflection. Habit is not just *a* guide, I believe Wordsworth is
saying. It is the most reliable guide we have.

Habit also does something that reason could not in any
circumstances do: it prepares an "after-joy"—the pleasure I
feel from acting generously—which nonetheless reason itself
can cherish. (Maybe reason cherishes it because I thereby seem
to become part of a life that is better for my being here. Reason
takes, as a measure of the individual act, the desirability of a
world of such acts, and sees that they are good. This is a
difficult point in Wordsworth's thinking and I leave it for now
without comment.) But the language of these lines brings to
light a certain circularity about the process of being converted
by the work of habit. For the word "cherish" has the same
source as *caritas*, charity. The person who gives in charity, by
learning what it is to cherish something, grows likelier to give
again. Wordsworth is offering an argument about the growth
of moral habits of conduct and reflection, and an argument
about the probable relations between them. He does not forget
that he is also describing a mystery. It will not do to summarize
the relations between habit and reason by saying, for example,
that rational social policy always requires a foundation in
customary feeling and social practices. That would suggest that
the only after-joy Wordsworth has in mind is to satisfy the
demands of social utility. I think, in fact, he means by joy
something like what he called in another poem "A pleasurable
feeling of blind love, / The pleasure which there is in life
itself." This pleasure is not related to utility.

The central passage that I have been quoting concludes:
"And thus the soul, / By that sweet taste of pleasure unpursued
/ Doth find herself insensibly disposed / To virtue and true

goodness." Why must the pleasure be *unpursued*? The problem (Wordsworth must have felt) with an ethic of rational choice, which speaks of the pursuit of pleasure or the pursuit of happiness, is that it subtly or conspicuously includes the idea of a reward. Emotionally, such a reward may come in the form of gratitude. I give you something and you are grateful for it—properly grateful. The little pattern observable in such an exchange yields a moral fable attractive enough to have sponsored many eighteenth-century moral systems. This way of thinking implies a story of pleasure pursued, achieved, rewarded, and reciprocated. But according to Wordsworth all this is wrong, and not only wrong, it is corrupt and depraved. It makes of society a machine that is void of moral energy. He says as much in the two long passages of reprobation: the dismissal ("Many, I believe, there are . . .," line 133) of those who live indifferent lives of virtuous decency; and the oratorical warning ("But deem not this Man useless. . .," line 67) to "Statesmen"—the freeholders, or taxpaying citizens of Cumberland—who are liable to consider the beggar useless and therefore may be tempted to remove him from sight.

Both passages are directed against people whose error is their pursuit of a rational reward. Of the first group, upright livers who follow the moral and religious law and act in conformity with every prescriptive command they have learned, Wordsworth says that they have their reward: "Praise be to such, and to their slumbers peace!" By which he means to say savagely that their life is a slumber. These people are keepers of social propriety who go so far and no farther: usually, their family marks an outward limit of their affections; and if you said to one of them, Why no more than this? the answer would be, It is not for me to invent obligations. They believe with the peculiar hardness of the well fed that the reach of sympathy goes exactly the length of the duties laid on us by social convention.

The second group whom Wordsworth condemns, or in whom he tries to plant a fear of themselves, consist of political representatives and their counselors, the economists just then emerging as a distinct force in politics, who act in conformity not with an established order but a new principle of social organization. They believe in *calculable* utility, and for them a man like the beggar must seem an indigestible anomaly. Their solution is to set him apart in what Wordsworth calls a "HOUSE, misnamed of INDUSTRY": a workhouse, or poorhouse. A historical note may be needed here as background. In the late 1790s, an arrangement of public rates-paying called Speenhamland (after the town in which, in 1795, the judges of Berkshire met to codify a new economic policy into law) had set a minimum rate for common laborers. It was, in a sense, an early device of welfare, but it was much else. On the Speenhamland system, laborers were paid out of the poor rates, with the result that a beggar could be raised to the level of minimum subsistence; while, at same the uniform rate, a prospering laborer would often be forced down to the level of subsistence. This created an artificial equality between the laboring and the unlaboring poor. At the same time, for a beggar the price of assured subsistence was to be watched over and kept with others like himself. He would not be allowed to wander.

Wordsworth stands out against the economic discipline of such projects when, in imagination, he turns the beggar loose again at the end of the poem:

> And, long as he can wander, let him breathe
> The freshness of the vallies; let his blood
> Struggle with frosty air and winter snows,
> And let the chartered wind that sweeps the heath
> Beat his grey locks against his withered face.

To be vexed by the wind and frost is a blessing, compared to the fate of being restrained by the charter of a poorhouse. So the poem repels every moral pretension of those who refer all conduct to a principle of economic utility. It appeals from them to a different kind of people, who have only one thing in common: that their feeling for a man like the beggar has brought into their lives an impalpable good. They themselves cannot quite explain the interest that his existence has provoked in them. Some of these people Wordsworth describes as "lofty minds / And meditative," who received, from their knowledge of this man "That first mild touch of sympathy and thought, / In which they found their kindred with a world / Where want and sorrow were." But others more complacent—the "robust and young," the "prosperous and unthinking"—equally behold in him "A silent monitor, which on their minds / Must needs impress a transitory thought / Of self-congratulation."

Now a monitor is something that watches, something that reflects back a meaningful image, and in an earlier usage something or someone that warns or admonishes. We might suppose that it is the better-off sort of people who watch over the beggar. By the surprising placement of the word "monitor," however, Wordsworth replies that there is a sense in which he watches, and even watches over, them. Unconscious as he is, how can the beggar have come to serve so impressive a function? Here is what I think Wordsworth saw. The beggar, by vividly calling to mind everything he stands for in a social order, recalls to others their own peculiar position in the same order: not their security alone, or their want of it; but the part that chance, or the fateful succession of accidents that we sometimes call "nature," has played in their own coming to be what they are. In his presence we all of us count our "charters and exemptions," the things that constrain us, and the things that leave us partly free. There is, of course, one great exemption even for the beggar—his being allowed to wander freely, undisturbed, in a congenial place. We have already begun to see how much Wordsworth makes of this. But in the passage I am speaking of now ("Some there are. . .," line 105), Wordsworth is careful not to exaggerate how much the beggar's presence can do. It brings to mind the "present blessings" of others. It does not and cannot give anyone the strength to preserve such blessings, to build them up as an assurance of future continuity.

Above all, Wordsworth says such a man is important to one class of persons, "the poorest poor." By giving to him, they come to feel gifted—a pleasure that the stringency in the rest of their lives does not much allow. This may seem a comfort that has almost the quality of an illusion. And yet the power of giving, and the thought that comes from doing so—"That we have all of us one human heart"—are for Wordsworth intimately connected with pleasure, with freedom, and with self-respect. And here I have to point out a most unusual feature of the poem, a conventional detail that becomes a stimulus to thought simply by being omitted. One thing "The Old Cumberland Beggar" does not contain is a scene of gratitude. Indeed, even the thought of gratitude does not arise. Wordsworth, in general, seems not to have believed that gratitude was a social or for that matter even a personal virtue: the odd ending of his ballad, "Simon Lee," is built upon the same suspicion. At the end of "The Old Cumberland Beggar" more particularly, we are aware of a reversal of expectation. Instead of seeing the beggar bless those who give to him, we see him blessed by the poet, speaking on behalf of all those others. "Then let him pass, a blessing on his head!" Nothing in the nature or character of the beggar has been singled out as "blessed." It is something about him and not something in the man himself that matters.

The old Cumberland beggar, then, is an emblem of alienation. Yet he sponsors the feeling of belonging to humanity which none of us would do without. It is a quiet suggestion of this poem, which becomes unmistakable when one reads it alongside other poems by Wordsworth, that any life at all, when its conventional accretions have burned away, might become the sort of monitor that the beggar's is. Perhaps, however, for the sake of starting an impulse of humanity, his life is more valuable than others just because it is less obviously valued. This is so radical and even improbable a message that many readers are tempted to sift the poem for an altogether different moral. I want therefore to close by warning against two possible misreadings that the poem may attract. One of these takes Wordsworth to be saying: Charity is good; the beggar is a prompter of charity; accordingly, he should be kept as he is whatever his sufferings, because the pains of one will have been more than offset by the pleasures of many from charity. If the poem said this, it would be pernicious, but in fact this is just the sort of weighing of utility that Wordsworth has denounced elsewhere in the poem.

But the supposition that it would have been plausible, if pernicious, for Wordsworth to argue something like this, comes from a prior belief that he must have been interested in the feelings of the beggar. Here once again we encounter the idea of balance or reciprocity. It is, to repeat, an idea about morality that had much currency in the eighteenth century, and from it Adam Smith evolved a definition of sympathy in which the giver and the receiver of sympathy, before they release their feeling into circulation, each alike takes stock of how much of the feeling the other may accept by the canons of what Smith calls "propriety." Wordsworth hated this prudent commercial morality. His revolution in poetry was all about doing away with this way of thinking forever. He is so sure that the humanizing power of sympathy has nothing to do with reciprocal feelings that he takes no interest at all in the inward state of the beggar. The only approach to a description of him that is not done from the outside comes in half a line near the end of the poem: "Few are his pleasures." That is as much as we get. If you look at the short poem called "Animal Tranquillity and Decay," which makes a sort of companion to "The Old Cumberland Beggar," you can see how consistent was Wordsworth's denial that a feeling *about someone* becomes deeper by pretending to be a feeling *from the other person's point of view*. The old man in that poem has been "led / To peace so perfect that the young behold / With envy, what the Old Man hardly feels." That is, they see in him the image of a tranquillity which may have nothing to do with his experience of himself.

Wordsworth cares about the personal and the social good of certain spontaneous actions that answer to certain natural feelings. He does not care about the way someone's inward feelings may correspond to someone else's. The old man of this poem is interesting for the response that he provokes: to say no more about him is perhaps a sign of respect, perhaps also of a temperamental coolness far from our usual ideas of sensibility. Anyway, Wordsworth does say no more. The man is seen from the outside. Not from the outside in, but from the particular to the general significance of the outside. This choice of tactics for representation has everything to do with Wordsworth's belief that gratitude, or any reciprocal feeling or action, can hardly be what matters in the social exchange that he recounts. It is the gratuitous, the unmotivated and unrewardable, sense of a person not easily assimilated to ourselves that here establishes one meaning of the idea of home.

Even in the 1790s, Wordsworth's politics are not to be found on any of the available maps. He is a radical republican in his conviction that "men who do not wear fine clothes can feel deeply"; a prophet against capitalism in his detestation of the new political economy; an agrarian conservative in the way of life he seems to hold out as an ideal. He becomes no easier to capture when one frames his thinking by the different concerns of our time. "The Old Cumberland Beggar" is, in about equal measure, a protest against the rationality of any laissez-faire system and a protest against the spiritual loss entailed by any enforceable policy of welfare. The poem remains a solitary exploration of the feeling one may have about a person in society—the sense of estrangement from our own place to which this feeling exposes us, and the queer sensation of being at home only in humanity. As for the "eye of Nature" under which the poem concludes, it too offers no final resting place for the understanding. Wordsworth implies that the eye of Nature may be no less arbitrary in its focus than the eye of the beggar as he moves with one step and another and another, or the eye of the poet himself as he starts the thoughts of this poem revolving. "I saw an aged beggar in my walk." "Him have I known." "He travels on." It is a slender knowledge on which to settle in one's relations to another person. Wordsworth seems to say that in thinking of the beggar, and in thinking of anyone, it is all we should ask or want.

Slavery, Alienation, and the Female Discovery of Personal Freedom

BY ORLANDO PATTERSON

No ONE would deny that today freedom stands unchallenged as the supreme value of the Western world. Not only philosophers, but ordinary men and women advocate it as something essential for their very existence as human beings. Most Westerners would agree with the philosopher Bernard Bosanquet that it is "the essential quality of human life, it is so, we understand, because it is the condition of being ourselves." It is the one value which many people seem prepared to die for, both by their words and their actions. My task is to explain why and how this extraordinary valorization of freedom came about.

To those who hold that freedom is a natural concept, something that all human beings, simply by being human, would naturally want, my problem must seem strange. The truth of the matter, however, is that there is nothing at all self-evident in the idea or, more properly, the high esteem in which we in the West hold freedom. For most of human history, and for many peoples in the non-Western world today, freedom was, and remains, anything but obvious or desirable. Other values and ideals are to them of far more importance, values such as the pursuit of glory and honor for oneself, one's family, or one's state, love of God, making money, experienc-

This chapter is adapted from FREEDOM: Vol. I: Freedom in the Making of Western Culture by Orlando Patterson, which was the 1991 winner of the National Book Award for Nonfiction. Copyright © 1991 by Basic Books. Reprinted with the permission of Basic Books, a division of HarperCollins Publishers.

ing nirvana, what have you. People in the West, of course, value these things too, but we also have the thing we call freedom, and we place it above all other values and ideals. We even divide the world into two great camps, the free world and the unfree, and our leaders declared, until very recently, that we are prepared to risk a nuclear holocaust in order to defend this near-sacred ideal we call freedom.

From the viewpoint of a comparative and historical sociologist, this is an incredible situation. Since valuing freedom is not a part of the human condition, not something we are born with, how, we must ask, did it ever come about that this value achieved the position of eminence that it did. To be more specific, my work over the past six years has been devoted to answering three questions: First, how and why did freedom become a value in the first place? Second, how and why did it become a supreme value? And third, why did it rise to supremacy only in the Western world?

What Is Freedom?

Freedom, I have found, is a tripartite value. Behind the numerous shades of meaning associated with the term are three ideas, closely related historically, sociologically, and conceptually, which may be called personal, sovereignal, and civic freedoms. Freedom since the fifth century B.C. has been, and remains, three notes or elements of a cultural chord. Personal freedom, at its most elementary, is a person's sense that he or she, on the one hand, is not being coerced or restrained by another person in doing something desired and, on the other hand, the conviction that one can do as one pleases within the limits of other persons' desires to do the same.

The second related kind of freedom which emerged in the West at about the same time as personal freedom is what I will call sovereignal freedom. This is simply the power to act as one pleases, regardless of the wishes of others, as distinct from the positive aspect of personal freedom, which is the capacity to do as one pleases insofar as one can. The sovereignally free person has the power to restrict the freedom of others, or to empower others with the capacity to do as they please with others beneath them. This conception of freedom is always relative. At one extreme stands the person who is absolutely free with respect to another, namely, the slavemaster; at the other extreme is the person who has no freedom with respect to another, namely, the slave in relation to his master. Between the two are all other human beings with more or less power with respect to others, including slavemasters themselves with respect to greater or lesser powers in their societies.

Civic freedom is the third note in the cultural chord of this triadic value. It refers to the capacity of adult members of a community to participate in its life and government. A person feels free, in this sense, to the extent that he or she belongs to the community of birth, has a recognized place in it, and is involved in some way in the way it is governed. Civic freedom implies a political community of some sort with clearly defined rights and obligations for every citizen. It does not necessarily imply a complete political democracy; full adult suffrage is a peculiarly modern variant of it. Civic freedom may be the exclusive privilege of a small minority of the total adult population. In ancient Athens, where it was first constructed, it was, as will be seen, an exclusive male club, denied to female citizens and all resident aliens. And in republican Rome it was even more restricted, being confined to male aristocrats.

Who were the first persons to get the unusual idea that being free was not only a value to be cherished but the most important thing that someone could possess? The answer, in a word, slaves. Freedom began its career as a social value in the desperate yearning of the slave to negate what for him, and for nonslaves, was a peculiarly inhuman condition. Now in saying this I am advocating nothing new. Many historians and philosophers have already noted that freedom started as a special legal status. As Bernard Bosanquet correctly observed, "It will not lead us far wrong if we assume that the value we put upon liberty and its erection into something like an ideal comes from the contrast with slavery." This contrast, he correctly insists, "we may take as the practical starting point in the notion of freedom."[1] What has not been recognized, however, is the critical fact that the idea of freedom has never been divorced from this, its primordial servile source. We are still powerfully drawn to the metaphor of slavery when we try to explain what we mean by freedom. And if not slavery, then some surrogate very closely identified with it: consider the fact that our former president, whose devotion to the ideal of freedom no one would deny, was fond of speaking of "evil empires" when moved to emphasize the freedom we enjoy.

To understand the origins and nature of freedom we must therefore first come to a better understanding of the condition called slavery. In doing so we grasp at once the relevance of freedom to the experience of home. Slavery is the permanent, violent, and personal domination of naturally alienated and generally dishonored persons.[2] It is, first, a form of personal domination. One individual is under the direct power of another or his agent. Usually this, in practice, entails the power of life and death over the slave. Second, the slave is in a perpetual condition of dishonor. What is more, the master parasitically gains honor in degrading his slave. Third, and most important, the slave is always an excommunicated person. He, usually she, does not belong to the legitimate social or moral community; she has no independent social existence; she exists only through and for the master; she is, in other words, natally alienated. The slave, in short, is the quintessentially homeless person. Homeless in the most fundamental sense of the term: kinless, rootless, a stranger forever, cut off

[1] Bernard Bosanquet, "Personal Freedom Through the State," in R. Dewey and J. Gould (eds.), *Freedom: History, Nature, Varieties* (New York: Macmillan, 1976), p. 191.

[2] Orlando Patterson, *Slavery and Social Death* (Cambridge: Harvard University Press, 1982).

not only from ancestors but from descendants: it is an invariant law of slavery that the slave has no rights whatever in her or his children and no claims on ancestors. The slave is absolutely alone, outside of history, outside of community. This is absolute homelessness.

In all societies the three constitutive features of the slave condition add up to a generalized conception of slavery as a state of social death. The slave is always conceived of as someone, or the descendant of someone, who should have died, typically as a result of defeat in war, but also as a result of poverty. His physical life was spared in return for his social death and his permanent subjection to the will of another. This universal way of rationalizing and symbolically expressing the condition of social death and absolute homelessness that is slavery has been best expressed by Locke: "having, by his own fault, forfeited his own Life, by some Act that deserves Death; he, to whom he has forfeited it, may (when he has him in his Power) delay to take it, and make use of him to his own Service, and he does him no injury by it."

It is important to understand that outside of slavery no individual in premodern societies had such absolute power over another. Michael Mann, in his *Sources of Social Power*, has demonstrated how in the long annals of human history one powerful theme stood out in all societies: the deep suspicion that persons held of concentrated power in one person. All power over any given individual was countervailed by the interest of other powerful persons in that individual. This is the meaning of kinship in kin-based societies. One big man's ambitions had to take account of another's, and there was always at least one big man in one's family. Home, kith and kin, supplemented always by the independent power of shamans and priests, effectively prevented the accumulation of excessive power over another. No one was free to do entirely as he leased with others. This only happened in the slave relation. Precisely because the slave was utterly kinless, which is to say, homeless, the master could exercise absolute powers of life and

death over her or him. It is the slavemaster who first discovers
the perverse pleasures of absolute freedom over persons, what
I call sovereignal freedom.

Slavery posed at least two fundamental problems wherever it
existed. One of these was more social or communal, the other
interpersonal. It is in solving these two problems that the other
two elements of freedom were created. The interpersonal
problem was that of getting the slave to serve the master
diligently. Having deracinated the slave and placed her in a
condition of permanent degradation and dishonor, how does
the master get so demoralized a person to serve him in any
capacity? The answer was dreadfully simple: motivate her with
the hope of escape from the condition of social death and
degradation, in other words, promise her freedom. It was in
this promise that the ideal of personal freedom was created.
Before slavery human beings never faced such a crisis and
therefore never felt the need for such a seemingly empty and
negative ideal. Before slavery what all persons wanted was the
security of attachment, greater engagement with the home and
community to which they belonged and which they took so
completely for granted that any escape from it was cause for
insecurity.

What also became problematic from the moment a slave was
introduced into a society, however primitive it might have
been, was the communal acceptance of the slave and of the
slave relation. How does a society, any society, come to terms
with the idea of socially dead, utterly homeless persons in its
midst? Why would a community, in the first place, permit such
a bizarre relationship? Clearly, there must have been something in the relationship which served the interests of the
community, some compensating factor. Put simply, what was
immediately gained was the status of the *freeman*. This is a
purely contradistinctive status; it makes sense only where slaves
existed. Now since the slave was homeless and kinless, it
follows that the first and most fundamental meaning of free

status should be that of belonging, being rooted in family kith and kin.

The linguistic evidence fully supports this hypothesis. Consider the origins of both our words for freedom: *free* is derived from Middle English *fre*, derived from Old English *freo*, which means "not in bondage, noble, glad illustrious."[3] *Freo*, further, is akin to German *frei*, ultimately derived from the Indo-European base *prei*, contracted from Sanskrit *prya*, "to love," and more immediately from the Germanic *frijaz* meaning, according to Calvert Watkins: "beloved, belonging to the loved ones, not in bondage." *Liberty* is derived, via Middle French *liberté*, from the Latin *liber*, meaning free, which is derived, along with the Greek cognate *eleutheros*, from the Indo-European base *leudh-ero*, meaning "belonging to the people." While the semantic development of the root *liber* is not entirely clear, it seems that in Latin there was an identification of the meanings "free" and "children."[4] The OED offers the following summary:

> The primary sense of the adj. [free] is 'dear'; the Germanic and Celtic sense comes of its having been applied as the distinctive epithet of those members of the household who were connected by ties of kindred with the head, as opposed to the slaves. The converse process of sense-development appears in Latin *liberi* 'children', literally, the 'free' members of the household.

What this brief etymological account makes clear is the intimate link between the meaning of the terms *freedom* and *slavery*, on the one hand, and, on the other, the closely related terms *family*, *kinsmen*, *household*, and *home*.

Three parties were immediately created, and brought in conflict in the slave relation: the slave, the master, and the freeman. And to crudely summarize the history of freedom: it

---

[3] *Webster's New World Dictionary.*

[4] Calvert Watkins, *The American Heritage Dictionary of Indo-European Roots* (Boston: Houghton Mifflin, 1985), p. 53; Ernest Klein, *Comprehensive Etymological Dictionary of the English Language* (Amsterdam: Elsevier, 1971).

was to motivate the slave that personal, negative freedom was created; it was to placate the freeman that civic liberty was first constructed; and it was in the expression of the absolute power of the master that sovereignal freedom emerged. The three were closely linked in the perverse dialectics of slavery.

Since slavery existed everywhere at some time, freedom made its appearance among all the peoples of the world, even hunter-gatherers. And yet it is only in the West that it became a dominant value. There are two reasons for this. One is the fact that it was first in the West that we find the historically unprecedented sociological phenomenon of large-scale slave societies. In most parts of the world where slavery existed it was of minor significance. The slave population would have been no more than 1 to 2 percent of the total; and the freed population minuscule. Sovereignal and civic freedom would have acquired some value in populations where the slave group was of some significance, and I suspect that this development took place very early in the history of the Indo-European peoples. Even so, it remained a minor value. Personal freedom, the third element of the chord, by the very nature of its origin would have been a despised ideal, the eccentric preoccupation of a lowly and demographically insignificant segment of the community.

Ancient Greece was the first group of societies in the world to become large-scale slave systems, in that slaves, by the end of the sixth century, played a critical, perhaps decisive role in the economic life of the urban economy, and reached proportions ranging between 30 and 33 percent. With the exception of politics and the military, Moses Finley has written, "there was no activity, productive or unproductive, public or private, pleasant or unpleasant, which was not performed by slaves at some times and in some places in the Greek world," and he concludes his classic paper on the subject with the following observation: "More bluntly put, the cities in which individual freedom reached its highest expression—most obviously Athens—were cities in which chattel slavery flourished."

All three elements of freedom flourished in Greece by the middle of the fifth century B.C. However, different segments of the population tended to emphasize one or other of these elements. Civic freedom, democracy, was the preferred element among the mass of native Greek men. Women, slaves, and resident foreigners were excluded from membership in the civic club that was Athenian democracy. I have shown,[5] along with others, that the growth of this exclusive club was not only made possible by, but dialectically derived from, the presence of slaves on a large scale in Athens. The aristocratic elite and their intellectual supporters—Plato, the Old Oligarch, Aristotle—despised democracy and advocated a sophisticated version of sovereignal freedom. The organic version of sovereignal freedom they developed was to remain a permanent and, for centuries, the dominant conception of freedom in the West. While we would like to exclude this conception of freedom from our view of the ideal today, there is no gainsaying the fact that it has a long and honored history in our civilization. The free man, in this view, is the most powerful person; the freest state is the most powerful state. One finds one's freedom in belonging to such a powerful community, an extended home, a public household, which excludes those who do not belong, are neither kith nor kin, enemies without as well as enemies within—slaves, metics, Jews, blacks, women out of their place, Turks.

From the start, two groups were committed to the celebration of personal freedom: precisely those excluded from the civic club and the aristocratic elite: women and foreigners, especially those who were once slaves and bought themselves out of slavery. Women play a special role in the history of personal freedom: it was they who first socially constructed it as a powerful value. This is one of the most

---

[5] Orlando Patterson, *Freedom*, vol. 1, *Freedom in the Making of Western Culture* (New York: Basic Books, 1991), pt. 2.

important findings of my forthcoming work. In the remainder of this paper I explain how this happened.

Women, Slavery and Freedom in Homeric Greece

While slavery was not of any structural significance in Homeric Greece, its cultural and psychological impact were undoubtedly important for all. And there was one important category of persons to whom enslavement and, antithetically, freedom were critical, namely, women. Freedom began its long journey in the Western consciousness as a woman's value. It was women who first lived in terror of enslavement, and hence it was women who first came to value its absence, both those who were never captured but lived in dread of it and, even more so, those who were captured and lived in hope of being redeemed, or at the very least, being released from their social death and placed among their captors in that new condition which existentially their whole being had come to yearn for.

In spite of the fact that one of the most memorable of the nonheroic characters of the *Odyssey*, the slave Eumaeus, is male, nearly all of Homer's references to slavery are to women, and all but one of his references to freedom involve women. The famous scene in which Odysseus, in disguise, meets and converses with his faithful old slave is as significant for what is not said as for what is said. At no time does Eumaeus yearn for his freedom, or express any regret at its loss. He is the model of the faithful slave. He does indeed make a celebrated comment on the effect of enslavement: ". . . Zeus of the wide brows takes away one half of the virtue from a man, once the day of slavery closes upon him."[6] The context in which the remark is made, however, must be emphasized. Eumaeus was referring to Odysseus's dying dog, Argos, which he claims had

---

[6] *Odyssey*, tr. Richard Lattimore (New York: Harper Colophon Books, 1975), 17:323–324.

been neglected both by the women of Odysseus's household and by the household slaves. Of the latter, he complains that they "are no longer willing to do their rightful duties" when "their masters are no longer about to make them work." It is not freedom, then, which constitutes half of a man's virtue, but men's "willingness to do their rightful duties." Eumaeus's enslavement has not prompted him to any existential discovery of freedom. He is still thoroughly wedded to the dominant value of his own former aristocratic class, having been the son of a king before his capture, and to the aristocrat to whom he is enslaved.

Contrast this now with Homer's references to freedom, all of them appearing in the *Iliad* (there is no reference with the root *eleuther* in the *Odyssey*). Three of the four significant references to freedom express the fear that was omnipresent in times of war—the loss of the freedom of the women of the city. In these three references the same formulaic term is used, namely, the loss of "the day of liberty." The day of liberty obviously implies the night of compulsion or slavery. Night has power even over the gods,[7] and is the most potent symbol of compulsion in archaic Greek poetry. We know from Hesiod that it was not only the mother of sleep and its brother, death,[8] but, significantly, also the mother of day.[9] Hidden in this earliest reference to freedom, then, is a powerful symbolic statement of its origin in the social death that is slavery.

Let us look briefly at the references to freedom. Achilles taunts Aeneas with the memory of how he chased him into Lyrnessos, stormed the place and "took the day of liberty away from their women and led them as spoil," even though Aeneas got away.[10] Hector, before killing Patroklos, shouted triumphantly:

---

[7] *Iliad*, 14:259.
[8] Hesiod, *Theogony*, 211–225.
[9] *Theogony*, 123–124.
[10] *Iliad*, 20:190–194.

Patroclos, you thought perhaps of devastating our city, of stripping from the Trojan women the day of their liberty and dragging them off in ships to the beloved land of your fathers. . . .[11]

But it is in Hector's relationship with his wife, rather than on the battlefield, that we find one of the most revealing passages on the subject of freedom. In what is perhaps the tenderest passage of the *Iliad*, Hector responds to the fears for his life by his wife, who pleads that she does not want to be a widow. He says that he understands her concerns, that it is not the men of the city he is worried about, should the Greeks win the war, since they will all be killed, but rather:

. . . the thought of you, when some bronze-armored Achaean leads you off, taking away your day of liberty, in tears; and in Argos you must work at the loom of another and carry water from the spring Messeis or Hypereia, all unwilling, but strong will be the necessity upon you . . . .[12]

The cumulative effect of these passages is clear. Personal freedom was a matter of major concern in Homeric Greece. Slavery was dreaded, and freedom was deeply valued. It was real not only in the constant threat of slavery, but also in the actual experience and negation of slavery.

For one thing, women were sometimes ransomed. The obvious fact should not be neglected that the Trojan War was fought over a woman. While Helen might have wantonly gone off with Paris, as far as the Greeks were concerned Paris's abuse of his host's hospitality was equivalent to the kidnaping and enslavement of his host's wife. For another, slave women were sometimes married and absorbed into their masters' households. This is implied in the fact that the children of slave women by their masters became the legal progeny of their fathers.

The female origins of freedom is reinforced by another

[11] *Ibid.*, 16:830–833.
[12] *Ibid.*, 6:454–458.

important fact about women in primitive and archaic societies. It was women who moved to their husbands' households. Further, where we find many small autonomous warring societies, women were invariably used as pawns and as a means of cementing alliances between these societies in much the same way that they were the means of securing alliances and harmony between feuding or potentially feuding clans within the same society. Thus in earliest times it was not movement from their families, or even from their societies, that women dreaded, for from infancy they would have been reared for just that. Home separation was then, as it remains today, a male anxiety. What women and the men of their families dreaded was the forced removal of women, the dishonor to their persons and their families, and the absence of any recognized place for them, or their children, in the society of their masters. Enslavement was the social death of forced illegitimacy. Once a man suffered such a death he might as well by physically dead since there was no prospect of regaining his honor, not in these earliest kinds of honorific societies. Indeed, as Gregory Nagy makes wonderfully clear, death for the epic Greek hero was not something reluctantly chosen as the lesser of two evils but something actively struggled for in order to gain the glory and honor that are "unfailing," immortal. It is for this reason that Achilles refuses to go back home and live a quiet old age, choosing to stay and fight in Troy and die young; in this way he becomes the epic hero, "destined for immortality in the form of a cultural institution that is predicated on the natural process of death." The greatest of heroes must die.[13]

Women, however, were not caught in this honorific trap. They were not expected to be able to defend themselves, hence they had suffered no irreparable loss of honor in their

---

[13] Gregory Nagy, *The Best of the Achaeans: Concepts of the Hero in Archaic Greek Poetry* (Baltimore: Johns Hopkins University Press, 1979), p. 184 and, more generally, chs. 10, 11, 12.

submission. Hence with them the possibility of the restoration of their status as legitimate members of their master's or their own former community existed.

In other words, gender expectations in early Greece made freedom a possibility for women, even as it closed it off to men. It was something for which women could yearn both openly and, like the chorus of slave women in Aeschylus's *Libation Bearers*, in their secret heart, in ways not open to Eumaeus, the male swineherd. It was simply not possible for a swineherd to become a prince again. Indeed, for the best of the Achaeans, it was not possible to go home again. Paradoxically, because women had less to lose, they had more to hope for. In that hope, and in its realization, was born the Western valuation of personal freedom.

The Female Force and the Ideology of Personal Freedom

As slavery and democracy grew in Athens, upper-class and urban middle-class women from Athenian citizen families were increasingly confined to the household, and there can be no doubt that their lives became far more circumscribed. The only certain benefit that civilization brought was greater legal protection, and that was largely a by-product of the desire of their menfolk to protect their property; in the seemingly more progressive case of the dowry, "to protect the interest of the father against the husband."[14] Young women had almost no freedom of choice in selecting their husbands,[15] and while they could, in theory, initiate divorce proceedings, this was rare. Nothing better expressed the real intent of Athenian legal protection of women than the fact that men who violently raped women were punished less severely than those who

[14] Marilyn B. Arthur, "Early Greece: The Origins of the Western Attitude Toward Women," in John Peradotto and J. P. Sullivan, eds., *Women in the Ancient World: The Arethusa Papers* (Albany: State University of New York Press, 1984), p. 34.
[15] W. K. Lacey, *The Family in Classical Greece* (Ithaca, N.Y.: Cornell University Press, 1984), p. 105.

seduced them, since the latter case entailed the corruption of the woman into a person who dared to exercise her freedom of choice.[16]

Several scholars have emphasized the fact that there was a close link between the condition of Athenian women and the growth of both democracy and slavery. The urban slave system made middle- and upper-class women largely redundant in the extrahousehold economy. Proper middle-class women were not even expected to go shopping, since the most modest of households could afford a slave to perform this chore. It is significant that one of the earliest acts aimed at democratizing the Athenian polity—Solon's abolition of ostentatious funeral processions—restricted the participation of women in funerals.[17]

In spite of all these curtailments, however, one should avoid going too far in the opposite extreme. First, the above generalizations apply largely to middle- and upper-class women in urban areas. Rural women of modest means, of whom we know next to nothing, would in all likelihood have continued to play an important role on the home farm. In the urban areas, poor women from Athenian citizen families did engage in the extrahousehold economy, especially petty trading. And noncitizen women—especially freedwomen—participated in many areas of the economy and were quite "liberated," both in economic terms and in their relations with men. Many were traders, craftswomen, and innkeepers.[18] Their role as courtesans and prostitutes is well known, although this is admittedly ambiguous evidence for greater personal freedom.

But to return to the middle- and upper-class women, we mut be careful not to exaggerate. People always fashion a social life, some meaningful fabric of culture, whatever their circum-

[16] Victor Ehrenberg, *The People of Aristophanes* (New York: Schocken Books, 1962), p. 196; Sarah Pomeroy, *Goddesses, Whores, Wives and Slaves* (New York: Schocken, 1975), p. 87.

[17] Pomeroy, *Goddesses*, p. 88. On the implications of the reforms of Solon relating to women see Arthur, "Early Greece," pp. 28–37.

[18] Ehrenberg, *People of Aristophanes*, p. 205. On the role of class in determining different attitudes to women, see Arthur, "Early Greece."

stances. Social and economic exclusion, and even brutal repression, do not necessarily imply a culture of poverty: consider the extraordinary cultural vitality of African-Americans, even during the period of slavery. As Ehrenberg rightly observes, "If a woman's life was restricted and ruled by strong conventions, it was by no means useless. Above all, the management of the household—that is to say, of a large part of a man's property—was in the hands of the wife."[19] Within the household, free women came in intimate contact with slave women. Indeed, slaves would have been the main adult company of nearly all such women, and one can easily guess at the implications of this close association. In addition to their slaves, women had the company of their children, upon whom they would have exerted more than normal influence in view of the absence of the father from the household.[20]

Men were fully aware of this other world which women created for themselves and expressed great ambiguity toward it. They felt threatened by what they imagined transpired in the female soul, and while such feelings reinforced the prevailing negative attitudes toward women, they also, ambiguously, implied a recognition of women as real, willful persons. Marilyn Arthur is persuasive in her conclusion that this ambiguity entailed "some movement toward the acceptance of women as full human beings," which was an improvement on the earlier aristocratic period:

> For the perception of women as a threat, and the hostility toward them as sexual beings, implicitly expects them to assert their claims in these regards, and implicitly understands the need to justify the prevailing order against such claims.[21]

And this brings me to the question of tragedy.

---

[19] Ehrenberg, *People of Aristophanes*, p. 203.

[20] On this I am in complete agreement with Philip Slater, *The Glory of Hera* (Boston: Beacon Press, 1968), though not necessarily going along with his Freudian interpretations.

[21] Arthur, "Early Greece," p. 50.

Tragedy as Cultural Evidence

It has frequently been observed that Greek tragedy presents us with a sociological and literary paradox: these dramas were written by authors living in a world of confined women, for an audience of males who seemed to hold women in contempt, yet they are overwhelmingly focused on strong female characters. How do we explain this? And to what degree can tragic drama be used as evidence for the condition of women or attitudes toward freedom in classical Greece? While nearly useless as evidence on social condition, classic drama is perhaps the perfect body of data for our understanding of fifth-century Athenian values and ideals concerning freedom and women. To be more specific, these dramas tell us a great deal about what men thought about women and freedom, and what they believed women thought about these subjects, much of which may well have been true. Greek drama was, in fact, a kind of natural poll of fifth-century Athenian values and ideals. To the historical sociologist of culture, their significance lies in the extraordinary access they give us to the deepest values and ideals, in all their intensity and contradictions, prevailing in fifth-century Athens. What Froma Zeitlin says of the *Oresteia* holds true for all these tragedies, that it "transcends aesthetic values, for it gives voice and form to the social and the political ideology of the period at the same time as it actively shapes the collective fantasies of its audience with its own authoritative vision."[22]

Women, if we are to believe these male authors, not only invented personal freedom, but brought something special to its expression, beyond the primal desire for the removal of brute constraint as the male slaves and freedpersons of the classical and later periods would come to define it. In all Greek drama, both tragic and comic, women stand powerfully, and

---

[22] Froma I. Zeitlin, "The Dynamics of Misogyny: Myth and Mythmaking in the Oresteia," in Peradotto and Sullivan, *Women in the Ancient World*, p. 159.

exclusively, for personal independence, for the voice of individual conscience against both personal and political tyranny, and for universal and natural, as distinct from manmade, justice, and for the freedom to worship their gods, and love whom they chose to love.[23]

It is significant that the tragic heroine is also often a slave: Cassandra in *Agamemnon*, the loyal Techmessa in Sophocles' *Ajax*, and most powerfully, Euripides' *Andromache* and *Hecuba*. This is even more the case in many of the minor female roles, but perhaps most important of all is the role of the female slave chorus in many of these dramas: the captive Trojan women in *Hecuba* and *The Trojan Women*; the chorus of captive Greek women in *Iphigena in Tauris* and in *Helen*; and the most significant for our purposes, the female slave chorus in Aeschylus's *Libation Bearers*. These are all cases of women who have been torn from their homes and come to the brutal discovery of freedom in the home of their conquerors. However, it is possible to become a slave in the land of one's birth; this is the most tragic kind of estrangement: to be made utterly homeless at home. The classic instance of this is Antigone.

However, even where the tragic heroine is a free woman, a queen in her own palace, the awareness of slavery and the antithetical passion for justice and freedom—raw, primal freedom—are ever present. It is from the chorus of free women in one of Aeschylus's earliest extant tragedies, *Seven Against Thebes*, that we get one of the most frightening, and accurate, statements of what slavery and the dread fear of it meant to ancient Greek women:

> Pity it were that this city, so ancient,
> should be cast to the House of Death,

---

[23] See, generally, H. Lloyd-Jones, *The Justice of Zeus* (Berkeley: University of California Press, 1971); and for a good recent discussion of the semantic field covered by the Greek term *dike*, see Simon Goldhill, *Reading Greek Tragedy* (New York: Cambridge University Press, 1986), ch. 2.

a spear-booty, a slave,
in crumbling ashes, dishonorably,
sacked by an Achaean, with the God's consent;
that its women be hazed away,
captives, young and old,
dragged by the hair, as horses by the mane,
and their raiments torn about them.
Emptied the city walls,
as the captive spoil, with mingled cries,
is led to its doom.
This heavy fate is what I fear,
It is a woeful thing for maidens unripe,
before the marriage rites, to tread
this bitter journey from their homes.
I would say that the dead
are better off than this.[24]

In Greek myth, Greek life, and Greek drama, we find not only that "servile power and female power are linked,"[25] but also that the two are linked with the strong desire for, and dangers of, complete personal freedom. The women of Euripides' *The Bacchae* are perhaps the best known in this regard. However, nearly all the women of tragedy, especially those who are slaves, express a powerful drive for personal freedom. Andromache remains defiant, boldly criticizes her jealous mistress for being "addicted to injustice," insists on sticking to her principles,[26] and dares Menelaus to kill her: "But not before you and your daughter [Hermione] feel the edge of my tongue."[27] The remarkable thing about Aeschylus's suppliant maidens is their aggressiveness in pursuit of their independence. They threaten not only suicide but sacrilege if they do not get their way. And what they want they are in no doubt about. It is to be removed from "the pride of men, pride well hated."[28]

[24] Aeschylus, *Seven Against Thebes*, 321–339.
[25] Pierre Vidal-Naquet, *The Black Hunter* (Baltimore: Johns Hopkins University Press, 1986), p. 211.
[26] Euripides, *Andromache*, 186–191.
[27] *Ibid.*, 459–460.
[28] Aeschylus, *The Suppliant Maidens*, 527–528.

Aeschylus's *Libatin Bearers* concerns itself with both types of
alienation: that of the chorus of foreign women, on the one
hand, and of Orestes and Electra on the other. The tragedy is,
above all, a play about the struggle for personal freedom and
the price one mut pay, the suffering, to achieve it. There are
other meanings of this tragedy, to be sure, perhaps even more
important ones. But the author is quite explicit in drawing our
attention to the fact that this is one of the play's significant
meanings. It is surely significant that all the characters,
whatever their outward status, claim to be slaves, or to have
experienced slavery. Electra says of herself that she has "been
sold" by her mother, is as someone kinless, and "now I am
what a slave is."[29] Orestes tells his mother before he kills her
that: "I was born of a free father. You sold me."[30] Most
important of all is the critical part of the Chorus, which
apparently shares with Electra the central roles in the play.

Now the remarkable thing about the Chorus is that it is a
group of slave women who have joined in a conspiracy to
murder their master and mistress with the objective of
achieving what they explicitly state to be freedom, both for
their free or half-free co-conspirators and, by implication, for
themselves. Once we realize this, something else immediately
becomes evident, namely, that everything the Chorus says has
a double meaning, one spoken as slaves revolting for another
set of masters seeking vengeance and the return of their
patrimony, the other spoken for themselves, as slaves hating
their own condition and their masters, any masters.

In the very first scene, the disguised Orestes sees them
coming with libations to the tomb of Agamemnon, and it is
significant that although they enter with Electra he only takes
note of them with the vivid description, "women veiled in
dignities of black."[31] And it is the Chorus that next speaks, not

[29] *Ibid.*, 132–135.
[30] *Ibid.*, 915.
[31] *Ibid.*, 11.

Electra. Further, the first thing they have to say concerns their condition of enslavement. Only later do we hear about their mistress's agony. They hasten out of the house "hurt by the hard stroke of hands."[32]

After setting the scene, they end with another lament on their condition:

> But as for me: gods have forced on my city
> resisted fate. From our fathers' houses
> they led us here, to take the lot of slaves.
> And mine it is to wrench my will, and consent
> to their commands, right or wrong,
> to beat down my edged hate.
> And yet under veils I weep
> the vanities that have killed
> my lord; and freeze with sorrow in the secret heart.[33]

That last sentence is one of the most loaded in all Greek drama, pregnant with a triple meaning. On one level they are simply mourning their cruel fate. And yet they claim to weep secretly for their murdered lord, the very man who enslaved them. This, of course, is in earshot of Electra with whom, very shortly, they will be joining in murderous conspiracy against their present masters. But this is not the end of it. What, we may ask, exactly is it that's veiled? What sorrow lies in the "secret heart"? Clearly, it is the desperate longing for escape, freedom from their horrible social death. These are no loyal slaves stupidly aiding one pair of future masters against the present. They have already gone through one exchange of masters as a result of the murder of the former by the present. They are hardly likely to go through it again, this time as co-conspirators with no reward in sight. Aeschylus's Electra is far too shrewd a character not to know this. She says to them:

We hold a common hatred in this house. Do not for fear of any, hide your thought inside your heart. The day of destiny waits

[32] *Ibid.*, 24–31.
[33] *Ibid.*, 76–85.

for the free man as well as for the man enslaved beneath an alien
hand . . . ."[34]

Indeed. But as if to hammer home the point that freedom, and
freedom now, is what lies centrally on the mind of the Chorus,
there follows a dialogue in which Electra asks, "Whom of those
closest to me can I call my friend?" to which the Chorus
responds with brutal candor: "Yourself first; all who hate
Aegisthus after that."[35] And lest anyone miss the point, Electra
spells it out: "You mean these prayers shall be for you, and for
myself?"[36] But she has gone too far. The secret heart of the
slave praying for freedom must be ever on guard. No free
person can be trusted, not even a closely watched, lonely
daughter psychotically bent on revenge for her murdered
father. For the time being Electra must settle for the cryptic
response, uttered from behind the veil once more: "You see it
now; but it is you whose thought this is."[37]

Once the plot is hatched and the slave chorus knows where it
stands, the women can be more open. Their excitement grows
as the plan to murder the usurpers progresses, and it is not
long before we get the distinct feeling that there is a certain
sweet tingle, in "love-in-hate" excitement in their expressions
of fear, like thieves breaking out of a maximum security prison
who have just killed the guard. Aeschylus leaves us in no doubt
that what excites them, what justifies their revolt, is the prize of
freedom. What they needed, they told Electra, was "some man
at arms who will set free the house, holding the Scythian bow
backbent in his hands, a barbarous god of war spattering
arrows or closing to slash, with sword hilted fast to his hand."[38]
Once again there is a strong duality of meaning here. To
Electra's ears this is simply a metonymical appeal to Ares, the

[34] *Ibid.*, 101–104.
[35] *Ibid.*, 110–111.
[36] *Ibid.*, 112.
[37] *Ibid.*, 114.
[38] *Ibid.*, 160–163.

god of war. But every member of Aeschylus's fifth-century audience would immediately have caught the second meaning, for the police force of classical Athens was made up exclusively of Scythian slave archers. It was a daring piece of irony for Aeschylus to have a group of slave women plotting murderous rebellion against their masters literally praying for the slaves who kept the public house of Athens in order to set them free with a barbarous spatter of arrows. The attentive theatergoer would also have remembered Electra's first words to the Chorus only a few minutes earlier. She had made her entry with the Chorus, had stood silently, dramatically, during the parodos, before the tomb of Agamemnon which was center stage, young, innocent, yet in her very innocence menacingly female, the embodiment of "the female force,"[39] capable of "innocent murder,"[40] a living womb, essential for life, set before its outward expression, a cavernous tomb (a man's house?), equally necessary for life. And her first words had been: "Attendant women, who order our house. . . ."

When, in the next instant, Electra discovers Orestes' lock of hair, the Chorus squeals: "My heart is in a dance of fear." Maybe; but they are also having the time of their wretched lives. As women, and as slaves, it is men who most strongly stand for what they are up against. The struggle for freedom is the resistance of the female force against the brutal assault of men:

> The female force, the desperate
> love crams its resisted way
> on marriage and the dark embrace
> of brute beasts, of mortal men.[41]

The celebrated choral ode to Zeus, in which the Chorus prays for Orestes' success in avenging the death of his father by killing his mother and her husband, is often taken by

[39] *Ibid.*, 599.
[40] *Ibid.*, 830.
[41] *Ibid.*, 599–602.

commentators as simply the traditional, and fading, Greek concept of justice through vengeance. But such an interpretation is meaningful only if we view the Chorus in its role as attendants. A different light is cast on the hymn when we view them as slaves who have joined in a palace revolt for the sole purpose of gaining their freedom, and I do not see how we can avoid such an interpretation since one of the most stunning expressions of freedom, as the antithesis of the dark tomb of slavery, lies at the very center of the prayer:

> And you, who keep, magnificent, the hallowed and huge
> cavern, O grant that the man's house lift up its head
> and look on the shining daylight
> and liberty with eyes made
> glad with gazing out from the helm of darkness.[42]

The "huge cavern" is a reference to the inner sanctum of the temple of Apollo at Delphi, and it powerfully echoes both the outer womb of Agamemnon's tomb and the inner womb of woman, fusing together the image of the female force. Hogan notes that Apollo and Hermes, referred to in the next stanza, "make a pair of sons of Zeus, one from light, the other from darkness, to guard the son of the house."[43] What is powerfully expressed in this unforgettable tripartite symbol is, of course, the tripartite chord of freedom: womb is generative personal freedom; Agamemnon's tomb is male force, freedom as deathly power; and Apollo's sanctuary is the Athenian temple of civic freedom. It is the female force, however, that generates the triad and remains its fundamental element. Freedom, the Chorus tells us, is "a woman's song":

> Then at last we shall sing
> for deliverance of the house
> the woman's song that sets the wind
> fair, no thin drawn and grief

[42] *Ibid.*, 807–810.
[43] James C. Hogan, *A Commentary on the Complete Greek Tragedies: Aeschylus* (Chicago: University of Chicago Press, 1985), p. 135.

struck wail, but this: 'The ship sails fair.'
My way, mine, the advantage piles here,
   with wreck
and ruin far from those I love.[44]

They pray again to Zeus as Aegisthus is being murdered by
Orestes. And once again, it is freedom that comes to their lips:
". . . our man will kindle a flame and light of liberty, win the
domain and huge treasure of his fathers."[45] And when,
moments later, he takes his mother inside to cut her down,
they break out into a joyful celebration, first of justice, which is
vengeance, but even more ringingly, of what that justice
meant:

> Raise up the high cry over our lordship's house
> won free of distress, free of its fortunes wasted
> by two stained murder,
> free of its mournful luck.[46]

Again the dual meaning; for if my reading is correct we must
now ask: whose distress are they really talking about, whose
wasted fortune, and whose mournful luck? When Orestes
begins to go through pangs of guilt over murdering his
mother, they reassure him that what he did was well done
because he "liberated all the Argive city" when he killed his
mother and her husband.[47] But of course, Orestes is not to be
let off so easily. The furies, all women, set upon him. There is
something almost detached about their advice to the tor-
mented Orestes that he should go to Loxias, whose touch will
set him free, and a note of contempt in their offhand "good
luck to you then" as he exists, pursued by the furies.[48] Why
should they care? He has served his purpose and won them
their freedom, a savior of sorts. Or, "shall I call it that, or

[44] Aeschylus, *The Libation Bearers*, 819–825.
[45] *Ibid.*, 863–865.
[46] *Ibid.*, 942–945.
[47] *Ibid*, 1046.
[48] *Ibid.*, 1063.

death?"[49] The male force that was a necessary agent of their liberation must now pay his debt of social life to the female spirits of vengeance. The savior's death was the price of their renewed social life.

I began by saying that the Chorus apparently shares pride of place with Electra in the *Libation Bearers*. That statement must be revised. Electra quietly vanishes halfway through this drama. And Orestes is a near faceless prop to achieve the goal of the real protagonist of the play. This is the Chorus, the actual libation bearers. In this regard the drama goes back to the very roots of Greek tragedy, which, it is known, grew out of choral performance. Do we detect in this formal regression a suggestion that what obsessed this first actor, this first personality in the history of Greek drama, now transposed to the drama of Greek history, was a woman, a slave, threatening chaos with her demoniacal striving for personal freedom? For this is not primarily a play about vengeance at all. It is a play about a group of foreign slave women struggling against slavery in its literal form and in its sexual form of male force. It is a play about their mounting excitement and joy as they find a way out of their social death. It is a play about a slave rebellion. It is a woman's song about personal freedom at its most pristine moment.

In Sophocles' *Antigone* we confront the most tragic form of alienation from home, that of the person who is made a stranger, an outcast in her own homeland. This is Antigone's fate, and it is no accident that her struggle with Creon has become a virtual charter myth of Western freedom, or as George Steiner puts it, "canonic in our Western sense of individual and society."[50] As rebel, woman, and slave—the ultimate male configuration of disorder—she comes to identity "right," "justice," and "law," unwritten, natural law, as the content of her personal freedom: ". . . it is within the intensely

---

[49] *Ibid.*, 1073–1074.
[50] George Steiner, *Antigones* (New York: Oxford University Press, 1984).

energized terrain of values and application covered, bounded by these three terms, that the worlds of Creon and Antigone clash."[51]

The symbolism of death and renewal which, in the domain of the divinities, exposes the tragic fate of Antigone, in the mortal domain represents the triumph of the value she has discovered, constructed, and defends. Death makes a "living corpse" of Creon's male force, his enslaving sovereignal freedom. But in the mortal domain, death for Antigone means the death of kinlessness, slavery, isolation, lovelessness, and homelessness. Death is the double negation that leads to social rebirth, renatalization, reconnectedness. Like the archetypal slave among the primitive Callinago Caribs who were forced to mourn their own social death by cutting their hair in the style of mourners,[52] she too is one of those who, as Creon—most appropriately—observes, must "sing the dirge for their own death."[53] And willingly she sings, as she walks to the death that will undo her homelessness and living social death:

> O city of wealthy men.
> I call upon Dirce's spring,
> I call upon Thebes's grove in the armored plain,
> to be my witnesses, how with no friend's mourning,
> by what decree I go to the fresh-made prison-tomb.
> Alive to the place of corpses, an alien still,
> never at home with the living nor with the dead.[54]

She will not, of course, experience this freedom in this life. But she will regain her natality, her connectedness with her kinsmen and home from whom she has been torn, in the next. The tomb becomes a "marriage-chamber" from which she is led "to my own people." Every African-American, every West Indian, will be struck with awe by these lines, for it was one of

---

[51] *Ibid.*, p. 248.
[52] Patterson, *Slavery and Social Death*, p. 60.
[53] Sophocles, *Antigone*, 882.
[54] *Ibid.*, 841–851.

the most passionately held beliefs in the mortuary practices of
the New World slaves that death would restore them both to
their freedom and to the African homeland from which they
had been severed.[55] Antigone's "eloquent espousal of early
death," writes Steiner, and he could just as accurately be
writing of the vast number of West Indian slave rebels who
committed individual and mass suicides in order to secure
their freedom and hasten the return home, "is, at once, a
defiance of the living, of those who set life above the eternities
of mortal law . . . and an assertion of personal freedom. To
choose death freely, to chose it early, is to retain mastery and
self-mastery in the face of the only phenomenon against which
man knows no remedy."[56]

In the mortal domain of his tragedy, then, Sophocles has
dazzlingly refigured the Persephone myth, making Antigone a
sacrificial virgin figure to the cause of personal freedom, who,
for her "self-sufficiency"[57] is buried alive in the male womb
that is Creon's civic tomb. She will find her freedom below; but
her self-sacrifice makes personal freedom a value for us,
energizes it with the demonic forces of her womanness and her
passion. In the face of the gods she dies a tragic, sterile death,
a woman who has failed to re-generate—for that is the literal
meaning of her name[58]—but in the face of men, she generates
the monumental value of personal freedom, and ennobles it
with the weight of her love and her life. The Chorus sings of
her creation as she walks to the sacrificial tomb:

[55] On these beliefs and practices, see, for Jamaica, Orlando Patterson, *The Sociology
of Slavery: Jamaica 1655–1838* (London: McGibbon & Kee, 1967).

[56] Steiner, *Antigones*, p. 264.

[57] Sophocles, *Antigone*, 876. See Charles Segal, "Antigone," in Erich Segal, ed., *Greek
Tragedy* (New York: Harper & Row, 1983).

[58] This is the meaning glossed by Seth Benardete from the literal meaning,
"generated in place of another," cited in Froma Zeitlin, "Thebes: Theater of Self and
Society in Athenian Drama," in J. Peter Euben, ed., *Greek Tragedy and Political Theory*
(Berkeley: University of California Press, 1987), p. 126. See also Goldhill, *Reading
Greek Tragedy*, p. 102.

You went to the furthest verge
of daring, but there you found
the high foundation of justice, and fell.[59]

But she will never be forgotten. Antigone lives forever in the
hearts of all women and men who cherish personal freedom,
both in its defiantly negative, and in its humanely positive,
aspects.

God's child and god she was.
We are born to death.
Yet even in death you will have your fame,
to have gone like a god to your fate,
in living and dying alike.[60]

[59] Sophocles, *Antigone*, 852–855.
[60] *Ibid.*, 832–836.

Rembrandt's and Freud's "Gerusalemme Liberata"

BY SANFORD BUDICK

W<small>E HAVE</small> before us a painting by Rembrandt (plate 1). Long after Rembrandt's death it was titled, on no external authority, *Jeremiah Lamenting the Destruction of Jerusalem*. Is this, indeed, a painting about the destruction of a home, a particular home called Jerusalem? Or is the painting, perhaps, about the *construction* of home, precisely at the moment of *blanking it out*? Indeed, might we view this as a painting which both discovers and creates home by placing itself within a thinking of home, which is where all homes necessarily begin? I will call the kind of thinking about home and tradition that, I believe, this painting dramatizes *a train of thought*, a *Gedankengang*. This is a word important to Freud,[1] whose own train of thought not accidentally coincides with that of Rembrandt. Indeed, Freud's train of thought even leads to the same scene of thinking as does Rembrandt's: the city of Jerusalem. Freud has something important to tell us about the concept of home, though his contribution to our thinking about home may be even more significant than Freud himself can possibly imagine. First, however, let me turn to Rembrandt's painting.

On first view, this painting seems straightforward enough. We have in the top left-hand corner a more or less clear depiction of the destruction of a city, which does, indeed, seem

---

[1] The recurring use of the word *Gedankengang* that I especially have in mind here, and that I discuss below, is that in *Beyond the Pleasure Principle*.

Plate 1. Rembrandt's *Jeremiah Lamenting the Destruction of Jerusalem.*

to be Jerusalem. In fact, as I have shown elsewhere, the identity of the city seems confirmed by a number of details in the right-hand corner of the painting: the bottle and the girdle, for example.[2] These objects have explicit iconographic identities in Jeremiah's prophecy. In the biblical text, the destructions of the bottle and the girdle are major prefigurations of the destruction of Jerusalem. The painting, therefore, lends itself to at least one fairly simple historical interpretation: since the city's inhabitants have failed to heed Jeremiah's prophecies, Jerusalem has been laid waste. The historical drama thus unfolding in the painting moves chronologically from the viewer's right to his or her left. But an obvious contradiction immediately presents itself. The Jeremiah who is now lamenting the destruction of Jerusalem, which, as represented in the painting, is now clearly taking place, sits alongside objects which belong to a different moment. These objects are not destroyed. How, then, are we to understand the story which this painting unfolds? Do these objects exist prior to the destruction of the city? Or have they been reconstituted, in some time after? In either event, why do they appear here, whole and unbroken, at the very moment of the city's destruction?

Let me turn to the figure of the old man at the painting's center; and let us now switch, as much as possible, to his perspective. As I have just suggested, temporally and imaginatively speaking, the bottle and the girdle to the old man's left are situated in a "before" or "after" the destruction. They therefore exist in anachronistic relation to the events at the old man's right. They exist, in other words, at an angle of withdrawal, as it were, from the catastrophe at the man's far right. There is a rift between these realms, precisely down the center of the painting. For a related reason, the diagonal figure of the old man, which has usually been seen as being itself the composition's major diagonal, is merged into the luminous diagonal space abutting the old man. This is the

[2] "Rembrandt's *Jeremiah*," *Journal of the Warburg and Courtauld Institutes* 51 (1988): 260–264 and plate 41. I am grateful to Moshe Barash for his comments on an early version of the following new pages.

space which runs through the points that we would expect to
be occupied by his right arm and right foot. Something is
missing in this painting, some factor of direct, historical
continuity (either from past to present or from present to
future), which is simultaneously some element of physical,
bodily, even spiritual wholeness of being. The prophet who
supposedly mediates destruction and redemption interrupts
this painting, as he himself is significantly interrupted.
Jeremiah, of all prophets the one most closely identified with
Jerusalem, both lends his dramatic presence to his beloved
home and, at the same time, is somehow absent from it.

Our experience of this painting, I suggest, is to a large
extent determined by the phenomenon of what is missing. The
extraordinary red-velvet modeling of the left leg and the lack
of visible right arm and right foot constrain our attention, on
the deepest levels of empathic perception, to adhere precisely
to a line plotted along points of absence. As the spokesman of
the Lord, Jeremiah has continuously suffered the fearful fate
of having his being taken over by the Lord. His being and
experience, I have suggested, are represented in this painting
as nothing less than the Lord's personification of Himself. In
the first verse of His speaking to Jeremiah, the Lord told him:
"Before I formed thee in the belly I knew thee; and before
thou camest out of the womb I sanctified thee, and I ordained
thee a prophet unto the nations" (1:5). "Then," Jeremiah
relates, "the Lord put forth his hand, and touched my mouth.
And the Lord said unto me, Behold, I have put my words in
thy mouth" (1:9). Jeremiah is as powerless to refuse his fate in
this scene now, near his end, as he was right at the beginning,
even before his beginning, in the womb. Now, however, the
Lord's takeover of Jeremiah has even more awesome consequences. For it absorbs him directly into the instrumentality of
Jerusalem's destruction.

This, indeed, is one of the terrifying secrets of this
mysterious painting. In *The Lamentations of Jeremiah*, chapter 2,
verses 3 and 4, we see that the Lord "hath drawn back his right

hand from before the enemy, and he burned against Jacob like a flaming fire, which devoureth round about: . . . he stood with his right hand"—his *withdrawn* right hand—"as an adversary, and slew all that were pleasant to the eye in the tabernacle of the daughter of Zion: he poured out his fury like fire." Just so Jeremiah sits in the only dwelling place remaining to him, with his right hand withdrawn, bent on this destruction. In Rembrandt's representation, the withdrawn right hand and foot are more the Lord's than Jeremiah's. (And, as we shall see, they may be someone else's as well.) Whatever this scene of the Lord and His prophet is, they are in it together. Who, then, is this man Jeremiah? And how, and in what relation to his Jerusalem home, does he exist in this painting? Indeed, what is the relationship between the far left- and far right-hand corners of this painting? Do these scenes duplicate and/or replace each other, bottles and girdles, destroyed and whole, yielding to cities destroyed and renewed, in all time and all place, in endless repetition of the destruction and reconstruc- tion—and destruction, again—of home? Then Jeremiah's muted lament might well be for what Freud will call "the repetition of the same fatality" (22),[3] the experience, always, of the inevitable destruction of home.

Let me return to the luminous diagonal at the old man's right. This diagonal, I argue, represents a space of separation which is painted out of, not into, the graphics of this painting. It is this space which resists the repetition of the same fatality that threatens to overtake this picture. Its relation to the rest of the picture is neither inversive nor subversive. It is pure disrelation, absolute zero, pure *negativity*.

By negativity I do not mean negation. Rather, I mean both

---

[3] Citations from Freud in English are from *The Standard Edition of the Complete Psychological Works of Sigmund Freud*, ed. and tr. James Strachey, 24 vols. (London: Hogarth Press and the Institute of Psycho-Analysis, 1953–74). The citations from *Beyond the Pleasure Principle* are from vol. 18. Citations from *Beyond the Pleasure Principle* in German are from *Sigmund Freud: Gesammelte Werke Chronologisch Geordnet*, vol. 13 (London: Imago, 1947). Page numbers are given in parentheses within the text.

an object and a condition of consciousness which are both unavoidable in human experience. We experience negativity whenever we come up against the implications, omissions, or cancellations that are necessarily part of any representation, or any writing, speaking, or thinking. These gaps indicate that all representations contain an unrealized dimension, so that each manifest representation has a kind of invisible, latent, dead double. Thus, unlike negation, this inherent doubling in representation defies representation. It forms the unrepresented and unrepresentable counterpart of every representation, every thought.[4]

The burden of such a negativity is at the center of Jeremiah's dramatized experience in this painting. With Rembrandt's genius for such experience, he explores the element of temporal discontinuity or anachronism which is so marked in the temporalities of the two scenes and which has other important counterparts within the painting. Rembrandt has contrived to view this old man against a depth of space that, on one side, has no depth at all, which is in fact not a defined space at all but pure nothing, zero. He has merged the old man into this empty space by the techniques of withdrawal and absence suggested earlier. Rembrandt thus views the old man binocularly, though one eye sees only nothing. This is not dialectical or stereoscopic vision. It is, rather, a way of seeing in which the continuing solidity of the principal object (ostensibly the old man) is continually withdrawn.

In Rembrandt's representation of Jeremiah this perception of always imminent, already immanent loss—which is the loss not only of Jerusalem or home but of one's own being—is a form of *hysterical seeing*. When we see objects in the world

---

[4] This paragraph is adapted from Wolfgang Iser's account of negativity in *The Act of Reading: A Theory of Aesthetic Response* (Baltimore: Johns Hopkins University Press, 1980), pp. 182 and 225–229 and a subsequent adaptation of those remarks in our introduction to *Languages of the Unsayable: The Play of Negativity in Literature and Literary Theory*, ed. Sanford Budick and Wolfgang Iser (New York: Columbia University Press, 1989), p. xii.

hysterically, as Rembrandt sees this old man, our experience too is a function of the interchangeability of world with this particular kind of nothing, which I called negativity. An immediate, universally shared crisis is therefore enacted in this painting. Indeed, the catastrophe of the virtually anaesthetic old man is far more inward than even a response to national disaster. What we observe in the situation of the old man against the abyss of the nothing is the very rupture of the ligature of self. If we imagine that such a ligature is produced by a subject's identification with the objects that he views, the old man's anesthetic appearance is the outward symptom of the particular way in which his meaning and his self have both been severed. The decay or half-life of the old man's being begins to bring his new elemental home into being.

The effect of the intervention of the nothing is to break Jeremiah's hold on life and to eclipse his own identity. Jeremiah suffers more than a deep depression or a passing phase. He has experienced his own demise as a subject. Through this extreme form of self-doubt, he has lost the ability or *forgotten* how to name objects, not least Jerusalem itself, lost in a corner. His experience—our experience—of the world's and our own negativity in this way is this zero within life. This zero or nothing, I have suggested, is not the negation or cancellation of life or self. It is only the expression of their inaccessibility to representation. Jeremiah and Jerusalem and home are not simply annihilated in this painting. They are given a new lease. It turns out that experiencing his own (and the Lord's) negativity is Jeremiah's one way of remaining at home in the world.

But, assuming that these observations are in some sense true of this painting, we must ask *where Rembrandt himself experiences its grave consequences, his own deep doubleness, his own half-time oblivion, his own going home.* The objective correlative of this experience of the painter must presumably be both the painter's enacting of his own utter doubtfulness and, at the same time, in its own right, a realm *beyond even Rembrandt's consciousness or intentionality,* a place that exists only in the train or wake of his thought, what Freud, I suggested, calls the *Gedankengang.* But what could such an area within Rembrandt's painting look like—an area which is both *Rembrandt's* and *not-Rembrandt's?* How can Rembrandt's staging of negativity make its appearance beyond himself?[5]

There is, I believe, just such a new world of this kind within this painting. This other world is produced by necessities of both the narrative and painterly forms that Rembrandt inherits from other hands. Here he acts passively, powerlessly, as a dual consciousness, both dead and alive. Here his right hand too, his painterly hand, is very much withdrawn.[6] By the same token, the viewer's consciousness of these phenomena of doubtfulness can also only be dual, hysterical. Our statements describing what occurs here can only be suggestive dualities, an uncertain measurement of uncertainty. Our capacity for this measurement becomes, I believe, a measure of our being at home in the world. Let us go then—Rembrandt, this interpreter, and other interpreters following along—to another, etherized place in this painting, a secret place and a secret experience divided, once again dualistically, in two.

I now draw your attention to the upper middle part of the painting, where there is apparently no form at all to see. I remind you of the first verse of the Lord's speaking to Jeremiah: "Before I formed thee in the belly I knew thee; and before thou camest out of the womb I sanctified thee, and I ordained thee a prophet unto the nations" (1:5). This

---

[5] Although Iser's views of cultural tradition are different from my own, he has recently formulated the notion of a "progradient" movement in literature that is relevant here: see *Prospecting: From Reader Response to Literary Anthropology* (Baltimore: Johns Hopkins University Press, 1989), pp. 280–283.

[6] Stanley Cavell first suggested to me that what I had called the withdrawn hand of the Lord is also, in some sense, the withdrawn hand of the painter, so that the hand of the painter who had painted this painting is not only unseen (that is a usual state of affairs) but also specifically retracted. For Cavell's remarks on Jeremiah's "acknowledgment" of the Lord's words and on the concept of "perpetual nextness," see *The Senses of Walden* (New York: Viking Press, 1972), pp. 16–17, 63, and 100–103.

instituting verse becomes the reference point for Jeremiah's great hysterical outburst in chapter 20:

> 14   Cursed be the day wherein I was born: let not the day wherein my mother bare me be blessed.
> 15   Cursed be the man who brought tidings to my father, saying, A man child is born to thee; making him very glad.
> 16   And let that man be as the cities which the Lord overthrew, and repented not: and let him hear the cry in the morning, and the shouting at noontide;
> 17   Because he slew me not from the womb; or that my mother might have been my grave, and her womb to be always great with me.
> 18   Wherefore came I forth out of the womb to see labour and sorrow, and that my days should be consumed with shame?

This outburst is awesomely hysterical. It is hysterical both because in it Jeremiah, of all people, imagines resistance to the Lord's irresistible intent, spoken through Jeremiah; and also because it lingers in self-decreating imagination, placing the speaker in a tomb before birth. In Rembrandt's world the cross-cultural name of the womb into which Jeremiah would die is the *hystera* or womb of classical *hysterica passio* or Melancholy or "anaesthesia." It is the immobile hysteria of being rendered insensible, as in *hysteriká páthe* (hysterical suffering) or *hysterikè pníx* (hysterical stifling). Hysteria, as you know, was especially, though not exclusively, associated with women and was thought to be caused by disorders of the uterus or *hystera,* so that male hysteria becomes a particularly fascinating phenomenon—for people like Freud and Rembrandt, at any rate. The conventional identification of the figure of Rembrandt's old man with the tradition of Melancholy now assumes determinative relevance. Rembrandt's painting of Jeremiah's hysteria, and his descent into the womb (which he asks might be his grave), erupts in this composition in a way that is quite uncontrollable, yet deeply skeptical, and even beyond belief. The being at home in the

Plate 2. Chaperon's *Melancholy*.

world—of the painter, as well as of the perceiver—is
significantly a function of this skepticism.[7]

Here we need to refresh our memories, in the works of
Rembrandt's contemporaries, of a particular feature of the
iconographic forms of Melancholy. I mean the evocation of the
hystera or womb by the placement of an urn at an angle (usually
to the right) to the melancholic-hysteric, who usually leans on
her left arm oblivious to the object, which is part of the
background of her affliction. The three compositions before
you (plates 2, 3, 4), each called *Melancholy*—one by Nicolas
Chaperon, one by Domenico Feti, and one by Giovanni
Benedetto Castiglione—each has the telltale *hystera*.[8]

---

[7] For some of Cavell's comments on "the truth of skepticism," see *The Claim of
Reason: Wittgenstein, Skepticism, Morality, and Tragedy* (New York: Oxford University
Press, 1979), pp. 446–451.

[8] These are reproduced from Raymond Klibansky, Erwin Panofsky, and Fritz Saxl,
Saturn and Melancholy: Studies in the History of Natural Philosophy, Religion, and Art (1964;
Nendln/Leichtenstein: Kraus Reprint, 1979), plates 134, 135, and 136, where,
however, no mention is made of the *hystera* feature of representing *hysterica passio*.

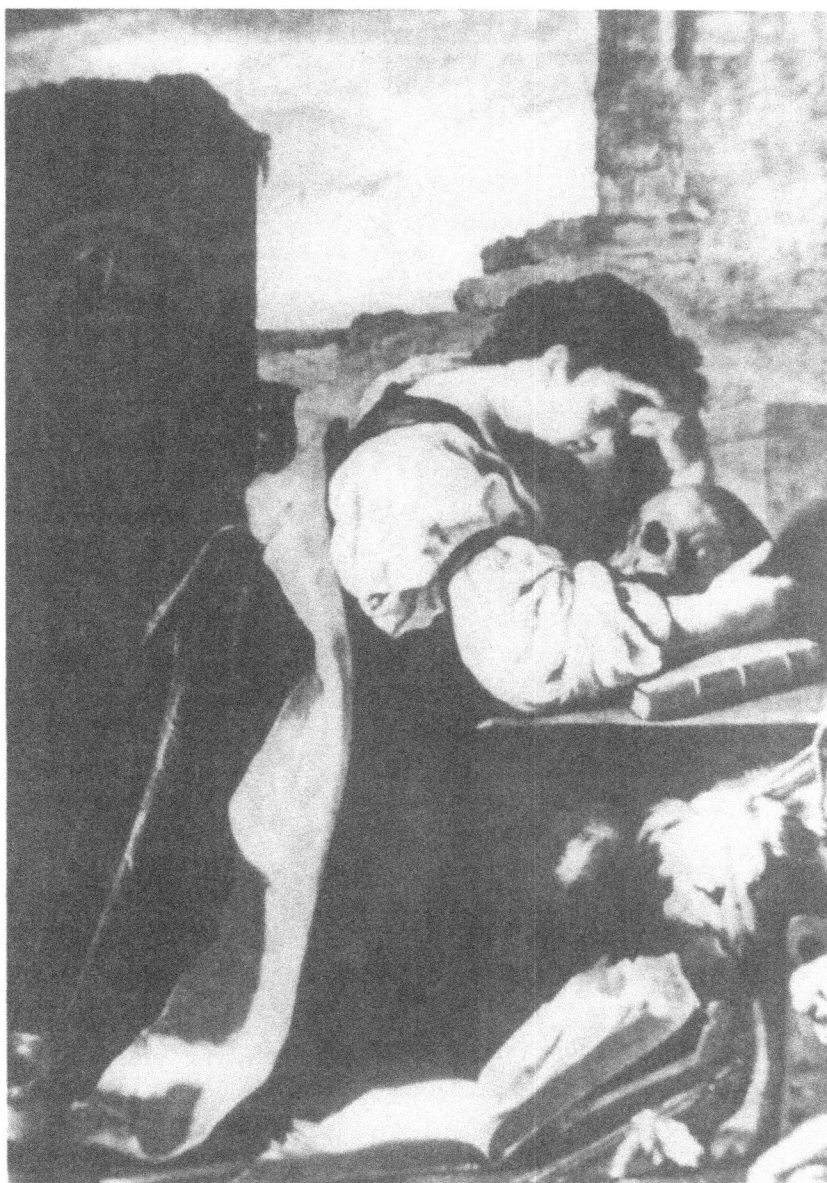

Plate 3. Feti's *Melancholy*.

Plate 4. Castiglione's *Melancholy*.

In the case of Rembrandt's hysterical Jeremiah, lost in a world of womb execrations, the womb, strangely enough, emerges from the space of interruption where there seems to be no form at all. And this womb is no urn metaphor for a

womb. It is a womb in itself, graphically (perhaps embarrassingly, obstructively) present, even if we experience its
emergence doubtfully, as if from the space of nothing. This
womb begins at the edge of a triangular bush. From there, at
the old man's right, it winds upward like a golden or brazen
funnel, beyond the edge of the frame.[9]

Let us assume we have seen this *hystera,* even if only
doubtfully. Do we then experience a connection between the
hysterical seeing of which the void is a central element and
the emergence, upon the same void, of this womb which is
the threshold of the nothing? What might be the relation of
turning to this womb and going home? The half-buried
presence of the womb suggests that we can only see it, and
say it, from below the threshold of any focusing, or homing
in, of consciousness. We can therefore put our question in
these other words: specifically in art, can a subliminal
connection be experienced between negativity or death-in-life
on the one hand, and the train of thought, beyond the
inclusive unity of the self, on the other? This painting seems
to suggest that, like Jeremiah and Rembrandt before us—and
like descending Homer, descending Virgil, and descending
Dante (and also, as I shall show in a moment, descending
Tasso and Freud)—we inherit our place in the train of
thought forged at this threshold, even if we cannot grasp it
or penetrate it in consciousness—or even in our unconscious.
Rembrandt's painting of Jeremiah escapes the repetition of
the same fatality only in the fatality—that is, the death—of
the self, within continued life beyond the self. Rembrandt's
Jeremiah experiences the staging of his own death-in-life in
this opening of the womb of negativity. This openness which
cannot be possessed is emphasized by the concentration of
Jeremiah's weight upon the book. For this writing, which is

---

[9] A more leisured meditation on the gender of this *hystera* would have to explore
Jeremiah's phrase "tabernacle of the daughter of Zion."

not Rembrandt's, already contains the whole of the scene before us, including its negativity and its wombs.[10]

If the present interpretation—this radical experience of negativity, this death within life—is correct, Jeremiah, the womb-anxious victim of hysteria, is represented beside a womb. This tracing of the womb represents only a doubtful space, rendered only by hysterical seeing. Jeremiah, and Rembrandt, and the viewer go dualistically from one hysterical seeing, from one such experience of death within life, to another. Yet even in their explorations of this *hystera* of negativity, they do not achieve individual consciousness of death-in-life. Their train of thought, like their withdrawn hands, only explores the home that bears thinking.

This is the same home which bears thinking in Freud as well. *Beyond the Pleasure Principle* represents a late and fascinating attempt on Freud's part to get beyond the fatal conditions of self-repetition. These are the same conditions of fatality which concern Rembrandt in his painting of repetitions. Freud's book is so complex and rich with regard to the issues that confront us in Rembrandt that on this occasion I cannot even hope to lay out the relevant Freudian terminology, much less begin to reconstruct his argument.[11] I now offer, therefore, only a fleeting glance at Freud's painting of a particular scene in his book. Something is amiss in this scene, something which, as far as I can tell, has not been noted before in print, though it must have been noticed silently by many of Freud's readers. In painting this scene, I want to show, Freud, like

---

[10] There is another womb on the other side of Jeremiah which I won't trace at this moment: in the tradition of Dürer's polyhedron in his *Melencolia I*, it is a *hystera* recreated in a repetition of angles, in this case angles which impinge on the frontal space of the book. These angles replicate angles formed by the old man's impingements on the empty space to his right. I have discussed this at greater length elsewhere (see next footnote).

[11] A different, longer version of the present essay, containing a more detailed discussion of relevant features of *Beyond the Pleasure Principle*, forms a chapter in my study of "place" as an interpretive concept (forthcoming, Yale University Press).

Rembrandt, "draws a blank" and thus effects the hysterical
seeing and death-in-life which, for both Freud and Rembrandt, makes possible inheritance, tradition, and, finally,
home.

I am referring to Freud's rendering of what he calls "the
most moving picture" of a fate that Freud calls the "repetition
of the same fatality" (22). This is the picture given by Tasso in
his epic poem *Gerusalemme liberata*. "Its hero, Tancred," Freud
writes, "unwittingly kills his beloved Clorinda in a duel while
she is disguised in the armour of an enemy knight. After her
burial he makes his way into a strange magic forest which
strikes the Crusaders' army with terror. He slashes with his
sword at a tall tree; but blood streams from the cut and the
voice of Clorinda, whose soul is imprisoned in the tree, is
heard complaining that he has wounded his beloved once
again" (22).[12]

What Freud sees in Tasso's emblem of Jerusalem is its tragic
"repetition of the same fatality." Yet what Tasso actually,
explicitly shows is the possibility for being *liberated*—or, to use
Tasso's own word, *sciolta* (12.71)—from that murderous
repetition.[13] Tancred has *not* wounded Clorinda once again.

---

[12] The poetic density of this incident is indeed "most moving" or "most gripping"
(*ergreifendste* [21]) since it repeats Dante's entry into the dark wood of error and his
descent to the realm of the dead. (Tasso calls it "this new Dis"—13, 27.) Nor does the
repetition stop there. Within the whole series of poetic descents which open up behind
Tasso's descents—Virgil's and Homer's most memorably—there is also the descent to
Plato's dark cave. Freud's later phrases concerning "a darkness into which not so much
as a ray of hypothesis has penetrated" (57) directly precede his invocation of Plato in
section VI. This is the place that "the poets" (45) and "the poet-philosopher" (58) know
best. Freud is "strengthened" (45) in his hypothesis of "the least rigid hypothesis" by
following the track of their descents—to the death instinct. The poets know that "we
cannot avoid contact" with this *hystera* which is "the most obscure and inaccessible
region of the mind." "Es ist das *dunkelste* und unzugänglichste Gebiet des Seelenlebens"
(p. 4; my emphases). *Beyond the Pleasure Principle* attempts to reach this dark *hystera*
only by "the least rigid hypothesis" of its *Gedankengang*. This is the hysterical
otherworld of the same poets who know the realm of Eros or the pleasure principle. All
who would explore this *hystera* must abandon (*hingeben*) all hope of penetrating to
saving knowledge.

[13] That the term *liberata*—and perhaps any single-stage adjective—was by Tasso
viewed as being inadequate for describing the making of home or "Jerusalem" may be

Freud—the Joseph of our civilization's dream life—has
forgotten Tancred's dream visitation, in which the soul of dead
Clorinda appears to Tancred and thanks him for having
liberated her forever and set her safely apart from the world of
the merely living.[14] This occurs immediately before the false
seeming in the wood. "You removed me," Clorinda says, "by
your mistake, from those who are living in the mortal world;
you made me worthy, by your act of mercy, to rise to God's
[womb] amid the blessed and immortal ones [*tu in grembo*
(womb/bosom/middle) *a Dio fra gl'immortali e divi*]" (*GL*,
12.92).[15] Freud tells us that Clorinda's soul is the transference
for Tancred's soul. Within the repetitions and working
through of his book, it is also the transference for the
"benefactor" who, Freud reports, repeatedly experiences fatal
relationships with his "protégés" (22), say of Freud with Jung
later in this book (52–53). Clorinda's soul cannot be, as Freud
imagines, imprisoned in the tree. Only its false, libidinal
semblance is there. Clorinda cannot be killed again because she
is already dead and free.

Like Dante's Beatrice in Dante's own tracings of the womb
descent (from which Tasso tries to inherit), Clorinda is beyond
the libidinal, beyond the life instincts, beyond the pleasure
principle; she is located, says Tasso's *Gerusalemme, in grembo*, in
the womb which is the exit point from life, within life. By

---

reflected in the fact that Tasso objected to *Gerusalemme liberata* as the title (chosen by
Angelo Ingegneri) for his poem. In other words, the homes produced by the epic
poem, the painting, and the *Beyond*, are first and foremost movements toward the
beyond.

[14] By calling Clorinda "that lovely liberated soul"—*la bella anima sciolta* (12.71)—
Tasso specifically makes her a prolepsis of Jerusalem's liberation from repetition of the
same fatality. Yet, as indicated above, the idea of that "liberation" was no simple matter
for Tasso. In the poem's final verses, the specific form this liberation takes is in
Godfrey's hanging up his arms in the Holy Sepulcher, in other words, at the
archetypical same-fatality which was paid down to break the repetition of the same
fatality. Citations from Tasso are from *La Gerusalemme Liberata*, ed. Giovanni Getto
(Brescia: La Scuola Editrice, 1967). Translations in English are from *Jerusalem
Delivered*, tr. Ralph Nash (Detroit: Wayne State University Press, 1987).

[15] For another imagining of the *grembo*, see, for example, 14. 41.

virtue of this "transference" (which is Freud's repeated framing term, before and after his explication of the exemplum), Tancred has also reached the *hystera* or womb of his own death-in-life. We are reminded here of the imagined, womb-like destination which sets Freud on his journey at the beginning of *Beyond the Pleasure Principle*. He speaks there of "the most obscure and inaccessible region of the mind, [with which] we cannot avoid contact" and which, paradoxically, might be reached, he says, only by "the least rigid hypothesis" (7). In citing the experience of Tancred and Clorinda, Freud unwittingly instances not a repetition of the same fatality, but a liberation from repetition and the pleasure principle into just such a womb-like "region of the mind."

Within the context of the line of thought of *Beyond the Pleasure Principle,* how are we to regard Freud's remarkable misremembering of his carefully chosen scene? Can we simply ignore it as a mistake, when Tancred's liberating "mistake," as Clorinda calls it, is itself the text Freud has unwittingly singled out for attention? This, after all, is a book in which Freud speaks "unwittingly" as a matter of principle (see 43 and 59). What are we to think of a dramatically wrong turn in a book that takes us on a death drive, beyond the pleasure principle, toward a newly liberated home?[16] Is it possible that Freud is

---

[16] Two other remarks by Freud concerning "Jerusalem" should be taken into account here. The first concerns the repetition of the very same fatality—in the same historical epoch as the incident from Tasso—described in *Civilization and Its Discontents:* as an example of *Homo homini lupus* Freud there instances "the capture of Jerusalem by the pious Crusaders" (*Standard Edition*, 21: 111–112). The second remark, made shortly before the composition of the *Beyond,* is far more complex and does not admit of a univocal interpretation. It involves the opposition between repetition of the same fatality and a new "experiment." Yet Freud does not explain what he regards as the experimental dimension of this nonrepetition. This remark occurs in a letter to Karl Abraham on Dec. 10, 1917: "In the struggle between the Entente and the Quadruple Alliance I have definitely adopted the viewpoint of Heine's Donna Bianca in the disputation at Toledo: '*Doch es will mich schier bedünken* . . . ' [the silent part of the well-known quotation is *Dass der Rabbi und der Mönch / Dass sie alle beide Stinken*]. The only thing that gives me any pleasure is the capture of Jerusalem [in early December] and the British experiment with the chosen people. [Freud is referring to the Balfour Declaration, Nov. 2, 1917.]" Cited from *A Psycho-Analytical Dialogue: The Letters of*

also signaling, beyond himself, his own liberation from the repetition of the same fatality—from the repeating Oedipal fatality of the pleasure principle which, in various incarnations, destroys homes everywhere? Precisely at the place he calls his *place of breaking off* in the book Freud will muse, "It may be asked whether and how far I am myself convinced of the hypotheses that I have set out in these pages. My answer would be," he continues, "that . . . I do not know how far I believe in them. . . . It is surely possible to [abandon] oneself [to] a line of thought" (59), to a *Gedankengang* (64).[17]

I would like to propose that in his portrait of Tancred and Clorinda Freud both suppresses and signals—via Tasso's well-known text—the way in which, in *Beyond the Pleasure Principle,* he must abandon himself to this train of thought. In drawing a blank about the *grembo* or womb—of escape from repetition—within this scene of allegedly inescapable repetition, Freud draws a blank in another sense as well. He draws—or unwittingly draws attention to—the blank or womb-like negativity which, in Tasso, Dante, and Rembrandt as well, maintains the motion of the train of thought from one consciousness to another. Like Rembrandt he draws this *hystera* by withdrawing his hand and foreshadowing the abandonment of his self, will he nill he, to the train of thought. The *hystera* and this particular kind of hysteria make all the home to which flesh can be heir. If earlier and later in his career, Freudian "figurative language" (60) (the basis of figuration itself in Freud's terms) was only imaginable as the phallic, penetrative life of the pleasure principle, now, in this moment of Freud's transference from Clorinda in the womb of negativity, a new-ancient figuration is brought back into being. Freud

Sigmund Freud and Karl Abraham, 1907–26, ed. Hilda C. Abraham and Ernest L. Freud (New York: Basic Books, 1965).

[17] In *Beyond the Pleasure Principle* Freud's other, closely related uses of the word *Gedankengang*—which Strachey translates "line of thought" (he uses this phrase on two occasions, pp. 58 and 60, when Freud's word is not *Gedankengang*)—are to be found in *Gesammelte Werke,* 18: 39, 60, 61 and *The Standard Edition,* 18: 37, 56 (twice).

discovers this womb through what he himself calls his "least rigid hypothesis" concerning what might be "beyond" the pleasure principle.

Within the train of thought, or home, into which he has thrown himself, a part of the unwitting Freud has escaped the repetition of the same libidinous fatality by exposing himself to another, more immediate fatality: the fatality of a death-in-life. If this exposure is, as some may feel, a form of self-castration, it is also, in any vocabulary, an immensely constructive act. Propelled by this hysterical, second consciousness (which is beyond even his unconscious), his train of thought has hypothesized a further *hystera,* beyond the thinking presently being thought. Freud's early interest in male hysteria[18] has thus been brought to term, but only in an hysterical breaking off. The train of thought—home, tradition—survives as the explorative matrix which no one penetrates. We only think it hysterically, dead within continued life, according to this least rigid hypothesis.[19]

---

[18] For Freud's early comments on male "hysterogenic zones" in "an area of the abdominal wall corresponding to the ovaries," see "Observation of a Severe Case of Hemi-Anaesthesia in a Hysterical Male" (1886) and "Hysteria" (1888): *Standard Edition,* 1: 30 and 43.

[19] Taken together with the story of the benefactor and his *protégés,* the message sent to "innovators like Jung" (52) by this *poetische Darstellung* and its dualistic hypothesis (of the fatality which is within life) may be understood as follows: 'Your monistic libido (53) does not reach where I presently am, where you as reader [whose "predilection" (24) or *Einstellung* (23) like my "prejudices" (59) or *Vorlieben* (64), formed by the withdrawn hands of the *Gedankengang*] must also be. I can appreciate your good work in the *Gedankengang* along which I too die and live exploratively. [Freud's discourse descends to a footnote praising Jung's good work just at this point.] Your monistic, Oedipal libido need not affect us otherwise. And one thing more: if you wish to explore my status as dualistic consciousness, as hysteric, which is informed by the connection between hysteria and death-in-life, you are free to explore the *poetische Darstellung,* the picture from which I have withdrawn my hand.'

HOME AS PLACE AND CENTER FOR PRIVATE AND FAMILY LIFE

The history of the concept of home is bound up with family and gender roles. As the functions of the home and its relationship to the family change over time and across cultures, tensions between prescriptive ideals and social realities are increasingly a source of stress.

Introduction / BY ALAN TRACHTENBERG

In this era of the "homeless" when exile and dispossession press everywhere on our minds, what remains of the innocence once attached to the idea of home as the central place of being, the citadel of the private and the sacred vessel of the domestic? Not only do images of the unsheltered and the disconnected assault our eyes and minds everywhere, but the cardinal propositions of the passing bourgeois era no longer claim the kind of allegiance and assent once thought natural and universal: hearth and threshold, private homes privately owned, fathers and mothers in their place, children secure in the home-based knowledge of what a man is and how a woman differs, holding themselves in readiness to assume the prescribed roles of fathers, mothers, homebuilders and homekeepers. Such families may not have had happiness in common, as Tolstoy said, but they did have togetherness under a single roof, within a central and centering place. So it is widely believed, and widely lamented that the picture no longer holds.

Today images of well-accoutred family places and domestic communities shaped by absolute gender roles and sanctioned by sentiment seem outlandishly retrograde, unacceptably patriarchal, and embarrassingly naive. And yet, does not a residue of such sentiment persist in our cultural memory of imagined havens of warmth, shelters against the storm? Is it possible to think about what "home" means without succumbing in some degree to nostalgia for the once-sanctified bourgeois family of European and American cities? Isn't this at least one of the images we unthinkingly set out to recreate when we imagine homes for ourselves, when we go about converting real space into a representation of the homeplace?

We may think of home, and take solace and moral courage in this, as a universal. But the historical, the contingent, habitually shows up in our thinking, typically as the conceptual form of unacknowledged desire. We think of "home" much as we practice it, as timebound social beings. Any discourse on meaning must eventually accommodate itself to historical practices buried within outwardly pure concepts and definitions.

And so the shape of the symposium tracks an arc of critical thought: in an inversion of Marx's architecture, superstructure has preceded base. But "base" is much too pale a category for the kind of work performed by the papers which follow. What unifies them is the historian's obsession with how things have been, the actual specificities of practice, of realizations and constructions in praxis, and the anthropologist's sense of praxis as culture. The key issue here, in my view, is the relation engaged in each paper between the material and the conceptual, between the home as apparatus, as physical form accommodating and shaping social behavior, and home as cognitive experience, as idea and representation. "Home as equipment for living" might cover the issues and the points of view developed here. This restatement of the panel's undertaking may better clarify the *practical* emphasis, which is to say that to see home as praxis is also to see, or prepare ourselves to see, the multiplicity of forms and ideas which have woven themselves into the word. The perspective delivered by the panel as a whole is *comparative,* and thus a defense against the innocence of mistaking where and how we live for home-as-such.

Prescribing the Model Home

BY GWENDOLYN WRIGHT

Every society tends to approach home and family with an implicit ideal about both, an inspiration simultaneously universal and quite particular, at once architectural and cultural. To a great extent, the two intersect and fuse together into an archetypical setting: the "model home." This topic may seem unduly commonplace, commercialized, and materialistic. Yet it can help to reconsider the relationships between abstract images and physical space, between universal truths and personal experience, between ideals and obstacles. The model home functions as a powerful ideology within a society, in part simply because it seems so familiar and obvious, so accessible and desirable. An object and ideal, seemingly without controversy, this notion of home contains and obscures innumerable conflicts.

The "model home" is, first, a physical prototype. It exists as an object: both an ideal place conjured up in our mind's eye and multiple architectural interpretations of that ideal seen in the landscape. Produced over and over again in a similar manner, the home can then be exchanged or sold within a particular market system. This is true whether the basis of the market is the appreciation of real-estate investments or the enhancement of a family through new daughters-in-law; whether the imagery desired emphasizes continuity (the "traditional" house of folk cultures) or innovation (our own fascination with fashion and technological improvements).

The home therefore exists within a given market system,

providing a primary vehicle of economic value and transfer, as well as a more elusive affirmation of the supposed logic of that particular market. The multigenerational dwelling plays such a role in so-called "traditional societies" based on exchange economies and family enclaves; and the Western counterpart buttresses the mystique of the free market. The single-family house remains the very epitome of what that system claims to offer. We see around us both the potency of the image and its dark underside. Homelessness can be publicly tolerated under capitalism, simply because there is the possibility of homeownership.

I am also speaking of a "model home" in the way most of us would tend to use the term: a place filled with requisite and familiar things—sacred icons or consumer goods—fetishes that attest to the family's virtue, their status, their stability. The model home, itself an architectural object, contains a plenitude of smaller objects, ranging from strictly practical to purely ornamental. In between one finds a multitude of goods deemed "functional"—though they may create the need they serve—or "beautiful."

Commodification is undeniable: an ambiguity between objects and aspirations, choices and expectations. The fact that people in this country buy so many objects for their homes, hoping to enhance them, does not make all objects meaningless. Yet consonant meaning must always be generated, and continually reappraised, by individuals.

The ideal of home, while universal, exists simultaneously as a deep-rooted individual concept—at once fantasy, memory, and longing—and as a cultural norm. One speaks quite easily of "the American dream home" or the "traditional" Dogon houses in Mali. Embedded within the spaces, between the objects, of all homes are implicit roles for men and women, for individual and community, for majority and minority groups within any society.

I am going to concentrate my remarks on the continuities, transformations, and tensions in the American ideology of the model home. The very word "home" is unique to the English language, after all, albeit with potent similarities to the German *Heim,* offering protection and familiarity, and allusions to the walls of the Old English *hus,* where goods were safely stored and husbanded. The etymology of *"hus*-band" evoked a man bound to the house through ownership; the "housewife" connected through relationships of marriage and helpmate. One can then trace the dichotomy as it evolved from the Latin *domus:* the symbolic power of "domain" and "domination"; or the parochial, innocent handicrafts called "domestic," the nurturance and submission of "domestication." Gender roles are unequivocally polarized under the roof of home.

Generations of Americans have tended to see their homes as statements about their status and their domestic life, as settings that revealed the kind of family who lived there. The home has continued to function as a mirror, reflecting a family portrait for the nation and for individuals. The household's major financial investment functions as assurance of good credit, peaceful domesticity, and class stability—the principal proof that one is financially secure, tasteful, and close-knit.

The right home still seems a way to achieve all that one longs for: a balance of successful achiever, interesting individual, and (for many of us) warm and accessible parent. To the architect, the builder, and the real-estate dealer these are client aspirations. Architectural definitions of "home" exist as a delicate balance of stylistic traditions, current fashions, and social or economic constraints. The market as a whole strives to know and control those desires, balancing predictability with a continuous infusion of minor innovations. In contrast, the architecture profession inevitably strives for new forms of expression befitting new ways of life. For a century now, the avant-garde has shown an adamant preference for unprecedented formal experiments, notably in house design. The profession as a whole tends to consider housing problems outside its domain, since they cannot be resolved in purely architectonic terms. Few architects are willing to accept the idiosyncratic and often rather conventional preferences of public taste, or the real economic limits of their clients.

If the nature of domestic concerns has shifted somewhat over time, many issues endure. Since the architectural formula for resolving them keeps changing in slight ways, it is difficult to confront the elusiveness of the goals. Are rooms our culture's fetishes, magically protecting family members? The Victorian house had its sunny nursery for health and well-being; the progressives endorsed separate bedrooms for each child to encourage independence; suburbanites in the 1920s wanted a basement recreation room to counterbalance insidious temptations outside the home; a generation later, the family room, with its television set, ensured togetherness; today's children need computer, video, and musical technology to connect safely, from within the home, with their youth culture.

Residential design after the Civil War (those houses we speak of as "Victorian") first purported to describe "individual" interests, taste, and social rank. The middle-class suburban home signaled the family's competing desires for uniqueness and social acceptance. Ironically, it was an outpouring of industrially produced goods and building elements that allowed for such expression: rugged construction materials and deep colors alluded to a love for nature; Japanese scrolls and casts of Greek statues attested to cultured education; each bay window or porch became evidence of something within—a piano, an embroidery corner, a niche for reading, a library—making that space exactly right for the activity and, in the process, proudly asserting it to passers-by.

During this same era interior decorators emerged as specialized professionals who could help coordinate such messages. In *Godey's Lady's Magazine,* one decorator likened the parlor to "the *face* of the house—the most noticeable part—and that from which visitors take their impressions of the whole." Residential architecture and decor were anthropomorphized.

The pervasive notion of a "model home" does not

necessarily imply a status quo. Yet Americans have often found it difficult to accept variations of their basic paradigms. Let me offer several examples. Henry David Thoreau's experiment at Walden centered, in the most conspicuous sense, upon a different notion of domestic comfort. "Most men," he wrote, "appear never to have considered what a house is, and are actually though needlessly poor all their lives because they think that they must have such a one as their neighbors have." Later in passing, he speculated on the housewife's isolation: "There is as much secrecy about the cooking as if he had a design to poison you." Thoreau, it seems, still posed the dilemma in terms of the husband's overseeing all the rooms of a conventional mid-nineteenth-century dwelling.

Most nineteenth-century building-and-loan companies were based on tight-knit ethnic communities. When these institutions approved financing for new cottages—indeed, such companies often initiated small developments—they did not question rooms for boarders, for these were commonplace among the immigrant working class; and they frequently chose to forgo such amenities as street paving, rather than tax the community beyond their means. As a result, these neighborhoods often *looked* unseemly to middle-class suburbanites in more idyllic residential communities. They could not comprehend the choices being made.

American homes have, of course, incorporated some modifications in gender roles. Certainly the most progressive and commercially successful examples occurred in the early decades of the twentieth century. Women's magazines like *Ladies' Home Journal* and *House Beautiful* endorsed "minimal houses" with simplified, built-in interiors, specifically in order to give women time to pursue jobs or volunteer work outside the home. Rational plans, efficient technology, and easily cleaned surfaces seemed the key. (One woman even suggested a kitchen that could be washed down with a hose.) Bungalow courts provided space for communal child care and social life. Professional services in urban "apartment hotels" included laundry, child care, and cooking. A dinner order could be delivered to your door—or to lobby-level restaurants and public dining rooms for entertaining.

In the aftermath of World War I, many communities chose to outlaw apartment buildings, shared houses, and homes smaller than a minimal size. The rationale was often phrased in terms of a risk to property values, a danger that permitted such zoning controls in the courts. But that comprises only one part of the story. One must unravel a sequence of associations. The correlation of certain dwelling types with independent, "nontraditional" women made them highly suspect. Americans feared the collapse of their idealized image of family life and gender roles. Homes that challenged these ideals were perceived as a danger to a residential "neighborhood," and hence to the value of the property.

Even where they gained acceptance, efforts to reform concepts of the home have often turned out to be limiting. Habitually they sought not so much to expand the sense of possibilities as to replace one ideal with another—whether teaching middle-class taste to the immigrant poor or insisting on collective space as the authentic expression of feminist values. The model home continued to be a potent, almost magical setting that could transform behavior or assure correct behavior in those already enlightened.

A simple story may clarify this point. It comes from a brochure promoting the benefits of kindergartens in the 1890s. Two poor Italian children attended a Boston kindergarten class, where their teacher gave them a flower to take home to their tenement apartment. The children presented the flower to their mother, who put it in a glass on the windowsill. The window pane was too dirty to let in light, so she cleaned it; when the sunlight shone through, she realized that the entire room was filthy and cleaned everything. That evening the children's father came home from the corner tavern and, startled by the transformation of the apartment into a "home," declared solemnly, "I'm going to give up drinking and get a job."

Certainly most Americans could anticipate how this story was going to end. Our culture's ideas about home are passed down through such morality fables and fairy tales, through advice books, popular magazines and newspapers, television shows and movies, laws and public programs. The messages can be poignant, reassuring, and inspiring. Yet, as with all myths, there are underlying lessons about deceit, danger, and the toll of breaking a rule or convention.

What does one learn by considering government housing programs as a form of cultural narrative, recounting assumptions about transformation and continuity in the home, along with political and economic realities? Urban renewal in the 1950s was based on the assertion that poorly constructed dwellings, unkept facades, and overcrowding constituted a dangerous evil called "blight." To classify even a quarter of the buildings in a neighborhood under this rubric presupposed the inevitable contamination of the others—a "domino theory" of housing. This danger in turn justified eviction and condemnation of all the dwellings, freeing the land for so-called "higher uses" such as luxury housing and office buildings. Where public housing was constructed, the favored prototype was a group of tall, spartan towers, separated from their surroundings by major traffic throughways, again in an effort to segregate residents from "contamination." Poverty could be banned, cordoned off, but never eliminated.

Likewise, the appearance of a "nice home" can cover over emotional and physical violence within all sorts of households. Appearance can lead us to expect that family life *should* work out because the setting *looks* right. That response can hold residents entrapped, making them feel personally inadequate for not living up to expectations, as well as blinding outsiders to the good or bad that may be taking place behind the walls of a dwelling.

We need to untangle our own culture's complex ideology of home: the expectations, the desires, and the systems interlaced within the images. "Home" is both an imposed ideal and a potent cultural, as well as individual, ideal. One must keep each dimension in mind, refusing to relegate the private domain of home solely to the forces of patriarchy or consumerism; yet never forgetting that, like all ideals, "home" is not necessarily all we would have it mean.

So let me continue to scan certain moments in the history of the American home, citing some of the main currents and the variations. I want to suggest why it has been and continues to be so hard to live up to the aspirations implied in our American ideal of home, and how this disparity affects us. The first step is to examine the interaction between architectural innovation and cultural ambition that fuels the market for renovations and new homes. It is then possible to disaggregate three forces. First is the artistic vision of a cohesive, unified design in which the whole is greater than its parts, and therefore a necessary aspiration for the architect and client. The second is the pressure to have the right stylistic statement, technological improvements, and other formalistic elements as evidence of one's domestic circumstances and status. Third is the pervasive sense of inadequacy about actual economic and familial circumstances, causing many people to overinvest in their homes.

These pressures impose a Procrustean "fit" on individual families and on the society as a whole. One group under constant pressure has been the middle class, always struggling to assure stability, and, in the process, establishing standards for others. In a culture that does not want to acknowledge class differences, the home becomes a highly charged symbol of status. In a country still deeply ambivalent about gender and racial equality, defense of home and community can mask intolerance.

The attachment to a single and singular solution, one specifically adapted to the needs of the middle class, then leads to conflicts about housing reform. Debates about policy tend to pit those who are concerned about the need for shelters and subsidized homes for the poor *against* those who worry that the market can no longer produce "affordable housing" for the majority of citizens. Can we afford to fight against one another about *which* kind of homes are the most problematic or most necessary?

Many categories of influence help define our notions about the home and family we should have. None of them suggest much sensitivity to variation, and even less to those who, by choice or circumstance, are outside the mainstream set of norms.

First is the market itself. Since the mid-nineteenth century, builders' and decorators' "pattern books" and specialized magazines have endorsed housing in cultural terms. Texts like *Homes for the People in Suburbs and Country* (1856) declared simplified structure and innovative detailing to be expressions of democratic equality. After World War II social scientists and marketing researchers studied the suburbs, seeking to define the "average family," its preferences and habits. Their samples were scarcely representative of the country as a whole, nor did the choices offer much diversity—beyond simple stylistic classifications like a "modern" or "colonial" facade. The results were used to buttress the notion that anyone who wanted an apartment or a "used house," as the description put it, was surely abnormal. Observers who noticed the homogeneity of the suburbs, the uniformity of class, age, and dwellings, felt sure that this setting would undermine Americans' individuality. Critics, too, reiterated the widespread belief in the power of the home environment to determine character.

Reformers have used domestic architecture—or at least an image of the clean, well-lit, demure home environment—as the sole indication of acceptable domestic feeling and its beneficent effect. Conservatives focus on references to a privatized abode, enclosing the family; progressive reformers prize collective space to promote shared work and social attachments. Neither side tends to grant the possibility of legitimate emotional attachment to settings that do not fit their ideal. In 1913, for example, the social worker Edith Abbott, a well-meaning woman by all accounts, wrote in her diary about the destruction of Chicago's Plymouth Court and the eviction of its Italian residents. "It was strange," she mused, "to find people so attached to homes that were so lacking in all the attributes of comfort and decency."

The government's intervention has expanded and now contracted in this century. During the 1930s, when the New Deal sought to recharge a crippled building industry, some programs ventured into production, providing apartment buildings as "temporary" homes for stable, two-parent working-class families (a prerequisite for acceptance into public housing) who had lost their income because of the Depression. Later public housing opened up to the very poor and single-parent families; in fact, to assure that private home building and real estate would not be affected, residents had to have an income at least 20 percent below the local estimate for a family to afford market-rate rents. Yet the most pervasive evidence of state involvement in defining the ideology of home remains the indirect endorsement of middle-class residential suburbs through highway building, FHA guidelines, income-tax deductions for residential mortgages, and the like.

Another source of influence is the architecture profession, inevitably drawn to argue that only trained architects can achieve character in homes. Uniqueness is a goal, most likely an expression of the designer, with the client filling the role of an intelligent person who knew whom to commission. We buy good taste and architectural distinction.

Indeed, Frank Lloyd Wright insisted that he was expressing the needs and taste not of particular clients but "a type of client"; since real people were always less perfect than this idea, he nailed the furniture to the floor, hoping to keep it in the right place. Less daring designers made their versions of these claims. In the 1920s architects assured the public that historical styles—Cotswold cottages, diminutive Tudor estates, Spanish colonial ranch houses—could maintain individuality and refinement in a world dominated by industrialization. Without the architect's trained eye, however, without his knowledge of details and proportions, his ability to synthesize historic forms with modern conveniences, the entire process of representation could fall apart. In psychiatry or domestic architecture, true individuality required professional intervention.

Some categories are benign, though they also hide the potential for both homogeneity and discrimination embedded in Americans' cultural norms about home. There are many subtle variations in houses by region, class, or ethnicity throughout the United States. Circumscribed within the dominant culture are myriad pockets of difference. Often such pockets offer welcome visual delight in a homogeneous modern environment, and a proud testimony of particular aesthetics and social patterns within each unique cultural heritage. Yet sometimes these communities, whatever their class base, are blatantly exclusionary. Even the less affluent districts can reveal a pervasive tendency to hide inequalities, to fuel hostilities, or to gentrify, all in the name of protecting difference.

Finally, one must again speak of separate psyches, longing for stability in a world that is often alienating, eager for the comforts and pleasures of home—sensual, familial, or merely private—yet fearful that these joys will prove ephemeral. And so we seek stronger evocations of the self or the family we want in our homes, gestures to buttress what we want to be.

The notion of the perfect fit between the person or family and the dwelling can easily become a form of bondage, preventing recognition of problems in our own lives, and in the multiplicity of family lives in our society. Confronting the problems of those for whom "home" is lost or denied can intensify the potency of this ideal, making one's own "perfect home" seem all the more essential and precarious. This fear prompts large numbers of Americans to turn away from the injustice they see around them.

Americans often allude to the "right to a decent home" as a national birthright. Yet, contradictorily, providing such homes is not a responsibility of the state. Our definition of citizenship, while no longer tied to property rights, puts the burden on the individual. Home conveys other privileges as well: privacy, freedom from intrusions, autonomy for the family and for consenting adults. Our belief in the power of these rights, protected within the home, makes us all too tolerant of abuses in the public sphere. These convictions are so entrenched that we hold on, even when reality flies in our faces: when it is difficult for many people to afford the homes they might want, even with reasonable expectations; when many families are pressured to the point of domestic abuse; when communities turn against outsiders as if they were intruders; when tens of thousands of people sleep in the streets. It can only be a personal failing, on our part or on theirs. This is a painful cycle of associations.

And so, as we explore the widespread and immensely unsettling problems of homelessness and exile from home, we must also bear in mind the more mundane, quotidian, and potent images of what home should be, asking how they inspire us, and how in turn they can constrain us.

We need to make demands on those who define and produce the physical stock of homes. The range of possibilities provided by our housing market is far too limited; those of architects are often prohibitively expensive fantasies. The government refuses to question the myths of the market's logic and the culture's equality that provide the foundation for its housing policies—or lack of them.

Another aspect of our dilemma is more difficult to challenge: the desire for an intimate and reassuring fit between our homes, our neighborhoods, and our dominant cultural values. Americans tend to personalize any difficulty in achieving this goal. One result is a widespread sense of dissatisfaction about the quality of our actual abodes, accompanied by unrelenting pressure on the family life we expect our homes to generate. Another is the exorbitant cost, in social and fiscal terms, of homogeneous residential neighborhoods that purport to safeguard this idyll of domestic stability. And finally there is the sense of being overwhelmed or threatened by the blatantly visible disintegration of this ideal with increased poverty, domestic violence, and homelessness. We tend to blame ourselves for not knowing how to respond, or to blame those who suffer most for not assuming adequate responsibility.

In fact, Americans have never had a uniform vision of home or uniform accessibility to good homes. This plurality and this differentiation of forms is increasing today—as are the patterns of family life. Yet we find it difficult to adapt, in part because of the ongoing belief in the power of a model home and its availability to good citizens. This disparity affects all Americans, making it difficult for them to find—or to share with others—the protection, comfort, and shelter we all need.

The Home and the Family in Historical Perspective

BY TAMARA K. HAREVEN

In our town, and I think in the American nineties generally, home was the most impressive experience in life. Our most sensitive and our most relaxed hours were spent in it. We left home or its immediate environment chiefly to work, and neither radio nor phonograph brought the outer world into its precincts. Time moved more slowly there, as it always does when there is a familiar routine with a deep background of memory. Evening seemed spacious then, with hour upon hour in which innumerable intimate details of picture, carpet, wall paper, or well-known pointing shadow were printed upon consciousness.

The home came first in our consciousness and thus in our culture, clubs, civic life, business, schools, society being secondary, and success there, except in money making, a work of supererogatory virtue. The woman who could not make a home, like the man who could not support one, was condemned, and not tacitly. Not size, nor luxury, nor cheerfulness, nor hospitality made a home. The ideal was subtler. It must be a house where the family wished to live even when they disliked each other, it must take on a kind of corporate life and become a suitable environment for its diverse inhabitants. . . . There was a rhythm in the pre-automobile home that is entirely broken now, and whose loss is perhaps the exactest index of the decline of confidence in our environment.[1]

The idealized memory of the meaning of home that Henry Seidel Canby, former editor of the *Saturday Review,* presents in his memoir of growing up in Wilmington, Delaware, at the turn of this century is typical of the strong identification of

---

[1] Henry Seidel Canby, *The Age of Confidence: Life in the Nineties* (New York: Farrar & Reinhart, 1939), pp. 51–54.

conceptions of the home with the family in Western society. Over historical time, however, "family" and "home" were overlapping concepts, but were by no means identical. The close identification of home with family is a relatively recent phenomenon that can be traced to the late eighteenth or early nineteenth century. The concept of the home as the family's haven and domestic retreat emerged only about one hundred fifty years ago, and was, initially, limited to the urban middle classes. In order to understand the development of the home as the family's abode, as a reality and as an ideal, it is necessary to examine the relationship between household, family, and home as they changed over time.[2]

First, the ideal Western family of the past, in which three generations coresided harmoniously in the same household, has been proven to be a myth. It is part of what William Goode referred to as the classic ideal of "Western nostalgia."[3] Actually, historians of the family have identified the persistence of a nuclear household structure in Western Europe since the sixteenth century, and in the United States since the times of settlement. More recently, historians have found that a nuclear household structure has predominated in England and Italy since the twelfth century.[4]

The persistence of a nuclear *household* pattern in Western society has significant implications for our understanding of the role of the home and its emergence as a way of life and a

---

[2] Tamara K. Hareven, "Family Time and Historical Time," *Daedalus* 106 (1977): 57–70; Lawrence Stone, *The Family, Sex and Marriage in England 1500–1800* (New York: Harper & Row, 1977).

[3] William Goode, *World Revolutions and Family Patterns* (New York: Free Press, 1963), p. 6.

[4] Peter Laslett, *The World We Have Lost* (London: Methuen, 1965); Peter Laslett and Richard Wall, eds., *Household and Family in Past Time* (Cambridge: Cambridge University Press, 1972); John Demos, *A Little Commonwealth: Family Life in Plymouth Colony* (New York: Oxford University Press, 1970); Philip J. Greven, *Four Generations: Population, Land and Family in Colonial Andover, Massachusetts* (Ithaca, N.Y.: Cornell University Press, 1970); David Herlihy, *Medieval Households* (Cambridge: Harvard University Press, 1985); Richard Smith, "Kin and Neighbors in a Thirteenth Century Suffolk Community," *Journal of Family History* 4 (1979): 219–256.

symbolic concept. Membership in a nuclear household rested on the principle of the residential separation of the generations. Marriage meant establishment of a separate household by the new couple, even if the older generation was living nearby. In rural society aging parents often lived on the same land with their married children, but still in separate households. This commitment to the separate residence of the family of origin and the family of procreation should not be misconstrued as a commitment to privacy. Contrary to prevailing myths, preindustrial households rarely included relatives other than the members of the nuclear family, but they often contained unrelated individuals whose presence in the household reflected the various special functions that the family held.[5]

In preindustrial society there was a significant difference between the family's domicile—the household—and the *home* as it became idealized later in Western European and American society. In addition to serving as the family's place of residence and the focus for the family's various domestic activities such as eating, sleeping, and child rearing, the household was the site of a multiplicity of activities. It served as the site of production, as a welfare agency and correctional institution, as an educational institution, and as a place for religious worship. Rather than catering strictly to the needs of the family, the household served the entire community, by taking in dependent members who were not related to the family and by helping maintain the social order.[6]

Accordingly, household membership was not restricted to individuals related by ties of blood and marriage. The household also contained unrelated individuals such as servants, apprentices, boarders and lodgers, and "unfortunates" from the community, such as orphans, elderly, the sick and infirm, delinquents, and mentally ill who were placed with families by the

[5] Demos, *Little Commonwealth*; Peter Laslett, "Characteristics of the Western Family Over Time," in Peter Laslett, ed., *Family Life and Illicit Love in Former Generations* (Cambridge: Cambridge University Press, 1977).
[6] Demos, *Little Commonwealth*, pp. 182–185.

local authorities. Even though extended kin were not present in the household as a general pattern, household membership was sufficiently flexible to accommodate extended kin at certain points over the family's cycle, especially when aging parents were too frail to live by themselves and needed to coreside with their children. Membership in preindustrial households differed, therefore, considerably from that in contemporary ones in several ways. Age configurations of household members were different from those in contemporary households. In some cases, the oldest child was an adult ready for marriage and the youngest child still an infant at the breast. Unlike in "isolated" nuclear families today, apprentices, servants, lodgers, and other unrelated individuals shared household space with the family, worked together, participated in various daily activities, and sometimes slept in the same rooms.[7]

The family in preindustrial society was characterized by *sociability* rather than *privacy*. As Philippe Ariès has emphasized, by contrast to the conception of the home in contemporary society as a private retreat from the outside world, in preindustrial society the family conducted its work and public affairs *inside* the household. Households were teeming with various activities, and family members, even couples, could hardly retreat into privacy within the crowded household space. The head of the household's various business associates and other individuals actively involved in the family's economic or social activities were often present in the household. Ariès provides a vivid description of life in the "big house" in preindustrial France and England. As long as family life was characterized by sociability, the household did not serve strictly as the family's private retreat. Rather, the family's public and private activities were inseparable, and the family's domestic life was often conducted with strangers present.[8]

[7] *Ibid.*, pp. 62–81.
[8] Philippe Ariès, *Centuries of Childhood: A Social History of Family Life*, tr. R. Baldick (New York: Vintage Books, 1962).

By contrast to the private home characteristic of our times, the "big house" in the past was opened to nonrelatives who were engaged in familial activities and fulfilled public functions. "It was the only place where friends, clients, relatives and protégés could meet and talk. . . . People lived on top of one another, masters and servants, children and adults, in houses open at all hours to the indiscretions of the callers. The density of society left no room for the family. Not that the family did not exist as a concept," but its main focus was sociability rather than privacy. As the family gradually emerged as a private entity focused into itself, sociability retreated into the background.[9]

Spaces within the "big house" were not differentiated into family space and public space. No rooms were specifically designated as bedrooms. Beds stood in public areas of the house, and family members slept behind curtains while social activities including outsiders were going on in other parts of the same room. Similarly, in colonial America bedchambers were not separate or private. Individuals and couples had to share beds with relatives or with unrelated individuals. Colonial American court records, especially those dealing with divorce, abound in various such graphic descriptions, all confirming the lack of privacy that families and unrelated individuals experienced when residing together in the relatively small and crowded houses in the prerevolutionary period, and the exposure of various individuals, including children, to the most intimate activities.[10]

Some court records contain detailed testimonies on the sexual activities of various members of the household, as observed by family members, servants, boarders, or visitors. In his study of privacy in colonial America, Flaherty cited several such cases. For example, Moses Atwater, of New Haven county, described

[9] *Ibid.*, p. 404.
[10] David Flaherty, *Privacy in Colonial America* (Charlottesville: University of Virginia Press, 1972); Nancy Cott, "Eighteenth-Century Family and Social Life Revealed in Massachusetts Divorce Records," *Journal of Social History* 10 (1976): 20–43.

the goings-on between Elizabeth Howe, a boarder in his household, and Ellixander Kane, a transient lodger:

> Their came Ellixander Kane A Tranchant [transient] Person to our House Desiring to Lodg theire and he being Weary he went to Bed in a bed on the floore Right before the fire which was made up for our Brother John Winston and after Kane had been abed Sum Time he asked Elizabeth How to Come and Lye with him She having before moved her Cheair Close to his bed Side at which Request she Lay Down by him [;] after Sum time we asked hur to git up and Attend order in the family but Shee gave no heed to it but seemed to fane hurself Aseleep. Afterwards Wee Would have hur git up that our Brother might Go into his bed but Wee could not prevaile with hur So he was forst to Seek other Lodging, and Afterwards wee went to bed in the same Rume at a Small Distance from said Kanes Bed: and after wee had been a bed Sum Time theire was Sutch actions Between them that we feared thare was unseemly Carriage between them and in the morning when we got up She was in Kanes bed.[11]

On another occasion, two different lodgers testified about the conflicts of their master and his wife in their bedchamber. From their room that was above the master's bedroom one of the witnesses could hear the wife's refusal to have sexual relations with her husband. He had "heard them discuss together and had heard her say, if he would not let her alone, she would get out of the bed and lye on the floor."[12]

The concept of the home as a private retreat first emerged in the lives of bourgeois families in eighteenth-century France and England, and in the United States among urban, middle-class families in the early part of the nineteenth century. Its development was closely linked to the new ideals of domesticity and privacy that were associated with the characteristics of the modern family—a family that was child-centered, private, and in which the roles of husband and wife were segregated into public and domestic spheres, respectively.

[11] Flaherty, *Privacy in Colonial America*, pp. 68–69.
[12] *Ibid.*, p. 69.

The husband was expected to be the main breadwinner and worker outside the home, and the wife a full-time housekeeper and mother. This new separation of domestic and public spheres led to the rearrangement of the family's work and living patterns within the home. While earlier all family members, including children worked together, or participated in various activities, even if they did not work, in the new setting the world of work became separate from family activities.[13] Family time became restricted primarily to the home, and leisure became an important aspect of domestic life. Reading, embroidering, viewing art, and listening to music had become important pastimes in the home.

Following the removal of the workplace from the home as a result of urbanization and industrialization, the household was recast as the family's private retreat, and home emerged as a new concept and existence. Eventually other agencies took over the functions that had been earlier concentrated in the family. Factories and business places took over the work and production functions of the family, schools took over the family's formal educational functions, and asylums and correctional institutions took over the family's functions of welfare and social control.[14] The separation of the workplace from the household and the transfer of various other functions and activities of the family to outside institutions resulted in the emergence of the home as a specialized site for the family's consumption, child-rearing, and private life. The display of the family's domestic life-style through the architectural style of the home and its furnishings and appointments became of extreme importance

---

[13] Barbara Welter, "The Cult of True Womanhood 1820–1860," *American Quarterly* 18 (1966): 151–174; Mary Ryan, *Cradle of the Middle Class: The Family in Oneida County, New York 1790–1865* (New York: Cambridge University Press, 1981); Carl Degler, *At Odds: Women and the Family in America from the Revolution to the Present* (New York: Oxford University Press, 1980).

[14] Demos, *Little Commonwealth;* see also Christopher Lasch, *Haven in a Heartless World: The Family Besieged* (New York: Basic Books, 1977); David Rothman, *Discovery of the Asylum: Social Order and Disorder in the New Republic* (Boston: Little, Brown, 1971).

in the self-characterization of the urban middle-class family in Western Europe and in the United States.[15]

Among such families "home" began to assume an enormous symbolic meaning, distinct from the household, from the early nineteenth century on. As Michelle Perrot put it, "The house was where the family gathered, the center and the symbol of its success." In France, Perrot observed, "the word *'interieur'* now referred not so much to the heart of man as to the heart of the household, and it was there that one experienced happiness; similarly, well-being was now conditioned on 'comfort.'" While earlier the family interacted with the community and the house was open to the outside world, now the house was closed off: "A house was like a private kingdom, whose owners sought to appropriate nature by growing gardens and building greenhouses to abolish the seasons; to appropriate art by amassing collections and staging private concerts; to appropriate time by collecting family souvenirs and memorabilia of journeys; and to appropriate books that described the earth . . . ." While earlier the boundaries between the home and the public world had been extremely flexible and, at times, invisible, now there emerged a preference for making the home the center from which the world is viewed and enjoyed: "People experienced a keen desire to know and dominate the world without leaving home."[16]

In the private home that emerged in the middle of the nineteenth century, household membership had become restricted to the nuclear family, except for servants. Unlike in earlier periods, apprentices, boarders or lodgers, and dependent community members virtually disappeared from middle-class households. Even the role and social origins of servants changed in relation to the new functions of the home and the

[15] Michelle Perrot, ed., *A History of Private Life*, vol. 4, *From the Fires of the Revolution to the Great War*, tr. Arthur Goldhammer (Cambridge: Harvard University Press, 1990); Dolores Hayden, *The Great Domestic Revolution: A History of Feminist Designs for American Homes, Neighborhoods and Cities* (Cambridge: MIT Press, 1981).

[16] Perrot, *History of Private Life*.

family. In preindustrial households, the servants were "life-cycle" servants—young people who were sent to serve in other people's households for educational purposes as much as for service. Such exchanges usually occurred within the same community. On the other hand, servants in nineteenth-century families were usually migrants or immigrants to the city, whose main function was to work in middle-class or upper-class households. For the majority of young women servants, domestic service was still restricted to a life-cycle stage but was now clearly defined as a form of employment rather than as temporary residence for purposes of socialization.[17]

In this new domestic regime it became inappropriate for middle-class women to work outside the home. "Our men are sufficiently moneymaking. Let us keep our women and children from the contagion as long as possible," wrote in 1832 one of the main advocates and advisers on the cult of domesticity, Sara Josepha Hale, editor of *Godey's Lady's Book*. Women's main responsibility and all their energies now had to focus on the home and the family, and especially on children. Homemaking became an occupation in itself, one that demanded physical and material resources, planning, and the persistent following of changing fashions. As one writer in mid-century put it, a house "is not only the home center, the retreat and shelter for all the family, it is also the workshop for the mother. It is not only where she is to live, to love, but where she is to care and labor. Her hours, days, weeks, months and years are spent within its bounds; until she becomes an enthroned fixture, more indispensable than the house itself." Homemaking was idealized as part of the cult of domesticity, and was accorded special social status. The complicated tasks of home management required specific advice in how-to-do-it manuals and etiquette books.[18]

---

[17] Lucy Salmon, *Domestic Service* (New York, 1890); Blaine Mckinley, "Troublesome Comforts: The Housekeeper-Servant Relationship in Antebellum Didactic Fiction," *Journal of American Culture* 5 (Summer 1982): 36–44.

[18] On domestic-advice literature, see: Welter, "Cult of Domesticity"; Kathryn Kish

Women were expected to be the perfect designers, executors, and custodians of the new domestic retreat. Housework and cooking became, therefore, extremely significant for the maintenance of the perfect home, which, in turn, was viewed by reformers as indispensable for the nation's prosperity and survival. Even the most trivial tasks were considered to be of utmost importance. "It is within your power to create a domestic haven in the lowliest cottage," wrote Daniel Wise. Various magazines, especially *Godey's Lady's Book*, as well as numerous cookbooks and advice books provided guidance aimed at enabling housewives to achieve perfection in their domestic tasks. The printing industry became significant in circulating and diffusing an enormous body of advice literature contained in popular magazines and manuals, which were directed at guiding the new custodians of the domestic sphere on the performance of their roles in appointing and maintaining the home and on their familial roles and child-rearing.[19]

The domestic ideal in American society was strongly linked to an idealization of the home as a utopian retreat from the outside world. Ironically, even though this concept of the ideal home was developed by urban reformers, moralists, and writers, it emphasized the pastoral ideal of rural society. From the early nineteenth century on, a host of popular writers extolled the ideal home in sermons, novels, and advice literature. "They asserted over and over that the home was a distinct sphere, an enclosure emphatically set apart from activities and priorities of the world," wrote Kirk Jeffrey. Associated with this idea was "an affirmation that, ultimately

Sklar, *Catherine Beecher: A Study of Domesticity* (New Haven: Yale University Press, 1973). For domestic-advice literature of the first half of the nineteenth century, see Lydia Sigourney, *The Western Home and Other Poems* (Philadelphia: Parry & McMillan, 1854); *Goodeys Lady's Book* (Philadelphia, 1840–60); Lydia Maria Child, *The Mother's Book* (Boston, 1831); Ann Kuhn, *The Mother's Role in Childhood Education: New England Concepts, 1830–1860* (New Haven: Yale University Press, 1947):35.

[19] Daniel Wise, *Bridal Greetings: A Marriage Gift* (New York, 1850), p. 84; quoted in Kirk Jeffrey, "The Family as a Utopian Retreat from the City: The Nineteenth Century Contribution," *Soundings: An Interdisciplinary Journal* 55 (Spring 1972): 35.

the individual found meaning and satisfaction in his life at home and nowhere else." The home began to be viewed as a utopian community, as a retreat from the world—one that had to be consciously designed and perfectly managed. The idealization of the home as a haven was a reaction to the anxiety provoked by rapid urbanization, resulting in the transformation of old neighborhoods and the creation of new ones, the rapid influx of immigrants into urban areas, and the visible concentration of poverty in cities.[20]

The anxiety emanating from the dramatic transformation of urban life was also linked to the internal changes within the family, especially to the separation of the workplace from the home and the removal of children's formal education from the family to the schools. Both of these processes led to the spatial and temporal segregation of family members from each other during the day. These changes were expressed most dramatically in the changes in the "dinner" schedules. From the middle of the nineteenth century on, the family gradually ceased to have its main meal at midday. Husbands began to eat their midday meals in restaurants, and the family dinner was shifted to the evening, except for Sundays.

Since city dwellers could not return to live in the country, they enshrined the home as a rural retreat from the city *within* the city. Hence the garden with its hedges, gates, and walls was of great significance in sheltering the home from the outside world, as well as providing an illusion of serene pastoral settings. As one clergyman wrote, the home was "a safe and alluring shelter for *yourselves* amid the vicissitudes of life, becoming more and more the abode of peace and love as the world grows dark without."[21]

The view of the home as the family's private retreat was closely linked to the new definition of woman's separate

[20] Jeffrey, "Family as Utopian Retreat," p. 24.
[21] William M. Thayer, *Pastor's Wedding Gift* (Boston, 1854), p. 36; quoted in Jeffrey, "Family as Utopian Retreat."

sphere, which glorified the role of the wife as a homemaker and full-time mother. In American society, the cult of domesticity that characterized this transformation in women's roles placed women on a pedestal as the custodians of the home and segregated them in their domestic sphere, while the public sphere was allotted exclusively to men. The cult of domesticity and the values associated with it were closely linked to the new family type and the ways of life that had become characteristic of the urban middle classes by the middle of the nineteenth century. The home became an essential aspect of the identity and self-definition of the middle class.[22]

The emergence of the home as a specialized retreat for the family was part of the process of industrialization as well as urbanization. Accompanying the cult of domesticity emerged a large industry that catered to the new consumer styles in the furnishing and appointment of the home by providing various appliances and gadgets. Industrialization had a dual impact on the redefinition of the family's role and on the accompanying emergence of the home as the family's private retreat. First, industrialization led to the separation of the workplace from the home and to the transfer of the welfare, educational, and correctional functions from the family to other institutions and agencies. Second, industrialization contributed to the creation of the necessary technology, communications, and transportation aimed at facilitating the furnishing and running of the new-style home. A variety of new appliances and gadgets made their way into the home from the middle of the nineteenth century on. These inventions became important not only as labor-saving devices but as status symbols of the efficient, well-ordered home. Initially, the most important invention was the cooking stove, which replaced open-hearth cooking. The stove revolutionized cuisine, and opened up a new range of

[22] Welter, "Cult of Domesticity"; Nancy Cott, *The Bonds of Womanhood: "Women's Sphere" in New England* (New Haven: Yale University Press, 1977); Ryan, *Cradle of the Middle Class.*

possibilities in the simultaneous preparation of a variety of dishes on the top of the stove, rather than the one-pot meals cooked in the hearth. In addition, a whole slew of gadgets and implements, such as apple corers and slicers, vacuum cleaners, laundry strainers, and other devices appeared on the market and made their way into the middle-class home. Ruth Schwartz Cowan claims that these new appliances, rather than saving housewives' time, actually caused "more work for mother," because they provided the opportunity for more complex preparations, which required increased time and labor investment on the women's part, and a decrease in the involvement of men in household work.[23]

Even if the new appliances did not always result in labor saving for women, they were of great symbolic significance in expressing the specialization in the functions of the home, along with those of the family—a specialization that required new codes of behavior, modes of production and management, and, therefore, new roles for women. The home was not just a sentimental entity, as the nineteenth-century cliché ("Home Sweet Home") would suggest. It also became an institution of industrial capitalism, with its characteristic equipment, organization, management, and cast of characters. Accordingly, the wife was cast in the role of a "home manager," who was judged not only for the making of the home and maintaining its aesthetic and nurturing atmosphere but also for the efficiency and frugality with which she managed this complex enterprise.[24]

It is precisely for this reason that in the late nineteenth century the home, like the office and other institutions, was subjected by reformers to scientific management. As a result, the concepts of industrial efficiency were applied to the home. Housework began to be viewed as a kind of enterprise that was subject to rules of efficiency similar to those of industry.

---

[23] Ruth Schwartz Cowan, *More Work for Mother* (New York: Basic Books, 1983).
[24] *Ibid.*; Hayden, *Grand Domestic Revolution.*

Efficiency in home management had gained extreme significance in its own right, exceeding practical considerations. The first reformer to emphasize and formulate this concept and to popularize it was Catherine Beecher, who defined the role of the housewife as a "home minister" and "skilled professional." In her *Treatise on Domestic Economy for the Use of Young Ladies at Home and at School,* first published in 1841 and reprinted in numerous editions, Beecher extolled the domestic superiority of women. Even though women's work was unpaid and segregated to the home, it was to be considered professional and important in its own right, and had to be provided with the necessary props and equipment in order to be accomplished effectively.[25]

Beecher's blueprint for the professionalization and "industrialization" of the home was epitomized in *The American Woman's Home* (1869), which she co-authored with her sister Harriet Beecher Stowe. The model home that they designed in this best-selling book was very much a product of the industrial age, both in its conceptions of specialization and efficiency and in the multiplicity of technological equipment they advocated for domestic use. In the new model "cottage" that the two sisters designed, the parlor was named "home room," the kitchen the "workroom," and the dining room the "family room." Ironically, the Beecher sisters placed their model cottage in the suburbs and disposed of servants. They anticipated a pattern characteristic of our times, where the kitchen was to be elevated to the level of the dining room, with the servantless wife cooking in full view of the guests while wearing her party clothes.[26] The main difference with our times

[25] Catherine E. Beecher, *A Treatise on the Domestic Economy for the Use of Young Ladies at Home and at School,* rev. ed. (New York: Harper, 1846).

[26] Catherine E. Beecher and Harriet Beecher Stowe, *The American Woman's Home* (Hartford, Conn., 1869). For a discussion of Beecher's designs of the ideal home and woman's role within it, see Hayden, *Domestic Revolution,* pp. 55–58; Catherine E. Beecher, "How to Redeem Woman's Profession from Dishonor," *Monthly Magazine* 31 (November 1895): 710.

was that the two sisters did not assign any collaborative or assistance role to the husband.

The new specialization in the functions of the home and the family also necessitated corresponding architectural designs. Architects joined the trend by busily developing blueprints for new styles of homes that were to accommodate the new domestic life-style. The domestic architecture that emerged in the United States in the middle of the nineteenth century, featuring Gothic revival cottages, Italianate villas, and bracketed cottages that were published in builders' guides between 1840 and 1860, translated the domestic ideal into architecture in several ways: These cottages were aimed at segregating the home from the outside world, thus securing privacy for the family. Within the home spaces were organized in a manner that separated the family's private activities from the public ones such as receiving guests. The parlor became a central space for the family's social activities and entertainment. The kitchen, which had been previously outside, was brought inside, alas, into the basement or the back of the house. Nevertheless, the kitchen became an important component of the home. The parlor was decorated by the family's heirlooms, portraits, lace and embroidery, shadow boxes, and artwork.[27]

The new type of home was intended to serve the specialized activities of various family members. This was reflected in the design of separate rooms for children, for women's activities such as sewing, and for men's activities including libraries and study rooms. Each child was to have a separate bedroom in order to foster the child's attachment to the home. As one writer insisted, ". . . satisfying this home-feeling will also contribute to their [the children's] love of the homestead." Without it, it is only their *father's* [sic] home, not theirs. . . . But,

[27] Clifford Edward Clark, Jr., "Domestic Architecture as an Index: The Romantic Revival and the Cult of Domesticity in America, 1840–1870," *Journal of Interdisciplinary History* 7 (Summer 1976): 33–56.

by giving them their own apartment, they themselves become personally identified with it, and hence love to adorn and perfect all parts."[28] Special attention was given to providing young women and young girls with separate rooms, as an encouragement to spend more time at home: "the young girl that, finding no intrinsic pleasure at home, nor regarding it otherwise than as the sphere of her domestic duties, would seek away from its shelter, and with other companions [find] pleasure and excitements neither so wholesome or refining as a fond parent would wish."[29]

In his analysis of the new spaces, designed in the domestic architecture which emerged in the middle of the nineteenth century, Clifford Clark concluded that "the design of the second floor, with its emphasis on creating a separate space for each member of the family . . . implies that the family was not an organic unit but rather was made up of separate, unique individuals who each had a specific role to play. . . . " Interaction within the family, like the public interaction with guests, was to take place primarily in specifically designated areas—the dining room, porch, and back parlor (family room). In these areas, family interaction became organized around certain rituals—meals, musical events, and games. Clark concluded that the design of the house implied that "the family was an organization which was not an end in itself, but rather a vehicle for promoting the development of each of its members."[30] The new domestic style required two types of privacy: privacy of the family from the community, and privacy of family members from each other *within* the home.

[28] Orson S. Fowler, *A Home for All* (New York, 1856); quoted in Clark, "Domestic Architecture," p. 50.

[29] Gervase Wheeler, *Rural Homes* (New York, 1851), p. 277; quoted in Clark, "Domestic Architecture," p. 35.

[30] Clark, "Domestic Architecture," p. 52; Andrew Jackson Downing, *Cottage Residences: A Series of Designs for Rural Cottages and Villas* (New York, 1842); *Godey's Lady's Magazine* published a series of revival designs, see George L. Hersey, "Godey's Choice," *Society of Architectural Historians Journal* 17 (1959); see also Clifford Edward Clark, Jr., *The American Family Home* (Chapel Hill: University of North Carolina Press, 1986).

While the ideal middle-class domestic home is linked in the contemporary popular image with suburbs, as suggested above, initially the ideals of domesticity were played out in the city. The new middle-class home was designed as a response to urbanization as a retreat from the world of work and from the hustle-bustle of urban life. At the same time it depended on urban services, conveniences, and public activities in order to achieve domestic refinement. Popular writers such as Catherine Sedgwick, who portrayed the newly idealized home life, placed the home firmly in the city. Sedgwick and other writers emphasized the redeeming moral virtue of the home in the urban environment. Despite the corrupting influence of the city, they claimed that the domestic world could transmit its values to the urban environment and maintain purity within it. But as the nineteenth century progressed, the ideals and life-style of domesticity were transferred to the suburbs and became identified with suburban living.[31]

Urbanization contributed to the advancement of domesticity by providing the concentration of necessary shops and services for its maintenance. As landscape designer Frederick Law Olmstead pointed out in 1870, "Consider what is done . . . by the butcher, baker, fish-monger, grocer, by the provision vendors of all sorts, by the iceman, dust-man, scavenger, by the postman, carrier, expressman, and messenger, all serving you at your house when required; by the sewers, gutters, pavements, crossings, sidewalks, public conveyances, and gas and water works."[32] The city was more generally desirable to women, because it provided them with access to services and shopping facilities. It also put them in close contact with various social networks, sewing circles, and reform

[31] Catherine Sedgwick, *Home* (New York, 1835). On the suburban ideal, see Robert Fishman, *Burgeois Utopias: The Rise and Fall of Suburbia* (New York, 1987).

[32] Frederick Law Olmstead, *Public Parks and the Enlargement of Towns* (Cambridge, Mass., 1870), pp. 7–9; quoted in Hayden, *Grand Domestic Revolution.* p. 11. See also David Handlin, *The American Home: Architecture and Society, 1815–1915* (Boston: Little, Brown, 1979).

associations, which helped them escape the confines of domesticity.

Why women eventually accepted suburban living, when the city provided both easy access to supplies and services as well as sociability and entertainment, is an important question in itself. From the 1870s on millions of Americans began to move to the suburbs to fulfill their dream of a tranquil domestic life removed from the city. The movement was pioneered by the wealthy upper class and upper middle class, who moved into elegant "Victorian" houses in romantic settings. From the 1880s on, middle-class families who responded to the propaganda for suburban living and to new housing opportunities made possible by the architectural and building professions began to populate the rapidly expanding suburbs around major cities. For the middle-class suburban families, residence was not identical with home ownership. In Boston and in other cities around 1890 only one fourth of the suburban residents owned their houses. Suburban living held, however, the promise of eventual home ownership. Most importantly, it represented an escape from the city and segregation along class and ethnic lines in "serene" settings.[33]

The development of domesticity as a suburban phenomenon, which flourished in the late nineteenth century, according to Margaret Marsh, was a response to the masculine domestic ideal, which by that point in time emphasized the virtues of a suburban retreat from the pressures of city life: "The new domestic ideal centered firmly in the suburbs, represented family pride, family identity and togetherness in face of an urban society that promised individual achievement, anonymity and excitement." By the eve of World War II, she claims, "a new suburban domestic ideal had materialized—an ideal that both reorganized domesticity to

[33] Gwendolyn Wright, *Building the Dream: A Social History of Housing in America* (New York: Pantheon, 1981); Kenneth Jackson, *The Crabgrass Frontier* (New York: Columbia University Press, 1985).

make it independent of the notion of separate masculine and feminine spheres and one which redefined the suburbs to emphasize 'place' more than the ownership of property."[34] As urban life became more bewildering, because of a high concentration of immigrants and poverty, domestic life in the suburbs had become idealized as an escape from the city.

The new domesticity in the suburbs led to the isolation of women and children from urban life, and eventually to the entrapment of women in suburban domestic life-styles. In a provocative study of family structure in a Chicago suburb, Richard Sennett pointed out that suburban life entrapped men as well. From a comparison of the career patterns of men who were living in nuclear households with those residing in households including extended kin in addition to the nuclear family, he concluded that men who were members of intensely nuclear suburban households experienced lower occupational mobility because they were isolated from the diversity of urban life. The sources that Sennett had available to him (the 1880 Census Household Manuscript Schedules) were insufficient to sustain this generalization, because they were limited to one point in time. The issues he addressed were of significance, however, because they raise a fundamental question as to when domestic privacy becomes a form of confinement for the individual rather than a nurturing environment. Philippe Ariès introduced this question when he lamented the loss of the "big house" and the isolation of the modern family in its domestic retreat:

> The modern family . . . cuts itself off from the world and opposes to society the isolated groups of parents and children. All the energy of the group is expended in helping the children to rise in the world, individually and without any collective ambition, the children rather than the family.[35]

---

[34] Margaret Marsh, "From Separation to Togetherness: The Social Construction of Domestic Space in American Suburbs, 1840–1915," *Journal of American History* 76 (1989): 506–527.

[35] Richard Sennett, *Families Against the City: The Suburban Homes of Industrial Chicago* (Cambridge: Harvard University Press, 1970); Ariès, *Centuries of Childhood*, p. 404..

The suburban form of domesticity had become entrenched in American society and predominated until the 1960s, despite various challenges by feminist reformers, especially Charlotte Perkins Gilman, who advocated the establishment of urban residential hotels with communal dining rooms for families so that working women would be free of housekeeping chores. Gilman expected that these apartment hotels would enable women to pursue professional careers along with motherhood without being confined to child-rearing and domesticity. The urban apartment hotel, she predicted, would also be a commercial success for developers:

> The apartments would be without kitchens; but there would be a kitchen belonging to the house from which meals could be served to the families in their rooms or in a common dining-room, as preferred. It would be a home where the cleaning was done by efficient workers, not hired separately by the family, but engaged by the manager of the establishment; and a roof-garden, day nursery, and kindergarten, under well-trained professional nurses and teachers, would ensure proper care of the children . . .

For people who preferred suburban life, Gilman also recommended a suburban counterpart to the apartment hotel, which involved the grouping of several residential houses, all kitchenless but interconnected by covered walkways with a central eating house.[36]

When discussing these trends, it is important to remember that the separation of the home from the outside world occurred initially in the lives of a small segment of the population, namely, the urban middle classes. In rural families, and in urban working-class families, the home was viewed less as a specialized retreat, and was open to a multiplicity of functions and activities as it had been in preindustrial society. Significantly, at the very time when middle-class women were being discouraged from pursuing gain-

---

[36] Charlotte Perkins Gilman, *Women and Economics: A Study of the Economic Relation Between Men and Women as a Factor in Social Evolution* [1898] (New York: Harper Torchbooks, 1966), p. 75; quoted in Hayden, *Grand Domestic Revolution*, p. 189.

ful employment, working-class women and children were being recruited as the primary labor force of the industrial revolution. Even after working-class families began to emulate middle-class domestic life-styles and furnishings, they continued to use the household space in a more diversified and complex way than the middle class. In rural families, the household continued to serve as the site of production in agriculture as well as in domestic industries. Family members worked side by side in related tasks, and there continued to be little separation between domestic life and work life.[37] In Western and Central Europe, prior to the industrial revolution rural as well as urban households in certain regions of Europe engaged in household production for external markets in the eighteenth and early nineteenth century. These industries, which were defined as "protoindustrial," employed the entire household unit. They used new machinery in the household in order to produce various items such as yarn, cloth, lace, gloves, and stockings for capitalist employers, who ordered the product, provided the raw materials, and then sold these products in national or international markets. Household production of this type was also carried out in rural areas in the United States, especially in New England. For example, the putting-out system for shoe manufacturing continued in rural New England until the middle of the nineteenth century. Thus, at the very time when the home emerged as a glorified domestic retreat in the lives of the urban middle class, the household continued to serve a variety of functions for rural and urban working class families.[38]

[37] Tamara K. Hareven, *Family Time and Industrial Time: The Relationship Between the Family and Work in a New England Industrial Community* (New York: Cambridge University Press, 1982).

[38] On protoindustrialization in Europe, see Rudolph Braun, "Early Industrialization and Demographic Change in the Canton of Zurich," in Charles Tilly, ed., *Historical Studies of Changing Fertility* (Princeton: Princeton University Press, 1976), pp. 289–334; Hans Medick, "The Proto-Industrial Family Economy: The Structural Function of Household and Family During the Transition from Peasant Society to Industrial Capitalism," *Social History* 1–2 (October 1976). For the United States, see Rolla Milton Tryon, *Household Manufactures in the United States, 1640–1860: A Study of Industrial History* (Chicago: University of Chicago Press, 1917).

The role of the home in working-class life has received less attention. Most historians have tended to generalize for the whole society on the basis of the middle-class experience. The process by which working-class families eventually adopted the new domestic life-style has not been documented. The common interpretation has been a "trickle down" theory, which assumed that middle-class ideals of the home gradually spread to the working class. Even after working-class families adopted the new concepts of domesticity, both home life and attitudes toward the home retained a different character in working-class life than in the middle class. For working-class families the home was not merely a private refuge; it was a *resource* that could be used for generating extra income, for paying debts, for staying out of poverty, and for maintaining autonomy in old age. Accordingly, their household membership continued to be more complex even in the twentieth century. Even though working-class families were also committed to the nuclearity of the household, they frequently took in newly arrived immigrants and, at least temporarily, shared housing with them. Privacy was less important than the flexible use of household space, which could be used to supplement the family's income or could be traded for services. Throughout the nineteenth century and early into the twentieth century a significant proportion of working-class households contained boarders and lodgers.[39]

The presence of boarders and lodgers in a working-class household was critical at times in enabling the family to pay for a mortgage and fulfill the dream of owning their home. As a form of exchange among families across society, boarders and lodgers replaced young adult children who had left home, thus enabling elderly couples or widows to continue to maintain their independence in their own home. In their enthusiasm for

[39] John Modell and Tamara K. Hareven, "Urbanization and the Malleable Household," *Journal of Marriage and the Family* 35 (August 1988): 467–479.

middle-class values, social reformers tried to denounce the custom of taking in boarders and lodgers as violating the privacy of the family. They warned that male boarders could potentially corrupt the young and seduce wives and daughters. In reality, in working-class families, boarding and lodging was a positive arrangement, an indispensable source of income and sociability, far more salient than the middle-class reformers' values of privacy.[40]

While homemaking activities and domestic rituals along with child-rearing commanded almost all the waking hours of middle-class women, working-class women could invest only a limited amount of time in the appointment and maintenance of the home and in child-rearing. In addition to spending an entire workday from sunrise to sundown in a factory or in other workplaces, working-class women did not have access to help by servants and to the household equipment that middle-class women controlled. Working-class women often alternated between factory work and home work (taking various jobs such as sewing or laundry into the home), and produced food and various items not only for their family members but for pay or barter as well. Privacy was of less concern to working-class families than solvency, the survival of the family unit, and the improvement of its life-style.[41]

In working-class homes there was little separation between domestic life and work life. The world of work spilled over into the household. In the major cities, "homework," such as garment finishing, engaged all family members in the household. Under such circumstances, the space in the home was used creatively, and was arranged and rearranged to fit

---

[40] Margaret F. Byington, *Homestead: The Households of a Mill Town* [1910] (Pittsburgh: University of Pittsburgh Press, 1974). Byington provides one of the most incisive and accurate descriptions of home life in the steel-mills district. But as a middle-class social investigator she also carried the bias about the negative influence of boarders and lodgers in the household.

[41] Hareven, *Family Time and Industrial Time;* Tamara K. Hareven and Randolph Langenbach, *Amoskeag: Life and Work in an American Factory City* (New York: Pantheon, 1978).

the various functions of the family as they came up. At supper time, bundles of garments or other sewing materials were removed from the table so that family members could eat their supper. Beds for lodgers or boarders, or for children, were opened up in the hallway or in the kitchen in the evening and were folded back again in the morning.[42]

Even within the memory of people now in their eighties, several siblings in large families would share the same bed, like the New England farm girls who had lived in boarding houses in the nineteenth-century textiles mills. Ora Pelletier, a former textile worker in the Amoskeag Mills in Manchester, New Hampshire, who grew up in company housing, recalled the experience of sharing her bed with other siblings in 1922:

> I remember during the strike my oldest sister had just got married, and my father and mother told her, "come back home with your husband." We had to pile up four in the bed instead of two so they could have a bed to themselves. Jeanette, Lucille, Irene, and I were in the same bed. One time, Lucille wanted Jeanette to give her the end of the bed, but Jeanette didn't want to. So Lucille got mad. She got out of the bed. We thought she was going to the bathroom. Instead she went under the bed and tied Jeanette's two braids to one of the posts, and when Jeanette went to turn around, her hair was caught there. The next night, after Lucille was in bed Jeanette stuck some gum in her hair. In the morning, my mother had to cut off half of the hair!
>
> We were so many at home, we didn't need any entertainment. We had our own. My mother would tell me to watch the others, to keep them quiet and keep them around so she wouldn't have to run after them. I used to put on a show for them. I'd put an old long dress on and get up there and sing. I'd sing opera. I had curls then, and I'd put my curls under my nose, change my shoes, and I would be Charlie Chaplin. I used to make them laugh.

[42] Elizabeth Shepley Sergeant, "Toilers of Tenements, Where the Beautiful Things of the Great Shops Are Made," *McClure's Magazine* 35 (July 1910): 231–232; S. J. Kleinberg, *The Shadow of the Mills: Working Class Families in Pittsburgh, 1870–1907* (Pittsburgh: University of Pittsburgh Press, 1989); Byington, *Homestead*.

Ora also recalled the sociability in her home despite the poverty and the long hours of work: "All the neighbors would come upstairs, and my mother would push the table and the carpets back, and they'd dance. Almost every night there was a party at the house. But my mother wouldn't let us go out dancing."[43]

Working-class families not only used the home as an economic resource and as a workplace, they also carried over the feelings of home into the world of work. "The mills were our home" is the recurring expression of nostalgia in the memories of former textile workers, who had worked in the Amoskeag Mills in Manchester, New Hampshire. Such workers managed to transform the factories into a home by clustering at work with their relatives and friends, and by using the space in the work rooms to prepare their lunches. Ora Pelletier recalled how her fellow workers temporarily transformed their workroom in the mill into a home at lunch time:

In a corner [of the sink room] was a great big, long sink. It always had a little water in it, and there was a steam pipe going into the water, so it was boiling hot. We'd bring soup, cans of corn, cans of tomatoes, and heat them in there for our meal. The Greek, Mary, used to bring eggs and put them in when she came in at seven o'clock in the morning, so she'd have hard-boiled eggs for dinner. And we'd swap lunch and everything.[44]

In other mill towns such as Pittsburgh, home life was less cheerful. As Margaret Byington, who investigated the steel-mill community for the Russell Sage Foundation at the beginning of this century, observed:

It is through the households themselves that the industrial situation impresses itself indelibly upon the life of the people. The environment of the home afforded by this checkerboard town tilted on the slope back of the mill site, the smoke which

[43] Hareven and Langenbach, *Amoskeag*, p. 243.
[44] *Ibid.*, pp. 183–184.

pours its depressing fumes to add their extra burden to the housewife's task, the constant interference with orderly routine due to the irregular succession of long hours—these are the outward and visible signs of the subordination of the household life to industrial life. The mill affects the family even more intimately through the wage scale to which the standards of home making, housekeeping and child rearing must conform.[45]

Housewives in Homestead were continuously fighting a loosing battle against the grime from the smoke and against poor sanitation and the absence of running water in their houses. Even in the Homestead company houses, which were considered the best workers' residences in Pittsburgh, Byington found that the water faucet was located on the back porch instead of in the kitchen, and that even when there was running water in the house, the only toilet was a privy vault in the back yard. In poorer tenements women had to haul water from the outside, and in many cases had to bring it up several stories three or four times a day. The sewage ran downhill from one house to the next, and seeped through the water wells of neighboring houses. Women frequently swept away the dirt from their unpaved yards, but even where they covered the bare earth with wooden slats, waste from the sewage came through on the boards, and was carried into the house. Byington provided a lasting description of the home life in Pittsburgh's poorer tenements:

> One morning I entered a two-room tenement. The kitchen, perhaps 15 by 12 feet, was steaming with vapor from a big washtub set on a chair in the middle of the room. The mother was trying to wash and at the same time keep the older of her two babies from tumbling into the tub full of scalding water that was standing on the floor. On one side of the room was a huge puffy bed, with one feather tick to sleep on and another for covering; near the window stood a sewing machine; in the corner, an organ,—all these, besides the inevitable cook stove upon which in the place of honor was simmering the evening's soup. Upstairs in the second room were one boarder and the

[45] Byington, *Homestead*, p. 179.

man of the house asleep. Two more boarders were at work, but at night would be home to sleep in the bed from which the others would get up.[46]

Even the poorest homes in Homestead, similar to the ones in Manchester, New Hampshire, displayed the family's attachment to its home and life-style. In one of the homes in a one-room tenement, even though the furniture was limited to the absolute necessities, it was hard to keep all the crowded belongings in order. "Nevertheless, the home is kept as neat as the circumstances permit, and the bright pictures on the wall are proof of a desire to make it attractive." The other family, who lived in a five-room house, had fulfilled the American dream of home ownership. In the front room with its leather-covered furniture hung sacred pictures which relieved the severity of the room with their vivid coloring, and revealed the "religious note in Slavic life, for if happiness is to stay with the family, the priest must come yearly to 'bless the home.' "[47] The families in Homestead, like the families in Manchester, New Hampshire, and in other American working-class communities, had a strong commitment to the "home," as Byington observed. Among the English-speaking families, she concluded: "More substantial proof of the instinct of home-making is shown in the often heroic efforts to buy a house."[48]

Among the English-speaking workers, families that had attained higher standards of living made a special effort to have a parlor or its semblance. "In one three-room house, where there were seven children, a room which had in it a folding bed, a wardrobe, the carriage where the baby slept in the daytime, and the sewing machine, was referred to with pride as the 'front room,' a phrase with a significance quite beyond its suggestion of locality." Residents invested much money and energy in making the front room the center of

[46] *Ibid.*, p. 53; Kleinberg, *Shadow of the Mills*, pp. 89–91.
[47] Byington, *Homestead*, p. 145.
[48] *Ibid.*, p. 152.

family life. "Here in the evening the family gathers about the soft coal or gas grate, while the mother sews and one of the older children plays to the father. Such 'front rooms' are the scenes of those simple festivities which enliven existence in this town." The family scenes and activities described here represent on a more modest scale the activities of middle-class families in the parlor or in the family room. In the four-room houses, the family ate in the kitchen.[49]

In the five-room houses, on the other hand, Byington found "an anomaly" known as the "dining room." This room is used for a variety of purposes, but rarely for meals. Interestingly, the family had achieved a real dining room in conformity with American ideals, and furnished it accordingly, but had neither the time nor sufficient space in the house to use it exclusively as a dining room. One of their daughters had learned in high school that the family should eat in a dining room rather than in the kitchen. She offered to help the family fulfill this middle-class script by serving the food. After several weeks the family returned to eating in the kitchen and to using the dining room for ironing, sewing, and various other activities.[50]

Even in the poorest tenements in New York's West Side, residents made a special effort to appoint and decorate their shabby and crowded dwellings. Mary White Ovington, one of the founders of the National Association for the Advancement of Colored People, was impressed by the efforts of black families to decorate a "home," sometimes with "cheap pictures, photographs, cards, vases, little ornaments," that the women, many of whom had been engaged in domestic service, received from their employers. These items, which their employers were happily rid of, nevertheless gave "an air of home likeness to the place." Ovington, who had visited many tenements of this kind, was moved by their residents' hospitality and homelike atmosphere:

[49] *Ibid.*, pp. 55–56.
[50] *Ibid.*, p. 55.

The Negroes' homes are often sadly cluttered, but they are rarely bare and ugly. With this love of pretty things goes a desire to live with something of form in the arrangement of the rooms and in the ordering of the meals. When breakfast or dinner comes you will almost always find the table set. I have been surprised to find in the most modest homes that the meal carried with it the air of a social function; the mother would use many dishes though she must take the time from her laundry work to wash them.[51]

Similarly, the poor Jewish home in which writer Alfred Kazin grew up in Brownsville, New York, left a lasting impression on his subsequent life. In that home the kitchen was the center of family life, and the various objects within became an unforgettable source of his identity:

The kitchen held our lives together. My mother worked in it all day long, we ate in it almost all meals except the Passover seder, I did my homework and first writing at the kitchen table, and in winter I often had a bed made up for me on three kitchen chairs near the stove. On the wall just over the table hung a long horizontal mirror that sloped to a ship's prow at each end and was lined in cherry wood. It took up the whole wall, and drew every object in the kitchen to itself. The walls were a fiercely stippled whitewash, so often rewhitened by my father in slack seasons that the paint looked as if it had been squeezed and cracker into the walls. A large electric bulb hung down the center of the kitchen at the end of a chain that had been hooked into the ceiling; the old gas ring and key still jutted out of the wall like antlers. In the corner next to the toilet was the sink at which we washed, and the square tub in which my mother did our clothes. Above it, tacked to the shelf on which were pleasantly ranged square, blue-bordered white sugar and spice jars, hung calendars from the Public National Bank on Pitkin Avenue and the Minsker Progressive Branch of the Workman's Circle; receipts for the payment of insurance premiums, and household bills on a spindle; two little boxes engraved with Hebrew letters. One of these was for the poor, the other to buy back the Land of Israel. . . .[52]

[51] Mary White Ovington, "The Negro Home in New York," *Charities* 15 (October 7, 1905): 25–26.
[52] Alfred Kazin, *A Walker in the City* (New York: Harcourt, Brace & World, 1951), pp. 65–66.

In their effort to impress American ideals of domesticity on immigrants, social reformers left nothing to chance. A 1909 textbook for teaching English to foreigners incorporated a lesson about the ideal home:

> This is the family, in the sitting-room.
> The family is made up of the father, the mother, and the children.
> That is the father who is reading.
> The father is the husband.
> That is the mother who is sewing.
> The father and mother are the parents.
> The sister is playing the piano.
> The brother is standing beside her.
> The family makes the home.[53]

Despite the differences between the middle class and the working class and between native born and various ethnics in the family's use of the home, as the twentieth century progressed, the significance of "home" in American society cut across all classes. For working-class as well as for immigrant families, heading one's own household was identified with autonomy. Establishment of a separate household by a newly formed family, as well as the maintenance of household headship in the later years of life, were sacred values and markers of autonomy in American society. Accordingly, home ownership was of great significance to all social classes.[54]

Nor were ideals of home ownership an American invention. They had been brought over to the United States by rural immigrants from countries such as England, Ireland, Italy, and Quebec, for whom the ownership of a plot of land or a

---

[53] Sara R. O'Brien, *English for Foreigners* (Boston, 1909), p. 55.

[54] Hareven, *Family Time and Industrial Time;* Conrad M. Arensberg and Solon T. Kimball, *Family and Community in Ireland* (Cambridge: Harvard University Press, 1968). For Irish immigrants' commitment to home ownership from the middle of the nineteenth century on, see Stephen Thernstrom, *Poverty and Progress in a Nineteenth Century City* (Cambridge: Harvard University Press, 1964); Sam Bass Warner, *Streetcar Suburbs: The Process of Growth in Boston, 1870–1900* (Cambridge: Harvard University Press, 1962).

house had been an ideal in rural society. French Canadian immigrants, for example, carried with them to New England portraits of their farm houses in Quebec, which had been painted by itinerant painters. Even though they had no desire to go back to the poverty on the farm which they had left behind, they hung these portraits in the factory tenements they were inhabiting in the United States, as a reminder of their "real home." Similar to the Slavs described by Margaret Byington, Italian immigrants brought with them the custom of the annual blessing of the home. The former Italian residents of Boston's West End returned habitually once a year to the empty parking lot where their homes once stood to perform this ritual.[55]

The care with which young women from peasant and working-class backgrounds assembled their dowry chests expressed a strong commitment to the interior of the home. While the linens, weavings, quilts, and coverlets which they accumulated were considered a commodity in the marriage exchange, the nature of the objects and the dedication with which they were made were intended for the domestic adornment of their future homes. Jane Addams and her fellow settlement workers at Hull House in Chicago often observed that even the poorest immigrant homes in Chicago or New York contained certain "folk objects" and family heirlooms that immigrants had carried across the Atlantic. Some of these artifacts represented ties with the immigrants' family traditions, mementos of ancestors or of personal events, rather than material value.[56]

This attachment to objects related to the home was particularly significant to people in their later years. Jane Addams recalled an old German woman who tried to hold onto a chest of drawers while two officials from the county

[55] Hareven, *Family Time and Industrial Time;* Marc Fried et al., *The World of the Urban Working Class* (Cambridge: Harvard University Press, 1973).
[56] Jane Addams, *Twenty Years at Hull House* [1910] (New York, 1981).

agent's office were trying to remove her to the county infirmary:

> The poor old creature had thrown herself bodily upon a small and battered chest of drawers and clung there, clutching it so firmly that it would have been impossible to remove her without also taking the piece of furniture. She did not weep nor moan nor indeed make any human sound, but between her broken gasp for breath she squealed shrilly like a frightened animal caught in a trap. . . . The poor creature who clung so desperately to her chest of drawers was really clinging to the last remnant of normal living—a symbol of all she was asked to renounce.[57]

In this brief examination of the emergence of the home as the family's domestic abode in reality and in ideal in Western society, I have tried to emphasize that in past the family's place of residence—the household—did not always carry the symbolic meaning of "home"; that, indeed, home was the invention of the middle class and was closely related to the emergence of the family as a private, emotional entity. By contrast to the middle class, working-class families continued to maintain greater flexibility and diversity in the use of their domestic space and ways of life. By the twentieth century the ideals of "home" had assumed powerful meaning in the domestic life of working-class families as well. Middle-class styles of consumption and furnishing permeated working-class families, but home life and the meaning of home in working-class families had different origins and a different character than in the middle class.

Ironically, despite the negative effect of excessive domestic privacy on the individual, middle-class reformers tried for over a century to impose on working-class and immigrant families the values and life-styles of the ideal middle-class home which they had devised. Working-class and immigrant families responded to these influences selectively: they adopted those

[57] *Ibid.*, p. 119.

aspects that suited their needs and their budgets, and blended them into their traditional culture, which they retained

The privacy of the home and the family have become central concerns in Western civilization. Some historians, like Christopher Lasch, have claimed that the family's private haven has been invaded excessively by modern bureaucracies and by the helping professions. Others, like Philippe Ariès and Richard Sennett, have emphasized the negative consequences of the family's retreat into domesticity and privacy, and its repressive impact on the individual. The first major critics of middle-class domesticity, however, were the women themselves, who had to carry out the high domestic ideals defined for them by the advocates of domesticity in the nineteenth century. Women responded to the pressures to create and maintain an ideal home in isolation from the rest of the world by taking the ideals of domesticity into the larger society, and by investing their energies in various reform movements and purity crusades.

The Idea of a Home: A Kind of Space

BY MARY DOUGLAS

THE MORE WE REFLECT on the tyranny of the home, the less surprising it is that the young wish to be free of its scrutiny and control. The evident nostalgia in much writing about the idea of home is more surprising. The mixture of nostalgia and resistance explains why the topic is so often treated as humorous. Dylan Thomas left home at an early age. His *Portrait of the Artist as a Young Dog* has a story about two men, outcasts from seaside suburbia, standing under the pier and wistfully speculating on what would be happening at home. Given that it is five o'clock in the evening, they know quite precisely that curtains are being drawn, the children being called in to tea, and even what tea will comprise. In *Less than Angels* Barbara Pym, that coolly detached recorder of homes, has an ironic passage about the suburban home of two sisters. After supper the dishes are cleared and the house made ready for night; every day before retiring one sister sets the table for tomorrow's breakfast, then both go up to bed; every night, before extinguishing the light, the other sister creeps down again to have one last look at the breakfast table in case something has been forgotten, and is very relieved if she manages to avert catastrophe by straightening a fork or adding a plate that should be there. These are affectionate images of home as a pattern of regular doings. Other images are frankly hostile. The very regularity of home's processes is both inexorable and absurd. It is this regularity that needs focus and explaining. How does it go on being what it is? And what is it?

Home certainly cannot be defined by any of its functions. Try the idea that home provides the primary care of bodies: if that is what it does best, it is not very efficient; a health farm or hotel could do as well. To say that it provides for the education of the infants hardly covers what it does, and raises the same question about whether specialized school or orphanages would not do it better. We will dismiss the cynical saying that the function of the home in modern industrial society is to produce the input into the labor market. As to those who claim that the home does something stabilizing or deepening or enriching for the personality, there are as many who will claim that it cripples and stifles. This essay makes a fresh start by approaching the home as an embryonic community. If it sounds platitudinous it is because many sociologists think of the embryonic community as modeled on the idea of a home. This relic of nineteenth-century romantic enthusiasm has been a stumbling block in sociology, where it is assumed too easily that the survival of a community over many vicissitudes does not need explaining. On this line of thought both home and community are supposed to be able to draw upon the same mysterious supply of loyal support, and further, their inner sources of strength are unanalyzable: thanks to a kind of mystic solidarity home and small local community are supposed to be able to overcome the forces of fission that tear larger groups apart.[1] This essay will approach solidarity from a more pragmatic point of view. It will try to answer the question, What makes solidarity possible? not by theorizing but by empirical observations on what strategies people adopt when they want to create solidarity

What Kind of Space?

We start very positivistically by thinking of home as a kind of

[1] Mary Douglas, *How Institutions Think* (Syracuse: Syracuse University Press, 1986), pp. 21–43.

space. Home is "here," or it is "not here." The question is not
"How?" nor "Who?" nor "When?" but "Where is your home?"
It is always a localizable idea. Home is located in space, but it is
not necessarily a fixed space. It does not need bricks and
mortar, it can be a wagon, a caravan, a boat, or a tent. It need
not be a large space, but space there must be, for home starts
by bringing some space under control. Having shelter is not
having a home, nor is having a house, nor is home the same as
household.[2] For a home neither the space nor its appurte-
nances have to be fixed, but there has to be something regular
about the appearance and reappearance of its furnishings.
The bedding in a Japanese home may be rolled away, and
rolled back, morning and night. The same with the populations; people flow through a home too, but there are some
regularities. Happiness is not guaranteed in a home. It is
possible to be happy in a hotel or a transit camp, but they are
nonhomes. Here is an instance of a happy, serviceable space
that fails the test.

> His Knightsbridge home was expensive, but it looked as if he
> were in the process of either moving in or moving out, and it
> had looked like that for the past sixteen years. . . . Vince was
> surrounded by packing cases, half laid carpets and paintings
> waiting to be hung. He was sitting in the middle of the floor,
> eating fish fingers, drinking whiskey and listening to a
> Linguaphone course.[3]

This nonhome was a fixed and solid building, full of domestic
things, but it was all beginnings and incomplete projects, with
no sign of coming out of the state of confusion that would lead
one day to the regular cycles of home life. So a home is not
only a space, it also has some structure in time; and because it
is for people who are living in that time and space, it has
aesthetic and moral dimensions. Compare the Knightsbridge

[2] This may come as a surprise to the judges in divorce courts who try to allot the
custody of children to the spouse who has a home.
[3] Francis Durbridge, *The Geneva Mystery* (1982).

nonhome with the African homes described by anthropolo-
gists.[4] The minimum home has orientation even if it lacks any
inside-outside boundary; usually it has both, so that the
cardinal points are not mere coordinates for plotting position
but "directions of existence."[5] Most of the homes we know are
not organized on lateral principles, right and left, but on a
front-back axis. Sometimes the orientation of a home marks all
four axes, back-front, up-down, two sides, and inside-outside.
Why some homes should have more complex orienting and
bounding than others depends on the ideas that persons are
carrying inside their heads about their lives in space and time.
For the home is the realization of ideas.

Virtual Space and Time

A fertile approach to the idea of home comes through the
philosopher Suzanne Langer.[6] She reproached philosophy for
separating artistic appreciation from the idea of rational thought.
She herself proposed to unite the various, divided cognitive
faculties under the single rubric of "presentational" thought.
This term she used for the perception of abstract analogies. She
focused on the rational activity of projecting or mapping on the
world analogic structures of bodily and emotional experience.
Since she was writing in the early 1940s, she was a long way
ahead of postmodern structuralism. Linguistics produced both
structuralism and semiotics, and came into anthropology and
literature through language. Langer couched her argument as
a protest against a too heavily language-based approach to rationality. So though she was actually leading semiotics before it

---

[4] Mary Douglas, "The Body of the World," *International Social Science Journal* 42
(August 1990): 395–399.

[5] James Littlejohn, "The Temne House," *Sierra Leone Studies* (New Series), no. 14
(December 1960): 63–67.

[6] Suzanne Langer, *Philosophy in a New Key*, 3d ed. (Cambridge: Harvard University
Press, 1957); idem, *Feeling and Form* (New York: Scribner, 1977).

was launched, in some sense when Langer was swimming against one kind of linguistics tide, from another direction a new linguistics tide was flowing in her direction.

Langer proposed that kinaesthesia works by creating analogic structures from one experience to another. Starting with music, and following the insights of German musicologists, she suggested that the distinctive characteristic of art forms was to create their own dimensions of experience, or to set up analogically and in a limited frame the dimensions of other experience. She used the terms "virtual" or "seeming" or a "semblance of" a commonly known dimension. By this usage, as she was at pains to say, she did not mean to draw a distinction between "virtual" and "real." Reality and unreality have nothing to do with her topic. Her ideas on analogic perception in art were forerunners of later work in philosophy on depiction and analogy. For example, she wanted to consider "presentational" thought because she rejected utterly the idea that representation was the artist's objective. She insisted that art is not a depiction, a copy of something else that is not art. Art for her is a communicative effort that makes specialized projections of the common dimensions of experience. This is why art should never be separated from reason if we are to understand rational processes. Here she would be close to Nelson Goodman's work on varieties of projection and notational schemes in science and art.[7]

Langer would also agree that analogies are not mere aids to theory. She would support Mary Hesse's argument against Duhem that analogies are not adjuncts to reasoning to be kicked aside by the scientist after the theorizing is complete in its mathematical form. The theory itself is a model as well as an elegant mathematical expression.[8] For Langer, analogies are not images; they are logical tools of understanding. She would be close to Mary Hesse's ideas of analogies in science as

[7] Nelson Goodman, *Languages of Art,* 2d ed. (Indianapolis: Hackett, 1976).
[8] Mary Hesse, *Models and Analogies in Science* (New York: Sheed & Ward, 1963).

working models, and of theories as analogies.[9] In philosophical theories of representation the sign is distinguished from something else that it represents. Unlike our real everyday experience of signs, the semioticians tend to start with identifying the sign as something static, fixed by convention, whereas it is only relatively stable, and easily transformed. Presentational thought, as Langer introduced it, is more open-ended, dynamic, more biologically based, freer from convention. It includes the maker of signs and the perceiver in one interaction. In human cognition it is a faculty for scanning a whole scene and its abstract structure.[10]

To some, Langer's writing on art will seem too mechanical, dealing as she does first with music, then with pictorial art, then with sculpture. But the formalism is necessary to an exposition of how we come to understand the categories of time and space. When she says "virtual time" or "virtual space," translate "virtual" into independent or autonomous. So music projects a virtual time, its own time, and each piece of music creates a separate autonomous time pattern of its own. Music gives a formal sample of the temporal patternings of the body, and the time patterns of the day; it is a presentation of patterned time, rife with tension and surprise, rousing and satisfying expectations of completion and return.[11] She invites

[9] Mary Hesse, *The Structure of Scientific Inference* (Berkeley: University of California Press, 1974).

[10] She also seems to anticipate much work in anthropology and psychology that emphasizes the perception of part to whole in physical and social relations: Mary Catherine Bateson, "Mother-Infant Exchanges: The Epigenesis of Conversational Interaction," *Annals of the New York Academy of Sciences* 263 (1975): 101–113; S. Runeson and Frykhol, "Visual Perception of Lifted Weight," *Journal of Experimental Psychology, Human Perception and Performance* 7 (1981): 733–740; Colwyn Trevarthen, "Communication and Cooperation in Early Infancy: A Description of Primary Intersubjectivity," in M. Bullowa, ed., *Before Speech: The Beginnings of Human Communication* (New York: Cambridge University Press, 1979); Colwyn Trevarthen and P. Hubley, "Secondary Intersubjectivity: Confidence, Confiding and Acts of Meaning in the First Year," in A. Lock, ed., *Action, Gesture and Symbol* (New York: Academic Press, 1978).

[11] Leonard Meyer, *Emotion and Meaning in Music* (Chicago: University of Chicago Press, 1956).

us to replace ratiocinations about time by the more empirical
work of modeling the experience of time.

Turning from time to space, Langer says that pictures
project a virtual scene: they make an autonomous projection of
visual depth and distance, and a projection of visual clarity or
confusion. A picture is a presentation of two-dimensional
space. Going on from two-dimensional to three-dimensional
space, she says that sculpture projects virtual kinetic volume; it
presents an independent model of the body's experience of
volume, weight, and motor control. Here she too briefly refers
to the relation between dance, music, and body, drawing on
the work of German musicologists and psychologists. Then she
goes on to architecture, alas, even more sketchily: architecture
is a "virtual ethnic domain." What does that mean? I suggest it
is the idea of home.

The ethnic domain is the domain of structured domesticity.
It projects the most encompassing set of analogies: like music,
it creates its own time rhythms; like a picture, it contrives its
own spatial effects and its own regulation of vision and
perception of distance; like sculpture it explores volume,
movement, and bodily behavior in the gravitational field. As
Langer says, architecture can also present the largest metaphors of society and religion; it can project meanings about life
and death and eschatology into the everyday arrangements
that it covers. In this vein, animal architecture of nests, lairs,
shells, hives, and warrens readily project the ethnic domain.
Hence the powerful attraction of popular zoology and
entymology; hence the beloved fiction about animal homes,
from the Jungle Books through Beatrice Potter's creations,
Salar the Otter to Watership Down and Mickey Mouse; hence
the grander mythic presentations of the ethnic domain under
the water or in the sky, and the peculiar fascination of the
homes of giants and dwarfs. In what follows, Langer's ideas
about presentational thought in the ethnic domain will be
applied to the production and use of a human home.

A Memory Machine

Langer's notion of virtuality suggests we should focus on the home as an organization of space over time. This reveals a distinctive characteristic of the idea of home. Each kind of building has a distinctive capacity for memory or anticipation. Memory institutionalized is capable of anticipating future events. Music is full of anticipation, with short and long cycles, but its time structure is independent of outside events. Everything takes place inside the musical composition. The home makes its time rhythms in response to outside pressures; it is in real time. Response to the memory of severe winters is translated into a capacity for storage, storm windows, and extra blankets; holding the memory of summer droughts, the home responds by shade-giving roofs and water tanks. Those are annual rhythms, but there are longer cycles, as testified by the standard pair of coffin stools always ready for the funeral wake in East Anglian houses. And shorter ones: to the onset of evening, the home responds with lighting; to strong light, with blinds. Children reading *Robinson Crusoe* are transfixed by his work of anticipation: candles, firewood, containers to catch and hold the rain, planks and other provisions from the wreck. The squirrel's autumn shopping cache, the storage arrangements of *Swiss Family Robinson*, the annual autumn shopping expedition in *The Little House in the Big Wood*, have the same essential appeal as the weekly shopping of the Yeoman's family before World War I:

> Tuesday had a special magic for me, when at four o'clock Mother and Father arrived home from market and unloaded the groceries from the high trap. Into the kitchen came a smell spicy as an Indian market. No sterile pre-packed food in plastic bags, but provisions selected by Mother like a connoisseur: cheese she had 'tasted', tea to her own blending, dates in large lumps carved from an even bigger block on the grocer's counter. I sniffed and guessed at the contents of the dark blue bags of rice, sago, spices, sultanas and other wonders. Out came biscuits in seven-pound tins, custard powder, candles, lampwicks, and

elastic for garters and bloomers: packet after packet! Surely we
should never want for anything again.[12]

Storage implies a capacity to plan, to allocate materials
between now and the future, to anticipate needs. A stocking-
up anticipates a running-down of supplies, which implies
continual reallocation, repair, renewal, in short an intelligent
plan. For the sake of the plan, space is differentiated, parceled
out, allotted to different intentions. This happens, obviously,
in a railway station or a hotel. What makes storage different in
a home is the scope of the intentions. A home has a much more
comprehensive expectation of service. People do not normally
expect to give birth or to die in hotels or railway stations, and
the management gets upset when they do. Even the
one-occupant home is a general service utility, an institution
whose uses cannot be defined except as a presentation of a
general plan for meeting future needs.

The Commons Dilemma

The well-stocked home presents in small the essential
problem of the commons. Its reserves are going to be a
common resource for the denizens of the home if they can
restrain their impatience. With only one person, the free-rider
problem is essentially the same, as Jon Elster has shown in his
discussion of weakness of will where he transfers the conflict
between persons to the conflict of wants within the person.[13] If
the homesteader consumes all his reserves in time of plenty,
the home will be unable to supply his future needs.
Unscheduled dipping into the larder, like the farmer eating
the seed corn, incurs moral judgment on individual weakness
of will. If the homesteader's desire are in conflict, it is the same

[12] H. St. G. Cramp, *A Yeoman Farmer's Son: A Leicestershire Childhood* (Oxford: Oxford
University Press, 1986), p. 67.
[13] Jon Elster, "Weakness of Will and the Free-Rider Problem," *Economics and
Philosophy* 1 (1985): 275–306.

as if, wishing to give up smoking for his better health, he cannot resist a cigarette, or if wishing to lose weight, he cannot resist a cream bun. Opportunism traduces his overall plan. Stealing from the future prosperity of his own home, he free-rides on his own attempts to make himself a home,[14] but the free-rider is the same person as the one who is providing the good things. This is the beauty of the model: since whoever free-rides on the goods of his own community is going to lose by its destruction. Neatly centralizing the conflict within the person, Elster opens a way of carrying the analysis further. He shows that the unit of analysis can be either a person or a community. If the latter, we can move on to consider what strategies the members need to deploy to strengthen their will to be a solitary group. There is not much that is mysterious about how they achieve solidarity and much that can be counted and measured.

The home's capability to allocate space and time and resources over the long term is a legitimate matter for wonder. We are not surprised that the cupboard is often bare; what should amaze us is that it often contains an extraordinary variety of things that are going to be used through the year, mentally ticketed for different kinds of expected events. Even more amazingly, they have been stacked so that they can be found at the right times. The most precious, to be used on the grandest occasion, are safely on the highest shelves, out of reach because they are least frequently wanted, while the most everyday stuff, hardier and cheaper to replace, stands near at hand. The spacing of provisions provides another aide-memoire for the totality of life within the home. In a much longer essay it would be possible to compare homes on the basis of how strongly the members are committed to the production of a collective good, or how much of it they succeed

---

[14] The problem of weakness of will is usually treated as a problem within rational-choice theory about the possibility of an individual acting against his own preferred interests. See Russell Hardin, *Morality Within the Limits of Reason* (Chicago: University of Chicago Press, 1988), pp. 191ff.

in producing, and to say more about the other kind of homes which aim to produce spaces for individuals. For introducing the idea of the home as a collective good it will be enough to concentrate only on one kind of home, an extreme type in which the members have been working successfully for a long time on the common objective.

The budget is the main instrument of structuring the collective effort. Through the budget the collectivity lays its finger on every allocation and qualifies every decision. The budget slots make a screen through which every private plan must pass lest individual demands put at risk the resources mentally set aside for the rent, the mortgage, the child's education, the summer holidays, the rainy day. However unformed its goals may be, the home protects it general plan with mutually adjusted budget slots. Children's pocket money has to be scaled to the wife's housekeeping money; she is in charge of the common purse. It would be absurd for her to have less than they do. Between the children, differentials have to be respected: if the younger gets more than the elder, problems of equity raise their head, with loud argument about fairness and function.

For these reasons a home is a model for kinds of distributive justice. The reference to morality points a major difference between a home and a hotel. Both plan for the future, but the planning of the hotel follows criteria of cost efficiency. The reason why the home cannot use market reasoning is, to extend Suzanne Langer's term, that it is a virtual community. It is not a monetary economy, though a household could be. Suppose a group of people sharing the rent of a house, each with his or her own timed access to the cooker and corner of the larder, each coming and going independently of the others, each autonomously making plans and keeping careful check of requital for services rendered by the others—that would be a household. They would settle conflicts over scarce resources by bargaining on semimarket principles. They would argue about their claims in terms of functional priorities or in terms of relative contributions. Inputs would be measured against outputs. This is the kind of institution which the "human capital" theorists can analyze with ease. At the other end of the scale from market to nonmarket is the home, with its laughably complex, tyrannical rules, unpredictably waived and unpredictably honored, and never quite amenable to rational justification. The question for the theory of collective choice is how a home manages to demand and to get sacrifices from its members, how it creates the collectivity which is more than the sum of parts. In what follows the word "home" is treated as a collective good, and focus will be on how contributions are exacted.

A home is characterized by massive redundancies. As an institution compared with others, a home is definitely not-for-profit, and like other nonprofit institutions there are characteristic difficulties about justifying its operations. Whereas the charitable or learned foundation does have to give an account of its expenditures, fortunately a home does not. Its continuance is its justification. Ask a home owner how he or she budgets for the home's needs over the years and you will be answered with a groan or a laugh. Yet the need to make budgetary allocations is at the heart of the project. If only the home had very simple objectives, such as running trains through stations while picking up and delivering passengers, a budget would be feasible. It is practically impossible to make a budget for a home with multiple purposes and undefined goals. A home may be putting resources aside for saving; certainly, and over and above the scheduled saving it may make a profit, but it is unusual for it to recognize an annual profit, because of the very vagueness of its objectives. If there is an unbudgeted surplus from one year to another, it may be treated as a windfall, blown or distributed on the spot or put into the savings account. There are homes that are run for a particular purpose, as adjuncts to or ancillary to something else. For example, the Leicestershire yeoman farmer who ran his home and family for promoting the interests of the farm made a profit, but this was thought by the sons to be an inversion of the proper relation of the farm to the family.[15] Using Robert Merton's distinction,[16] the virtual community has no manifest functions and is dominated by its latent functions. Since these are hidden, it is well to ask how they are performed, how an institution which is largely latent in its purposes remains in being, and how the commons dilemma is resolved.

Coordination

The primary problem of a virtual community is to achieve enough solidarity to protect the collective good. If solidarity weakens, individual raids destroy the collective resource base. Though the home, like other not-for-profit institutions, is inefficient on market criteria, in another sense it is remarkably efficient. It does not need specialized administrative personnel because the claims of fairness diffuse the work of organization. Members continually make claims on resources, but they are not going to win a contest of conflicting claims by asking on their own behalf; the winning claim is made in the name of the public good and in the name of fairness, which in a home is reckoned to be a public good. Individual claims are conceded or rebutted on the same grounds. The theoretical solution of the distributional problem is fairness, but the practical solution is to make every member a watchdog on the public behalf, and to use coordination to do the rest. Coordination facilitates public monitoring and a high degree of visibility.

Coordination might seem to pose a problem of its own: it is not so obviously easy to arrange. But the home has an easy solution: its characteristic method of coordinating is to

---

[15] Cramp, *Yeoman Farmer's Son.*

[16] Robert Merton, "Manifest and Latent Functions," in *Social Theory and Social Structure* (New York: Free Press, 1968), pp. 73–138.

maintain open, constant communication about fair access to resources. Like fairness, coordination is regarded as a public good. How can the home be run if no one knows who is coming and who is going? It is not a hotel, goes the complaining refrain. Coordination is achieved in three ways: coordinated work is on a functional basis, coordinated access to the fixed resources is governed by rotation, and distributions of movables by synchrony, which ensures visibility. As in other institutions, work tends to get allocated in lumps, according to space used and periodicity of tasks.[17] Someone doing one task, say in the kitchen, might as well save on transaction costs by doing others in the same place, say the kitchen, if they occur at the same time. So the home has a tendency to develop a simple division of labor, by age and sex.

However, the functional basis only goes a short way to provide coordination. Rotation is the principle used to control access to fixed space, the bathroom for example, if there is one, the outside privy if there is not. Whoever tries to monopolize that specialized space gets fiercely criticized. The criticism is in the name of the collective good: what sort of home is it where one person can hog the bathroom? Who do they think they are? Have they bought it up? The same attack is made on other offenses against the collectivity: "Dropping your sweet papers on the floor . . . who do you think is going to clean up after you?" "Marching in and out, without so much as by your leave; do they think this is a hotel?" The idea of the hotel is the standard "Other," where every comfort has to be paid for, the mercenary, cold, luxurious counterpart against which the home is being measured.

The home's technique is to use synchrony and order to protect fair access to other goods, movables and perishables. Synchrony and order effectively combine to show up delinquency. Round the table each knows where to sit, the order of

[17] Mary Douglas and Baron Isherwood, *The World of Goods* (New York: Basic Books, 1979), ch. 6.

seating corresponds to other orderings, such as the order of chores, the order of privileges and birth, the order of bedtime. Rankings are scored in space. The positions indicate the fairness of the distribution of food. Anyone who tries to get in first to take the best food or larger amounts will hear about fairness. The problems of fair access and distribution are anticipated by synchronicity, and there is always post hoc criticism as a last resort. No one can get in first, or secretly, before the others, because everyone has to be physically present. Charity has to be discreet, even secret, but in a home gifts have to be delivered and opened publicly, so that everyone can enjoy the display of finely cadenced distinctions. Although all distributions are visible and publicly monitored, everyone will tell you that monitoring for fairness is not an intention. Indeed, when intentions are closely integrated none are primary. Everything that is done together in the home has multiple purposes. That is why it is of little use to ask members of a home why they do anything the way they do it.

Much of the burden of organization is carried by conspicuous fixed times. The order of day is the infrastructure of the community. In a home there is no need to look for someone: it should be possible to work out where everyone is at any given time, that is, if it is functioning well. But home is a fragile system, easy to subvert. It is generally well recognized that the main contribution of members to the collective good is to be physically present at its assemblies. An act of presence is a public service.[18] Absence is to be deplored. Perhaps the most subversive attack on the home is to be present physically without joining in its multiple coordinations. To leave erratically, without saying where or for how long, to come back and go upstairs without greeting, these lapses are recognized as spoliation of the commons. In one of her autobiographical essays Colette describes her mother coming into the garden and calling: Where are the children? No answer. They are up

---

[18] See the account of "consumption services" in *ibid*.

in the trees, stretched out in the boughs, or curled up in the grass, in the stable, hiding, sleeping, reading. She gets no answer, and her disregarded call bespeaks the weakness of that home shortly to be disbanded.

The time devoted to the common meal is a conclave, used for coordinating other arrangements, negotiating exemptions, canvassing for privileges, diffusing information about the outside world, agreeing on strategies for dealing with it and making shared evaluations. The conclave invents exceptions to its rules: permissions to be late, to skip a meal. A home is a tangle of conventions and totally incommensurable rights and duties. Not a money economy, the home is the typical gift economy described by Marcel Mauss.[19] Every service and transfer is part of an ongoing comprehensive system of exchanges, within and between the generations. The transactions never look like exchanges because the gesture of reciprocity is delayed and disguised. No one can know the worth of their own contribution to the home. It is not just that calculation is too difficult, but more that it suits no one to insist on a precise offsetting of one service against another. Debts are remembered well enough, but by keeping them vague there is the hope that repayment may be more than equivalent. Direct reciprocity is avoided. In the most extreme, perfectly abstract, complete instances of a home, there would be no free gifts, no loose ends, and nothing meaningless at all. Every smallest gesture would be laden with information, every greeting and every meal a celebration of the system itself. A virtual community is in place, from which vantage point clans, tribes, and phratries can be surveyed—and hotels.

From set times for meals flow further rules about timing. Not just mealtimes, but throughout the meal even, the synchronized attack with knives and forks on the plates is finely tuned. Members of a home eat level, drink level, get

[19] Marcel Mauss, *The Gift: The Form and Reason for Exchange in Archaic Societies*, tr. W. D. Halls (London: Routledge, 1990).

reproached for eating too fast or too slow. Synchrony guarantees fair distribution: no second helpings can be given until the last slow eater has cleared his plate. The home requires apology or explanation from one caught raiding the larder ahead of the mealtime or after it or between meals. Why was he hungry? Where was he last mealtime? The expectation of synchrony gives a right to a vast amount of information about members' doings.

Tyrannies of the Home

This is how the home works. Even its most altruistic and successful versions exert a tyrannous control over mind and body. We need hardly say more to explain why children want to leave it and do not mean to reproduce it when they set up house. When we add the possibilities of subversion, the case for rejecting the idea of the home is even stronger. The free-rider on the collectivity may be the authoritarian father, or it may be the youngest child, or the mother herself. There is no space here today to talk about the model subverted to an individual's private self-interest. Nor is it necessary to say much about the inadvertent interruptions of the proper flow of claims and counterclaims which block the perception of the collective good. For a thousand reasons, the home becomes inefficient in its own terms. It is rigid: mealtimes cannot be suddenly changed to accommodate a visitor lest cascading disorder overthrow its subsystems. Warmth and friendship may take second place in its priorities.

Apart from its tyranny over times, the home tyrannizes over tastes. In the name of friendly uniformity, the menus tend to be designed not to satisfy food preferences but to avoid food hates. One person's rooted dislike or medical prohibition results in certain foods being totally eliminated even if they are everyone else's favorite food, so in the regular menu everyone gets what they are indifferent to, and no one ever gets their favorite dish.[20]

The home also censors speech. It has slots for different tones of voice, conversational topics, and even language. In the name of the community, referred to as "we" or "everyone," neither shouting (because it dominates) nor whispering (because it is secret and exclusive) is allowed, and no private conversations at meals. The rank order which shows in the order of seating and the order of serving imposes restrictions on topics—"Not in front of the children"—or on language—"Not in front of your mother-in-law."[21] "Don't sing at the table," says the mother in The Little House on the Prairie, and then, realizing they are sitting by the wagon with no table, she amends it to a rule against singing at mealtimes.[22] Obscenities and talk about money problems at mealtimes are ruled out for different reasons. We have already said that though the family may depend on money coming in, in its internal dealings it is essentially a nonmonetary arrangement. A truce on money talk at table is a truce in the name of the home on all the private struggles that are going on to negotiate a share of the budget for particular projects. Finding the right time to talk about something can be quite a problem in a highly coordinated home.

The idea of the hotel is a perfect opposite of the home, not only because it uses market principles for its transactions, but

[20] G. Mars and V. Mars, unpublished manuscript on cultural theory applied to London families.

[21] An American sociologist commented that this description of the home as a system of rules and rankings was distinctly elitist. Particularly the control on speech recalls the family in the American south in which children had to wash their mouths with soap if they used foul language. It is necessary to say that the details of the rules vary slightly, but the general concern to make an equitable, structured space for living is reported for many civilizations. The examples from English autobiographies and children's stories quoted here are not upper class. In Africa the control on speech takes the form of prescribing categories of kin who are allowed to joke with one another, thus defining others before whom obscenity is ruled out.

[22] Laura Ingalls Wilder, Little House on the Prairie (New York: Harper & Row, 1953).

because it allows it clients to buy privacy as a right of exclusion. This offends doubly the principle of the home whose rules and separations provide some limited privacy for each member. Even when the space is at a premium, by conventions of eyes averted and speech controlled, privacy is cherished in the home. The home protects a person's body from voyeurism and intrusive scatology. Whatever the distinctions that govern the home's procedures, and for whatever reasons they are instituted, one of their effects is to honor a person's incumbency of space. To some extent the old, whose bodily infirmities belie their dignity, are protected from ridicule by the practice of ranked space and time. The child owes its safety from parental incest to rules separating bodies and times. To infringe these boundaries is to threaten the collectivity itself. This explains why the home generally makes a ban on obscenity. What forms are banned depends where the thresholds of privacy are drawn. Spoken or graphic obscenity invades the privacy which the community affords to its members, and will be put under control.

A Self-Organizing System

On this account, home as a virtual community is often absurd, and often cruel. We have tried to interrogate its life to understand community sources of solidarity. The result of the inquest is to show that those committed to the idea of home exert continual vigilance in its behalf. The vigilance focuses upon common presence at fixed points in the day, the week, the year, on elaborate coordination of movements and far-reaching surveillance of members' claims and counter-claims. If we were to follow further Suzanne Langer's ideas about virtual time and virtual space in artistic creation, we would try to draw a clear series of pictures of the assemblies and dispersals which pattern different virtual ethnic domains. If we had to choose an index of solidarity from the time-space structure of homes, the strongest indicator would not be stoutness of the enclosing walls but the complexity of coordination.[23] Complexity is more surprising than simplicity or confusion. From an information-theoretic point of view its presence needs to be explained. The persons who devote vigilance to the maintenance of the home apparently believe that they personally have a lot to lose if it were to collapse. This is the point at which biological pressures to provide for the care of the young have to be invoked. Other embryonic communities have more trouble about mustering solidarity and demanding sacrifice. To this extent the sociologists are right who attribute to primordial passions the survival of families and small communities.

We have been contrasting the home explicitly with a hotel, and contrasting a virtual community with a virtual market. The type of home that has been taken as exemplary has a lot of authority at its disposal, but it is not authoritarian or centralized. Everything happens by mutual consultation. Mutual adjustment of interlocking rules combines to meet functional requirements, personal claims on scarce amounts of time, space, and other resources. That is what makes this home so complicated, difficult to enter and difficult to change. This home emerges as the result of individual strategies of control defended respectively in the name of the home as a public good. Ideally the mother operates the system, so does the father, and so, undoubtedly, do the children. It is extremely coercive, but the coercion is anonymous, the control is generalized. The pattern of rules continually reforms itself, becomes more comprehensive and restrictive, and continually suffers breaches, fission, loss at the fringes.

It is not authoritarian, but it has authority. It is hierarchical, but it is not centralized. The best name for this type of organization is a protohierarchy. It is recognizable because it

---

[23] Jonathan Gross, "Measuring Cultural Complexity," in Mary Douglas, ed., *Food in the Social Order* (New York: Russell Sage Foundation, 1984).

springs up, spontaneously, to meet certain recurring conditions of organization. It is a multipeaked, rationally integrated system which we find in villages, districts, kingdoms, and empires. Highly efficient for maintaining itself in being, it is easily subverted and survives only so long as it attends to the needs of its members.

www.ingramcontent.com/pod-product-compliance
Lightning Source LLC
Chambersburg PA
CBHW032119020426
42334CB00016B/1008